LAST OF THE GUARDIANS

LAST OF THE GUARDIANS

A story of Burma, Britain and a family

DAVID DONNISON

With best wishes to
the Ashtons —
David Donnison

Superscript
The imprint of Cyhoeddwyr y Superscript Ltd,
404 Robin Square
Newtown. SY16 1HP

First published by Superscript, 2005

Copyright David Donnison, 2005

All rights reserved. No part of this publication may be
reproduced, stored in a retrieval system, or transmitted
in any form or by any means without the prior permission
of the publishers.

This book is sold subject to the condition that it shall not,
by way of trade or otherwise, be lent, re-sold, hired out or
otherwise circulated without the publishers' prior consent
in any form of binding or cover other than that in which it
is published and without a similar condition including this
condition being imposed on the subsequent purchaser.

The map on page 66 is an original creation for
this volume by Don Williams of Bute Cartographics:
don-williams@tiscali.co.uk

Design, typesetting and cover by Derek Copsey:
derek@derekcopseydesigns.freeserve.co.uk

ISBN 0954291395

Printed and bound by Antony Rowe, Eastbourne.

CONTENTS

What's writing really about?
It's about trying to take fuller possession
of the reality of your life

Ted Hughes

INTRODUCTION

Many people find there comes a time when they want to learn more about their origins and the influences that shaped their lives. For me this curiosity was sharpened by finding I was the possessor of memoirs written by my parents and two of my aunts, a set of journals I wrote between the ages of fourteen and twenty-one, and a large number of letters that members of the family wrote to each other between 1930 and 1980 – thousands of pages describing a world that has gone for ever. My curiosity became almost a duty when I found that my father, in his will, had asked me to be his literary executor. I began to seek out friends and relatives who could tell me more about our family and about Burma (now called Myanmar) where the main characters in this story had spent many years.

Those born and raised in the British Empire – whether they were British or citizens of the colonial territories – find they have been involved in two interlocking stories: their family's story and the story of an empire. They cannot tell one without bringing in the other. So my story is an account of an extended family who were shaped in many ways by their experience of empire, and an account of Burma under British rule, perceived through the lens of this family's experience. We already have shelves of books by, and about, imperialists. If this one adds something to that literature it will be because it tells the story of the children as well as the adults, the story of the family's law breakers as well as their law enforcers, and the story of the feelings they had for the native peoples they lived among. These feelings were to become very important in the closing stages of the story. Most of the books about empire dwell on the conquerors' triumphant years. This one, too, offers stories of that kind. But it also tells how and why imperial authority unraveled, and what happens to the people caught up in the conflicts and betrayals that lead eventually to the end of empire.

My parents' memoir, which they wrote together a dozen and more years after the story it tells came to an end, is the main source for this book which is more theirs than mine. But to intersperse long paragraphs they wrote through material from many other sources – as I at first tried to do - makes difficult reading. So, emboldened by my father's request that I act as their editor, I have freely selected and amended their words, without adding scholarly dots and brackets to show where the editing has been done. I have disciplined myself by imagining my parents to be looking over my shoulder. *I* can say whatever I like, and they would not agree with everything I have written. But I have attributed no words to them that they would have been unhappy about. Readers who wish to learn more about their version of the story can find the original memoir in the British Library which inherited it from the India Office Library where my father placed a copy. I have treated other memoirs and the books I have quoted in the proper scholarly way, quoting precisely from them, and inserting dots, square brackets, page numbers and footnote references wherever they are needed.

Since so much of this book consists of my parents' words, I have retained, throughout, the place names they used: "Burma", not Myanmar, "Rangoon", not Yangon, and so on. It would have been tedious, and somehow misleading, to do otherwise.

To unearth the truth and present it as clearly and fairly as possible has been a demanding, and sometimes a painful, task – a task I feel better equipped for if I keep my emotional distance from the characters in the story by writing about them in the third person. Thus I describe my parents as "Vernon" and "Ruth", not as "my father and mother"; likewise my sister and other members of the family. I also describe myself throughout the story as "David". Where I drop into the first person, that's me, reflecting or editorializing today. I take responsibility for anything "I" say, but do not have to justify what "David" says or does. Readers who get confused about the relationships involved in the story can consult the family trees on pages 34 and 35.

I could not have written this book without the help of many people. My sister Annis Flew, my cousin Bastien Gomperts, and my uncle Michael Barratt Brown have read and commented on every chapter. Other cousins and a "foster cousin" — Peter Bailey, Ursula Hodgkinson, Beryl Gale and Audrey Wilson - did likewise for some Chapters. John Okell, more expert about Burma than any of us, has kept me straight on many points. Ray Pahl, Paul Binding and Peter Marris gave perceptive editorial advice — all the more helpful for being sometimes contradictory. Don Williams crammed more information more clearly into a map than I had thought possible. Meanwhile Kay Carmichael, my wife, was the first to encourage me to work on this task, and has critically but lovingly talked through every chapter with me.

I

A BRIDE GOES TO BURMA

On 1 November, 1923, the *S.S. Pegu*, a passenger ship of the Henderson Line, was moored at a Birkenhead quay, raising steam to sail for Rangoon. A train had just pulled in, bringing passengers from London to join the ship, and a straggling line of them were beginning to mount the gangway from the dockside, carrying light bags. Their heavy trunks and boxes had been sent ahead days ago – labelled "Wanted on board", to be placed in their cabins, or "Not wanted on board", to be stowed in the hold.

Observe a couple in this advancing line: both of them small, in their late forties, hair already turning grey, but elegant in discreetly expensive coats and hats – David Singer, a London stockbroker, and his wife Isabel. With them comes their 23-year-old daughter, Ruth; taller despite her flat-heeled shoes, more robust, with bouncy black hair, naturally glowing cheeks and a hint of freckles. One day she will be my mother. She and her parents can be seen in the accompanying photographs.

Who was this young woman? What led her to leave her comfortable Hampstead home and the University of Cambridge, where she was training to be a doctor, to set out for a remote country and marry a rather unlikely man? And what did these young people think they would be doing there – helping to rule people who had until recently managed their own affairs pretty well?

A family's myth, like that of a nation or an empire, is created as much by the things its people forget as by those they remember; created, too, by the ways in which they interpret the things they remember. I will tell some of the memories passed on to me by my mother and her sisters, and add some of the things they and their forbears forgot or never knew — imparting as I do so (who could avoid it?) a selective spin of my own to the story. In the next chapter I will do the same for Ruth's fiancé, Vernon, and his family.

RUTH SETS OUT

Threading their way through the ship, Ruth and her parents found the cabin which was to be her home for the next month. Her trunk was already there. So was Mrs. Kier, who had been allotted the other berth in the cabin.

Introductions completed, the Singers hurried back on deck. Ruth's sister Eleanor was lying ill at home — as so often at times of crisis — and her parents had to get back to London to care for her. The trio stood awkwardly for a moment at the head of the gangway. "I was setting out on a journey of eight thousand miles to a country none of us knew", Ruth later recalled. "My father was deeply moved, but there was nothing we felt able to say. My mother, wishing no doubt to reassure me, said 'And remember, if you change your mind when you get to Rangoon, you can always come home again'. With that, she kissed me tearfully and they disappeared into the gathering darkness." It was a characteristic benediction for her daughter's marriage.

Once necessary unpacking had been done, Ruth curled up in her berth, the ship vibrating as engines began to rumble, and there she slept, and slept — for days. "Mrs. Kier must have asked a steward to bring me something on a tray from time to time for I never ventured on deck or went to the saloon".

The last weeks in her Hampstead home had been utterly exhausting. There had been goodbyes to exchange with relatives and friends — many of them dismayed and anxious about the venture on which she was embarking. There had been endless wedding presents to choose and to thank people for; all the things her parents expected her to take to the outpost in Burma to which she was going; clothes, for hot weather, for walking through the jungle, for social occasions and for getting married in. And table silver...

"My parents asked me what design I liked best. I disliked the elaborate 'queen' pattern of their own silver, much preferring the plain 'rat-tail' design, and felt sure Vernon would agree. So my mother ordered the silver and, coming home one evening, I went up to bed and found a large oak canteen on a chair in my room. I opened it and there lay the shining rows of spoons and forks for every occasion: the little gilt egg spoons, the shining round bowls of the soup spoons, a long, graceful gravy spoon, spoons for breakfast and spoons for tea, large forks for meat and small ones for puddings, sauce ladles and serving spoons and jam spoons, each gleaming in its own dark blue velvet niche. They seemed too lovely to touch. Could they really be ours? Yes – for there was a monogram engraved on each. I took one to the light, wondering what they had made of our combined initials – V&RD – which I had often inter-twined in well-designed monograms for this moment. My own future initials stared blankly at me under the light: RSD." Her mother had yet to accept Vernon's place in her life.

This silver was to travel with them for the next twenty years, till a day came when it was hurriedly wrapped in rough cloth and thrown into the rucksack that Vernon was to carry through the jungle, just ahead of the Japanese army. With Ruth already in India, he was unsure whether he would be able to get through to her, or would have to try for China where silver could be used as currency. After struggling in blinding heat for days along tracks leading towards India, he could carry the silver no further and stuffed it deep into a hole in a tree. Where it probably remains to this day.

Then there had been the farewell parties. "My mother arranged one for the friends and relatives of both families to dis-play our wedding presents and send me off. Singers and Donnisons had little in common, and without Vernon I felt pretty bored by the whole ritual; but at least it was another milestone on the way to my departure. As the numbers to be invited swelled, my mother decided there would have to be two parties, and to my horror I found she was inviting the social 'sheep' to the first and consigning the 'goats' to the second. Some of the goats understood very well what was happening and took great umbrage. My old governess, Miss Griggs, who for years had been the sanest influence in my life, refused to communicate with me ever again."

There had been poignant partings. "Margaret Hope (later Godfrey) for long my closest friend, came to say goodbye. We knew we would not see each other for many years, but we said little. Margaret conveyed her most powerful feelings without words. I sensed that she feared for me... wanted to warn me. When the time came for her to go I took her to the door and she went slowly down the steps to the pavement. Then she suddenly came running back, took something from her handbag and pressed it into my hand without a word, turned and ran back into the street and away. What lay in my hand was a little gilt powder compact, well used – just something of her own which would be a link between us. I kept it with me for twenty years till I could no longer find a refill to fit it."

The last days had been most exhausting of all – "my mother constantly standing around asking what I wanted to do with this and that. Warm clothes and my bicycle could be stored for the day when we came home on leave. But the disposal of my final laundry baffled me. I wanted to leave no trace of myself behind – and nothing so distasteful as soiled linen."

As the time for departure approached, Ruth's mother felt moved to give earnest advice. "Double beds were to be avoided. And if I became pregnant I must at once return home. To this I replied that we did not intend to have a baby for at least a year, and when that time came I would want more than ever to be with my husband. To this she said, darkly, 'Man proposes, God disposes'."

Her exhaustion eventually lifting as the Pegu entered the Mediterranean, Ruth came out on deck. The sea was calm, the sun was shining, and everyone about her seemed happy. She began making friends. Some of them – Mrs. McCallum, returning to her civil servant husband, and Maud Lister, going out to marry policeman Fred Wemys – were to become lifelong friends.

"I was entering a new community and learning its ways. There were rubber planters and missionaries, employees of big firms, policemen, army and civil service people, all in a one-class ship. Lots of Scottish names. Nearly all were going the whole way to Rangoon with a few travelling on from there to Singapore. Vernon had warned me that I should avoid falling out with anyone. I might meet them again among half a dozen European neighbours with whom we would have to live and work in some remote place for years to come.

"Mrs. Kier, my cabin mate, was the childless wife of a Malayan rubber planter. She was friendly, and in a way fascinating. I had never met anyone so hidebound by formality or with such stereotyped opinions – untouched by anything that had happened since about 1911. She assured me I would soon be wearing rouge to mask my growing tropical pallor. Her husband always said with pleasure how much better she was looking when she resorted to this subterfuge. (Only actresses and prostitutes regularly wore makeup in those days.) I could not imagine Vernon being taken in by a little rouge. The Singers – perhaps because of our Portuguese and more distant middle eastern origins – had vivid complexions which needed no embellishment. I found that I blossomed in the growing heat of the Mediterranean. When I removed my stockings and put sandals on Mrs. Kier was scandalised, but many of the younger women followed my example.

"I had a great time playing deck games and looking after toddlers – there were lots on board and their mothers welcomed my help. I sewed some last pieces of my trousseau and read Anna Karenina. My mother had given me a copy, saying that she had read it while expecting me, but I decided I would get it over now.

"I wanted to learn all I could about Burma and its people, but found that very few of the passengers spoke their language or were even aware of the country's native inhabitants. Except for Mrs.McCallum, who told me marvellous tales about a life she delighted in, visiting remote places with her husband, walking on rough tracks, the baby in his bassinette, transported, along with their baggage, on bullock carts. She told me about people working the soil who were utterly dependent on the seasons for the growth of their crops and their food.

"Our first call was at Port Said where I went ashore with old hands and followed tradition by buying a topee – a sun helmet – at Simon Artz. At Aden there was a letter waiting for me from Vernon, saying he had hopes of getting permission to come out in the pilot boat that would meet us at the mouth of the Rangoon river – but I must not count on this. Then came the long, hot voyage across the Indian Ocean. The novelty of the journey had worn off and it seemed interminable, despite games, dances and distractions of all kinds.

"At last we were approaching Rangoon – sweet, spicy smells of land reaching us from over the horizon. I tried to put aside my hopes of seeing Vernon before we docked and went to bed in my cabin for the last time. But I could not sleep. Some time after midnight I gave up trying, got up, put on my old Japanese kimono and went up on deck. There it was dark but cooler. The ship was slowing down. Then I saw lights from a smaller boat some way off. A huge lamp was hoisted over the Pegu's side and a rope ladder attached to the rail beneath it. Leaning over from the upper deck, I could see a rowing boat pull up at our side and figures appeared, climbing up the ladder into the light. I counted them, knowing that two other women were hoping their fiances would come out on the pilot boat. No sign of Vernon. I was beginning to turn away into the darkness when someone came up quietly behind me. And there he was. It was about 1am.

"We sat on deck till dawn as the Pegu gathered weigh and continued up river. Then I went down to my cabin to dress. Mrs. Kier expressed her regret that we were not yet married. Had we been, she would of course have vacated the cabin for us, but in the circumstances...."

THE SINGERS

Who were the Singers? Ruth and her three younger sisters all agreed who was the most revered member of their family: Simeon Singer, their grandfather. Indeed, I still occasionally meet people who clap me on the back when they discover that Simeon, who translated the Hebrew prayer book they use into English, was my great grandfather. "You have a great heritage my boy!" they say, and I feel ashamed that I know so little about that heritage, for most of Simeon's children – including David, my grandfather - abandoned their father's faith early in their lives. They remained loyal to the family. David, his sister and brothers, went to lunch every Sunday with Simeon and their mother in their tall, dark, heavily furnished home at 52 Leinster Square. They may have abandoned his faith, but they were proud of him and proud of being Jewish; and they passed his story on to my generation.

Simeon, they told us, was a Rabbi – the son of a Rabbi who came from Hungary via Denmark to find in London a more toler- ant world. In earlier years Simeon and his growing family had a hard time in a poor parish – the Borough, in Southwark. To sup- port them he got part-time teaching work to add to the money his congregation provided. But he was eventually appointed as the founding Rabbi of the prosperous New West End Synagogue in Bayswater where he became a leader of the Jewish Reformed syn- agogues that conducted their services in English and allowed men and women to sit together in the congregation. It was for them that he translated the prayer book.

He was a scholar, a reformer, a community leader and patri- arch. He also had political connections: his father was related to Isaac Singer, a prominent German socialist, and he was a friend of Theodor Herzl, founder and leader of the Zionist movement, who is said to have first outlined his plan for setting up a Jewish 'national home' when staying as a guest in Simeon's house.

It's time to slow this story down and sift fact from fiction. Simeon's translation of the prayer book is the most widely used,

Simeon Singer

Simeon's family: David Singer on ground at left.

but it was not the first. His father was a business man, not a Rabbi. Simeon and his congregation were on the liberal, comfortable, assimilating wing of orthodoxy, not part of the Reform movement which came years later. He was a Minister or 'Reverend'. Strictly speaking, there was only one 'Rabbi' in Britain at this time. And although Herzl was a friend, Simeon disapproved of Zionism. No matter: the myths we weave around our heroes are the more revealing for not being quite true.

THE ISAACS

David Singer's wife, Isabel, was an Isaac, one of three daughters of Stephen Hart Isaac, an Englishman, and his beautiful Portuguese wife — whose picture supports this claim. There was unanimity among my forbears about the hero on this side of the family too. He was Stephen's father, my mother's great grandfather, Samuel Isaac. Take a look at his picture too: a broad man with a big beard, luxuriant side-whiskers and a confident, smiling charm. Sam was known as "The Major". He was — we were all told — the engineer who designed the first big tunnel to go under a river: the four-mile long railway tunnel under the Mersey — a pioneering professional from the heroic age of engineering; and his son, Stephen, was an engineer too.

This story is also partly a myth.[1] For Samuel was not the engineer but the entrepreneur who spent years putting together the capital and building the enterprise that made the Mersey tunnel. He was a bit of a chancer, some would say, enjoying prominent roles and playing for high stakes. Advancing from trading to manufacturing — particularly of boots made with new, mass-production methods in a Northampton factory — he helped to found and lead the local Volunteers there (hence his title, "the Major"), built a fountain (now demolished) in the town's main square, played a leading role in the local synagogue, and tried, unsuccessfully, to get nominated as a Conservative Parliamentary candidate.

Samuel Isaac: "The Major"; Sime Isaac, Isabel's mother

Winning big contracts to supply the Army, Sam Isaac engaged – in those days probably had to engage – in dubious dealing (a big, unsecured loan to the official responsible) and was lucky to escape disgrace when that official decamped with the money and his mistress to America and the whole scandal was investigated by a Parliamentary Committee and a Commission. Excluded from further contracts with the British Army, Sam then supplied the Confederate side in the American Civil War – his blockade-running ships sometimes getting through, sometimes being captured. When the Confederates lost he went bankrupt because the bonds in which he had been paid became worthless. But he soon bounced back (the Isaacs always did) and eventually gained his greatest fame by building the Mersey tunnel. Gladstone, the Prince of Wales and other Royals attended celebrations of this achievement which included a procession through the tunnel and a banquet held in the middle of it. The first railway engine built to haul trains through the tunnel was named "The Major". (It now stands rusting in New South Wales.) He died, rich and applauded, with an imposing London home – and the tunnel company went bankrupt a few years later.

Sam had a brother, Saul, who worked with him in their early days, but set up on his own in Nottingham after the defeat of the Confederates. There he, too, went bankrupt, but soon recovered and acquired, as his main enterprise, a new coal mine on the edge of the town. He lived nearby in a great house surrounded by gardens, and became the first Jewish Conservative M.P., soliciting votes with an election address fulsomely supporting Church schools and other symbols of the establishment. (Disraeli was elected earlier, but his father had taken his family into the Anglican Church, so is not regarded as Jewish by Jews.)

Their cousin, Nathaniel Isaacs (he added an 's' to their name) was an even more colourful figure. He was sent off in 1822 at the age of fourteen to stay with an uncle in St Helena. The voyage, under a drunken and brutal captain, took four months. Three years later, at the age of seventeen, he made friends with a passing naval captain who took him to Natal — then barely explored by Europeans. There he fought in a local campaign, was wounded but recovered, made friends with Shaka, the Zulu chief, and secured a large grant of land from him. Thereafter, he did business in and around Africa for many years, generally basing himself beyond the areas where British officials regulated trade, and eventually came home to spend his affluent, declining years in Liverpool. (If all these cousins and uncles seem a bit confusing, their family tree will make things clearer. See page 34.)

Through the middle of the nineteenth century, Britain's Jews were concentrated in London, where there were thousands of them, with much smaller communities of a hundred or two — often less — in provincial cities. Most of these people were craftsmen and small traders. The leading figures in London were a "cousinhood" of rich, assimilated, respectable, intermarried families with worldwide connections — Rothschilds, Montefiores, Salamons... Towards the end of the century everything changed as successive waves of refugees poured into the east end of London from Russia and Eastern Europe — poor people speaking no English. Then, in the 1930s, came the refugees from Germany followed by others from all over occupied Europe.

Joseph Roth, in *The Wandering Jews*, a celebration of those who came from Eastern Europe, writes a tirade against comfortable, assimilated Jews who "no longer pray in synagogues... but in boring temples where the worship is as mechanical as it is in the better-class, Protestant Church... well-bred, clean-shaven gentlemen in morning coats and top hats, who wrap their prayer book in the editorial page of the pro-Semitic, liberal newspaper in the belief that it will attract less attention that way... And on top of that, they're proud of it! They're lieutenants in the Reserve..."[2] Those shafts were, I think, aimed at people like the Isaacs and the Singers.

The bewhiskered Isaacs — forceful, charming buccaneers — were ideally equipped to prosper in the time of Britain's most rapid industrial and imperial expansion. They lived on the fringes of the "cousinhood", striving to gain entry to it and to the English establishment. Starting as traders and manufacturers in places like Liverpool, Nottingham, Northampton or Chatham, and frequently operating in Britain's empire, they moved in their later years to big houses in London.

Comparisons with Melmotte, in Trollope's novel The Way We Live Now, and later with Robert Maxwell – "Captain Bob" – are irresistible. But we should not assume the Isaacs were any more unprincipled than the average entrepreneur of their times. It was a rough world in which they had to make their way, and those who lacked the ability, the chutzpah or the luck to cope with it had a hard time. Nathaniel Isaac "of Chatham", a younger brother to Samuel and Saul, was a small-scale dealer and Army supplier who got into difficulties, conned money out of various people, ran away to Dover when he realised that his misdeeds had been discovered, and poisoned himself in his lodgings before the police arrived. He was 22. Saul's elder son, Frederick Hart Isaac, shot himself (accidentally, it was said) in the grounds of his father's house on the outskirts of Nottingham at the age of sixteen.

Sam's son, Stephen Hart Isaac, Ruth's grandfather, was not in fact an engineer but helping to manage his father's coal mine when he married the beautiful Sime Seruya from Portugal (pronounced "Simmy"). They had two children and then his wife – staying with her mother in Lisbon to have a third baby – died in childbirth. Shortly after, Stephen too died, at the age of 27 –"of a broken heart" the family said; but his grand daughters grew up believing he killed himself.

Financially, Stephen's three girls were well provided for by older members of the family, but the loss of their parents scarred them and, in time, their children too. Isabel, Ruth's mother, was sent with her older sister Alice to be brought up by their Isaac grandparents (The Major and his wife) in London at 31, Warrington Crescent, Maida Vale. The new baby (named Simi after her mother) stayed in Lisbon where she was brought up by the Seruya grandparents. The two girls in London were raised by governesses under the spartan Victorian regime their elderly grandparents must have been familiar with. (Ruth later recalled a visit to the most important of these governesses, who seems to have favoured Alice over Isabel. By then long retired, she was "a Scottish lady... a critical, cold character of old-maidish habits and little affection".) Their grandfather died when Isabel was eleven or twelve, their grandmother grew frailer, and by the time she was fourteen Isabel was running the household – hiring servants, directing their labours, and sleeping in her grandmother's room so that she could be constantly available to care for her. Ruth recalled that "she never spoke of the house with any affection, although she lived there for more than twenty years".

Isabel and her sister were sent to Simeon Singer's Saturday scripture classes where they made friends with his two rather unruly sons, Julius and David. Isabel managed to get herself to a secondary school and then to London University's Bedford College for Women. She completed two years of a science course and left without any qualification. She was pretty in a dark, petite way, and made the most of social opportunities, forming a life-long friendship with Harriet Chick (later "Dame Harriet", a distinguished scientist who was a pioneer in the discovery of vita-mins). Meanwhile her sister Alice became increasingly involved in suffragette and radical politics, and Isabel too picked up some of these interests. Simi, who had grown up in Lisbon, came to London as a teenager and shocked the whole family with her wild and passionate Latin manners.

SINGERS: THE NEXT GENERATION

Isabel and Alice married the Singer boys. David, despite going to the City of London School, left at fifteen with no qualifications. He got a job licking stamps and running errands as a clerk in the City, and moved on two years later to a stockbroker's firm where his natural abilities were recognised and he gained steady promo-tion. He was the only member of his family who ever made serious money, and he became the lynch pin for his generation; caring for his mother after Simeon died, and supporting his brothers when they got into scrapes or needed help. He married Isabel in 1899 and Ruth was born next year. Five other children followed but two of them died, leaving four surviving sisters: Ruth, Eleanor, Barbara and Evelyn, each quite different, but all vivid, strong characters, and the three younger ones strikingly beautiful.

Their mother's affection-starved childhood had left her incapable of giving the simple, unconditional love that every family needs somewhere at its heart. She was restlessly demanding and censorious – and still was when, as a small boy, I used to go and stay with her thirty years later. Ruth suffered particularly. Perhaps because she had a pronounced squint in childhood and was less attractive than her sisters, perhaps because of the death of the longed-for brother who was the next in the family, she always knew she was "a perpetual disappointment" to her mother. "She delighted to recount the successes of her friends' children in contrast to my failures". Till her dying day Ruth would recall humiliating incidents of her childhood with undimmed bitterness.

Isabel's ultimate weapon when defied by her children was to threaten that a party or some other treat would be cancelled if the offender refused to obey. Ruth soon learnt the power that every small child has, and was prepared to forego anything – let the heavens fall – rather than give way. When, at the age of five, she was sent on her own to have dinner with her revered grandfather, the "Rabbi", he asked her to "thank God for my good dinner" after the meal, but she refused. They never said grace at home. Simeon said, "Very well, we will wait till you feel able to"– and they sat in silence till three o'clock before he conceded defeat.

Ruth developed real affection for Miss Griggs, the governess who was later so hurt by being invited to the goats' farewell party. She was a good teacher, but Ruth's sister Eleanor thought the poor woman gave Ruth little warmth, describing her as "a long, thin, breastless virgin". Years later, when she reproached their mother for neglecting Ruth, Isabel replied "But she had Miss Griggs" — "which was just the point" Eleanor commented.

The younger sisters seem to have developed a self-protective comradeship, or perhaps they were luckier with the nurses and governesses hired to look after them. Some of these women were good people, but one was a sadist who beat and terrorised her charges until another servant blew the whistle on her.

Gwendolen, the third Singer daughter, suddenly developed appendicitis at the age of five and was operated upon by a surgeon in a tail coat on the nursery table — the room specially sterilised for the occasion. (In those days the middle classes did their best to stay out of hospitals.) She died five days later. Next year, Eleanor, who had adored Gwen, developed similar symptoms which frightened the whole family — Eleanor most of all, I guess. She survived. But thereafter, as a "delicate" child, any hint of illness focused everyone's attention upon her and excused her all duties — a pattern which further alienated Ruth. (In fact, Eleanor was to live longer than any of them, dying in the year 1999 at the age of 95.)

This was a successful, intelligent family with "advanced" ideas — affluent, atheist, athletic (the girls and their parents learnt to swim, to ride bicycles, to ski and play all sorts of games) and politically progressive in a cautious way. David, his daughters believed, continued secretly to vote Labour, even when he became a member of the governing Council of the Stock Exchange - MacDonald Labour I guess. Isabel had her scarf of suffragette colours — which remained carefully folded in her drawer.

Living in a big house, first at 20, then moving to 19, Lyndhurst Road in Hampstead, the Singers must have seemed a very fortunate family. They had lots of servants, and were one of the first to have a telephone, electric light and a car — with a chauffeur to look after it. David liked the look of a Panhard but before buying it insisted that a driver should be sent with him to try it out. Turning out of Finchley Road into steep Netherhall Gardens, the car ran out of puff and stalled. There was no way it could be persuaded to mount the slope till the driver turned it round, put it into its lower

David Singer

21

Ruth and her Singer grandparents

reverse gear, and triumphantly backed up the hill. So David bought it.

But it was not a happy family. They had a growing number of unmentionable topics, including everything to do with sex and death – their grandfather's, and that of sister Gwen and their only brother Stephen (named after his Isaac grandfather). "Three days after he was born" Ruth recalled, "I was told that he had gone to heaven. A few days later I asked when he was coming back from heaven. It was conveyed to me that I had trespassed into some uncomprehended mystery – something which I ought to have understood that made grown-up people cry. Fear, horror and shame assailed me and I never mentioned the subject again. I still have no idea why he died." Later, during the war, the deaths of young men from neighbouring families who had been their friends were accepted in silence and never discussed. The mysteries of sex were revealed, however, when Ruth and Eleanor found a wonderful book in their mother's library called "*The Physiology of Human Reproduction*" which told all.

The girls' clothes were equally oppressive. Ruth remembered them vividly. "Although our dresses were beautifully made, specially for us, they were always hidden under an overall during the day or a pinafore in the evening. As for underclothes, we wore layers of them. In winter there was first a body belt of natural-coloured Jaeger wool, over which came a pair of long sleeved combinations of the same wool, with legs to the knee. Then came a home-made bodice of white cotton, to which buttoned white, calico knickers with frills round the knees. Suspenders attached to the bodice kept up the long black woollen stockings. For every day we wore blue serge knickers over white cotton 'linings' and probably a kilted blue serge skirt buttoned on to a second bodice, with a red or blue jersey on top. For best..." But need I go on? Little wonder that Ruth longed to be a boy.

David Singer, the girls' father – a gentle, hard-working, generous man – must have lived in an emotional desert. He eventually moved out to stay in his club during the week for considerable periods. Then, as one daughter after another became nubile, he seems to have developed an innocent passion for each of them in succession – and was quite hostile to some of their young suitors. For the rest of their lives each was convinced that she had been his special favourite.

Ruth made friends with the children of neighbouring families and eventually found marvellous freedom in a good boarding school – Wycombe Abbey – where demands on her to work were less severe than at home, and good teachers applauded her progress in just about every academic subject, and in music and games. It was an Anglican school to which the girls had to bring a prayer book and bible. Although her mother chose all the schools the girls went to she refused to buy these books for her – perhaps with a last twinge of remorse for abandoning Judaism. So Miss Griggs provided them.

DONNISONS COME ON THE SCENE

At Wycombe Ruth found she could make more friends, some of them for life. Margaret Hope, who gave her the powder compact as a parting gift, was one of these. Earlier, in her primary school, she had found a shy young boy of her own age – Vernon Donnison – who wore shorts and sandals. They formed an unspoken pact against the noisy crowd and went occasionally to each other's homes at week-ends. This link was maintained during school holidays through their teenage years.

The Donnisons lived down the hill in Highgate. Frank, their father, had inherited his father's shop in the City, selling pens, envelopes and notepaper with printed letter heads to passing customers and to firms such as the stockbrokers in which David Singer had become a partner. They lived in "a rambling old house on West Hill called 'Hohenstein'" Ruth recalled, "and had a wonderfully happy, free life and lovely games. I don't think they were ever told to be quiet, as we incessantly were. Vernon's little sister, Yseult, ran barefoot everywhere, and no-one was ever 'naughty' –

not even me. At home, try as I might, I earned that epithet every day, often without knowing why."

Ruth's contact with the Donnisons was renewed when, in her last year at school, their daughter Yseult came to Wycombe where her parents visited her on every permissible occasion – three times a term: quite unlike the Singers. Once they brought Vernon, by now a young officer in the Grenadier Guards on sick leave after getting diphtheria in France but due to return soon to the front.

From Wycombe Ruth moved on to University College, London, to work for the first MB examination and entrance to Cambridge. There, in the medical school, she made more friends. One of them was Annis Gillie, another first-year student (who later became a distinguished doctor) with whom she managed to sneak into operating theatres to watch the surgeons at work. Life at home, where she lived for the year, was as loveless as ever; but on Saturday nights she would go to the Donnisons where ten or twenty young people would gather for music and dancing – Vernon's father, Frank, playing wild, old-fashioned waltzes on the piano. Vernon would escort her home across Hampstead Heath. On 14 July, 1919, Ruth spent all the money she had taking him to the Russian ballet at the Alhambra Theatre. Afterwards they went out through London where "there were great crowds of happy people, some of them dancing in the streets".

Before starting at Cambridge Ruth was taken by her parents to spend several months in a *pension pour jeunes filles* in Paris, run by a duenna who promised to teach her charges French and introduce them to the culture of this great city. But as soon as parents had left Madame revealed herself to be "hard and mean", imposing "galling chaperonage" and forbidding any contact with the French. Many years at Lyndhurst Road had prepared Ruth for dealing with women like this. Despite her increasingly angry disapproval, Ruth sallied forth to meet friends of her family, learn French and explore Paris. The friends included the Tchaikovskys – the old man was a relative of the composer and a socialist moderate who had been deported by the Tzars and imprisoned by the

Bolsheviks. Ella Paresce was another contact; also a Russian – a fine pianist who taught Ruth much about music. And there was the Lwow family. Their father was in charge of a mental hospital and his two sons seem to have fallen for Ruth. She became engaged to Andre and I have the letter she wrote to her parents asking their blessing for their marriage. Vernon never knew about this and the plan was soon abandoned. Perhaps Ruth's father dissuaded her? Andre Lwow became a distinguished scientist and many years later Ruth saw the report of his Nobel prize in the Times. What Vernon recalled was that she came home, speaking good French with a Russian accent, adding that: "She had gone to France a somewhat four-square schoolgirl. She returned fined down, an attractive young woman, with a developing confidence and taste in matters of dress." He was now a student at Oxford.

At Cambridge, where Ruth entered Newnham College in 1920, she "had freedom such as she had never enjoyed before, living in a beautiful city; and above all there were friends... young, natural, enthusiastic and from cultured backgrounds." She struck another blow for freedom by switching to a natural sciences degree. Medicine could be tackled later. Her mother expected all her daughters to become doctors, and two of them did; but Ruth felt natural sciences would be more interesting and offer good ways of making a living. She was increasingly determined that she must soon find a way of leaving home. She also got involved in a lot of music, became President of the College Music Society, and for two years played lacrosse for Cambridge. A fellow student described her as one of those who broke away from long hair and long dresses to wear calf-length skirts and bobbed hair. With "dark curls and pink cheeks", clad in "dazzling orange", she must have been a striking sight. [5]

Love for Vernon was filling a growing part of her life, steadily enlarged by walking and cycling trips, joint family holidays, and an unforgettable ball at Oxford. They got engaged in 1922, provoking a good deal of dismay in both families, shortly before Vernon set off to join the Indian Civil Service. Ruth, with her

College's blessing, abandoned her plans for becoming a doctor and set off to join him the following year. She felt that as a woman with the rare privilege of a Cambridge education she should not lightly discard this ambition. So she brought her dilemma to her tutor who showed great understanding, assuring her that what she had learnt would be useful wherever she went. She set off next year, her course unfinished, to join Vernon in Burma.

Meanwhile, at home, Ruth's father had been carrying the burdens of family leadership. As his father Simeon had become established more money became available for the education of the younger children. Richard, David's younger brother, became a barrister but got into trouble of some sort that compelled him to emigrate to New Zealand. The Empire was always a refuge for "black sheep" in the Singer and Donnison families, but no-one ever explained what sins they had committed. David kept in touch with Richard, providing money occasionally. In time Richard did very well as a lawyer – representing people in the most scandalous divorces of that small society. Then his high spending habits, funded, it was said, by dubious use of clients' money, compelled him to take flight to Australia. There, in his last years, he made yet another career, taking the parts of elderly characters in some of the first Australian television dramas. The buccaneering spirit of the Isaacs seems to have re-emerged in Richard. Isabel would never allow her brother-in-law's name to be mentioned in the family. It was said that he had once made a pass at her.

Charlie, the youngest of David's brothers, presented a different kind of problem. He was a brilliant young doctor, fluent in Latin, Greek and Hebrew, who became fascinated by the history of medicine when he found in an antiquarian bookshop a volume that showed that the circulation of the blood had been discovered before Harvey's famous work which is usually assumed to have been the first to propose this theory. To pursue that ambition, Charlie – who had been earning a little money by serving as a ship's doctor – would have to become an academic, and in those days that called for a private income. Universities did not pay enough for a family to live on.

The wealthy Waley Cohens had a daughter, Dorothea – a chunky, spirited little woman who later became a scholar in her own right. But she was, in Ruth's brutal words, "the ugliest thing that ever stepped". (I remember her well and would find it difficult to contest that.) The Singers knew the Waley Cohens and David helped to negotiate a dowry from them that would make his young brother financially independent. Charlie said it wasn't enough, and the offer was increased… and increased… again and again. Ruth remembered her father stamping around the house in fury, saying "Charlie's a fool! Charlie's a fool! He'll never get any more!" Eventually he settled, signed a 68-page marriage contract, married Dorothea, and a great series of pioneering works on the history of medicine and science eventually appeared. Dorothea did quite a lot of the research that went into them. But Ruth could never take her uncle as seriously as the scholarly world did.

A BRIDE OF EMPIRE

It is time to return to Ruth and Vernon on the deck of the *S.S Pegu* with the sun rising on the Rangoon river. They came ashore at 9am. that morning, Sunday 2 December, and were met by one of Vernon's friends who had an ancient Ford in which he took them to the flat of a senior official; Reynolds, the Forest Secretary. He and his wife would be Ruth's hosts. Greetings and drinks completed, his driver took them out to the Mingaladon golf course where they went for a long walk – alone together at last, and in a very appropriate place: "Mingaladon", she said in her memoir, "means the hill of marriage". (Actually it means something more like "the city of good omens". No matter: the myth may be as important as the truth.)

Next morning was filled with shopping and a visit to the dentist for Vernon who rarely came to Rangoon from the distant District where he was stationed. Then in the late afternoon they remembered that for their wedding next morning they would need a ring, and hurried, just before closing time, to jewellers who eventually found one that would fit Ruth's slim finger. It was engraved for them and delivered by hand late that night.

"At 9 am. next morning we gathered in our hosts' flat – me in the long, white, embroidered silk dress my mother had insisted I wear for the occasion – together with the Registrar and five others. Oaths were administered, we signed and the witnesses signed, and in about three minutes, at a cost of four and a half rupees, we were man and wife. About 50 guests came to celebrate with us – mainly top officials of our host's seniority. It was daunting to meet so many important people. The wives had come to assess what kind of woman was to join their ranks but the men were more interested in local politics. We cut the wedding cake which my mother had had made for us: two tiers crowned by a white sugar elephant – her idea."

There followed much packing – mainly done by San Hla, Vernon's Burmese servant who had come with him to Rangoon. He had looked after Vernon like a father for the past year. "Suddenly he appeared, holding a little red velvet box in his hand and saying sternly to Vernon 'Last night there was a gold ring in this box. Now it has gone. What have you done with it?' We showed him it was safely on my finger and he forgave us.

"Then began the journey to my new home: first by car to a small launch in which we travelled for two days up river to Bassein – San Hla cooking for us in a tiny galley – and then for nine days in a larger houseboat, pulled by a launch tied alongside it. The Commissioner for the region, who was Vernon's boss, had loaned us the houseboat – and his wife had personally supervised its preparation for us, furnishing it with cushions, potted plants and even a black kitten for luck.

"The nine days we spent travelling to Kyonpyaw were a delightful introduction to my new country. Europe faded away behind us. Everyone we saw was Burmese. Gliding gently along the waterways we would stop now and then if Vernon had an inspection to make or if a local headman wished to see him. His chief clerk intercepted us, bringing a basket of papers which had accumulated while he was away. He also brought Boojie, Vernon's Bassein hound, to join us on the house boat. In the evening the brilliant daytime sky gave way to the short, cold-weather sunset, streaked with red, yellow and pale green. Fireflies flickered in the hedges along the banks of the river, and delicious cooking smells rose from thatched houses. Beyond them stretched always the paddy fields.

"Our only problem was the house boat's bedroom. It was broad enough, stretching right across the boat, but the beds were narrow, iron structures, bolted to the floor at least two yards apart, each tightly enclosed in a mosquito net hung from poles which squeaked horribly with every movement. I recalled my mother's dark warning that, where love is concerned, 'Man proposes but God disposes'. For the present it seemed that God and man were to be in agreement – but not with us."

CONCLUSION

These young people, aged 24 and 23, had left the London world of cash for the colonial world of power. The resources available to them, the people they could command and what they could ask of them, all depended less on money than on their position in a power structure.

What brought them together in this place? The story I have told may suggest some of the answers to that question. Here I shall focus on Ruth. She was deeply in love with Vernon, and remained so until she died 45 years later. Despite the long separations they had to undergo, I don't think either of them ever looked with serious sexual interest at anyone else. But that poses the same questions in a new way.

Why fall for this man? Because he was loyal and kind, enjoyed exploration, outdoor adventure, music, learning new languages - and getting to know new societies and giving them some leadership. All these were things that Ruth wanted too. He would also take her a long way from a home that offered her little love. (Her sister Barbara's memoir often refers to her in childhood and youth as "poor Ruth".) The younger Singer girls were happier than she was in Lyndhurst Road, but it may be significant that Eleanor, her next sister, went to work in California for a while and Barbara, the next, went to Berlin – both much further from home than they would seem today.)

Ruth was also making a choice about the kind of people with whom she wanted to throw in her lot. The repeated references in the story to friends who were scientists, musicians or scholars, to people she described as being "natural, enthusiastic and from cultured backgrounds" – all these were code words, not just for class but for a certain kind of middle class person. Two stories, recalled by her son David, provide a clue to their meaning. When he was about thirteen his mother said – only half in jest – that in her family "everyone had to get a good education. Otherwise you could only make money – like poor father." And when, on some occasion, young David expressed admiration for the Jews she replied, rather sharply: "But you only know the professors, doctors and musicians – nice Jews. There are Jews of quite different kinds – business people who are grasping and vulgar."

I'm sure she did not deliberately lie about Sam Isaac and his son Stephen being engineers and Simeon Singer's father being a Rabbi, when all three were business men. Nor, perhaps, did her parents. But somewhere in their minds lay the wish to suppress painful memories of the ruthless world their forbears had climbed out of to join the kinds of Jew – indeed the kinds of middle class people - they wanted to be. The horizontal distinctions of that time between different kinds of middle class people were as important as the vertical ones between different social classes. Apart from a few sons of well-established fathers, usually in the City of London, business scarcely ever recruited university graduates.

The tradition continues today. In his scholarly and heart-warming Simeon Singer Memorial Lecture, the Rabbi now in charge of Simeon's Synagogue lists his children. Those who entered, or married into, the liberal professions are each mentioned. David disappears among the remaining three who are "said to have gone into the commercial world".[+]

Why did Vernon and Ruth go to remote colonial places? For generations the British had grown up with the assumption that there were large parts of the world – most obviously in India, Africa, the West Indies and the white colonies – where they could travel freely and reasonably safely, speak their own language, find work and gain the help of friendly authorities if in trouble. Ruth's family had been on a long holiday to India, and they had friends there who used to call on them when on leave. They saw the Empire as a place that offered more adventure, more freedom and more fun than an office, a surgery or a college in a smokey British city. It also offered a refuge for friends and relatives down on their luck who needed to escape and start afresh. "Asylum seekers" in those days went from Britain.

The willingness of people who regarded themselves as politically progressive – radical even – to go out and rule other nations may today seem odd. But the Empire had its progressive myth – a story in which men much like Plato's Guardians had a duty to raise up the wild and ignorant people of the jungles and turn them into civilised men. Kipling's stories and poems are full of it. This was the early 1920s, before the British Government made a firm commitment to work towards a hand-over of power – which, it still assumed, would retain former colonies in what later came to be called the British Commonwealth of Nations. Canada, Australia and New Zealand were the white models for this process. It was not till the 1930s that large numbers of progressives began to link their campaigns for the liberation of oppressed people at home – women, the unemployed and casual workers – to campaigns for the liberation of colonial peoples. George Orwell began writing his fictional indictment of empire, *Burmese Days*, at this time; but he did not publish it till 1934 – in the U.S.A. The first anti-imperial article printed by the *Observer* – flagship of

Britain's liberal press – did not appear till 1942. Orwell wrote that too.[5]

All of this can be better understood as we turn, in the next chapter, to the training of an imperialist.

NOTES

1   For my story about the Isaacs and the Singers I owe a great deal to Michael Jolles' monograph on Samuel Isaac, Saul Isaac and Nathaniel Isaacs, 78, Greenfield Gardens, NW2 1HY, 1998.

2   Joseph Roth, *The Wandering Jews*, London, Granta Books, 2001; pages 21– 22.

3   Ann Phillips (ed.) *A Newnham Anthology*, Cambridge, Newnham College; page 139.

4   Rabbi Geoffrey L. Shisler, *The Life of the Rev. Simeon Singer*, London, New West End Synagogue, 28 March, 2004.

5   The reluctance of Western radicals to take up the anti-colonial cause was clearly set forth by Edward Said at many points in his book, *Culture and Imperialism*, London, Chatto and Windus, 1993.

RUTH'S FAMILY

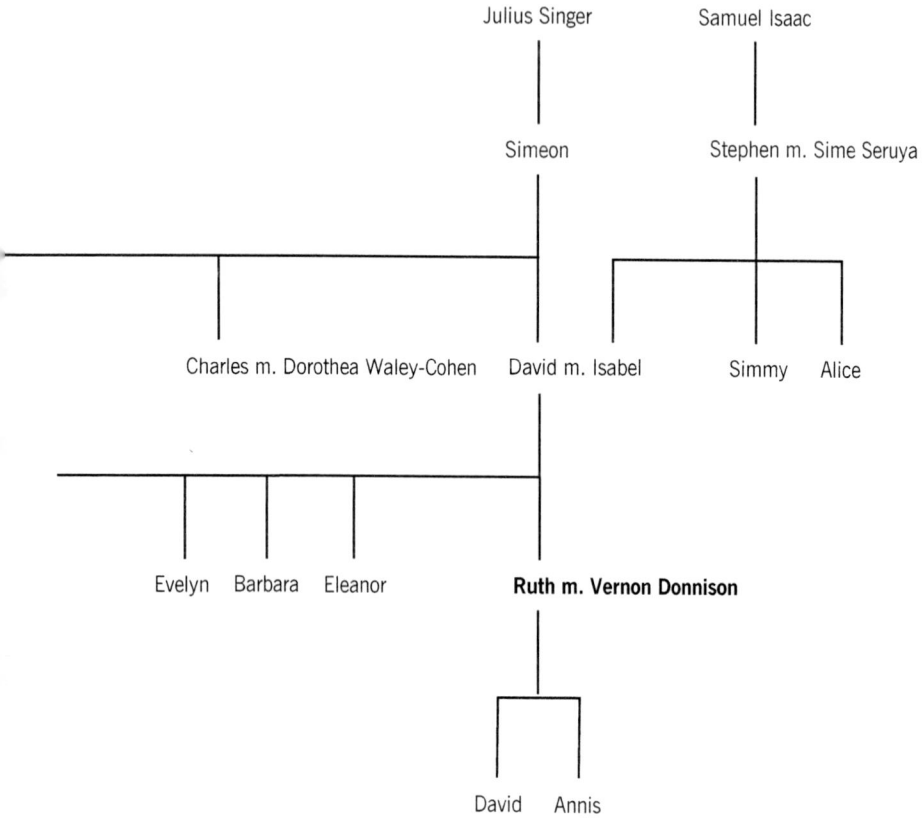

VERNON'S FAMILY

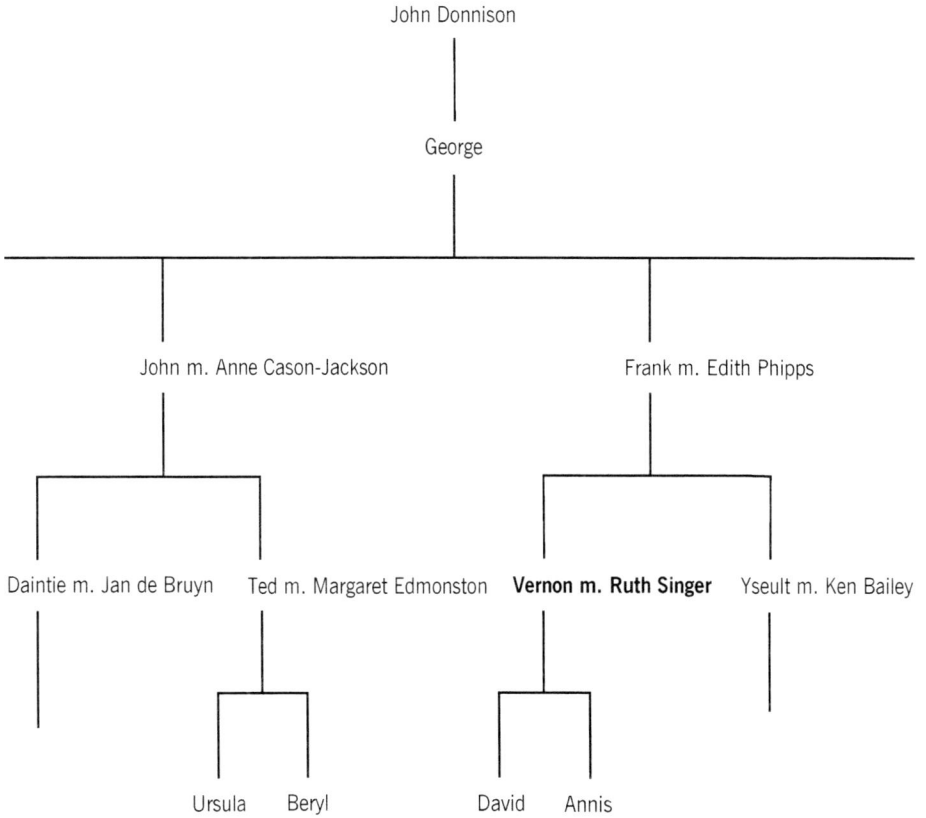

John Donnison

George

John m. Anne Cason-Jackson

Frank m. Edith Phipps

Daintie m. Jan de Bruyn   Ted m. Margaret Edmonston   **Vernon m. Ruth Singer**   Yseult m. Ken Bailey

Ursula   Beryl   David   Annis

II

AN IMPERIAL TRAINING

How did it come about that the shy ten-year-old boy sent to a progressive school, unusual in 1910 for taking girls as well as boys – the boy first noticed by Ruth because he was wearing shorts and sandals and had rather long hair – set out for Burma a dozen years later to play his part in running the British Empire? To answer that question we have to know something about his family, their origins and myths.[1]

THE DONNISONS

Frank Donnison, Vernon's father, was one of the oldest of the ten children of George Donnison. George had inherited the stationer's shop set up by his father, John, at 20, Wormwood Street in the City of London – close to Broad Street Station. It was a solid little business, for the Donnisons were wholesalers as well as retailers and printers as well as stationers, and George was eventually made a "freeman" of the City. When I came to live in London in the 1950s 'Jno. Donnison & Son' still marched in bold white letters across the shopfront, although it had become a branch of a larger firm many years before that.

Frank expected his brother John, named after the founder of the business, to take over the shop. But John, described to later generations as 'the black sheep of the family', went off to India. What exactly he had done to compel a flight to the Empire was never revealed to us: something, perhaps, which today would scarcely raise an eyebrow. He must have been a robust character,

George Donnison

George Donnison's family:
Edith & Frank in front at left; John standing by his father.

38

fort he settled in Bangalore, famous as an Army town in the south of India, and lived, unmarried, with the estranged wife of the Commissioner of Police. (A risky step, some would think.) Her name was Anne, and they had two children: a son, Teddy, and, eight years later, a daughter, Daintie. John was an athlete, being at one time tennis champion of Southern India. After working for a big firm he set up a shop of his own. He died of anthrax in 1920, caught in the classic way from the hairs of a shaving brush. Anne had by then taken up with another man – a policeman or army sergeant (perhaps both?) She lived on for many years, coming finally to London where she is remembered by her grand-daughters as a dark, forceful woman, partly Indian, who was said to have been matron of an Indian hospital ship during the first world war (or was that another myth?).

The shop in Wormwood Street must have done well under George's management because Frank was sent to Bishop's Stortford school which Vernon, his son, later described as "a minor public school of non-conformist outlook... very undistinguished and little known". Distinguished or not, its contribution to Britain's economy may have been greater than that of many more prestigious establishments. Among Frank's contemporaries there were a boy called Cooper, famous later for his Oxford Marmalade, and another called Colman, famous later for his mustard. After the first world war, Vernon, then in his early twenties, noted that the school had "emerged from its obscurity" – not because of the marmalade and mustard but because its boys had won "a number of 'Blues' at both Oxford and Cambridge" – meaning they had played the principal games in matches between these Universities. No other University counted.

The Donnisons lived on the sensitive, shadowy boundary between England's middle and lower middle classes. Frank, along with some of his brothers and sisters, spoke with the received pronunciation sometimes described as a public school or Oxford accent. Other members of the family "spoke common". All of them were chapel people – Congregationalists, who are a venerable group, founded in Cromwell's time. George must have played a respected part in their affairs for they gave him a silver salver, engraved with his name and their gratitude, which was eventually given to Vernon and may now grace a shelf in a Japanese family's home, or - more likely - a Burmese home since few of the Japanese escaped from Burma with their loot.

When he left school Frank wanted to be a musician. But, with John gone, his father insisted that he work in the family shop, which he reluctantly did, living at home with his parents and a crowd of brothers and sisters at 66 Grosvenor Road in Hackney, and bicycling to Wormwood Street each day. He hung on to his music, however, making almost a second profession of it. He gained qualifications as a pianist, became a Fellow of the Royal College of Organists, taught singing, and became organist and choirmaster for the Congregationalist chapel in Highgate which paid him £50 a year to add to the £150 he got as salary and commission from the shop.

The Donnisons seem to have been about as solid and unremarkable a family as you could find – living in London since the seventeenth century and probably earlier. That's why I know less about them than I know about the Singers. The further a family has travelled across the face of the earth, the more stories they have about their forbears, for it is the family's myths, not the place where they are living, that give them their identity.

EDITH

Edith, who was to marry Frank, was different: a woman wrapped in myth and mystery to this day. They met in 1887 when she was 21 and he was 24. She sang in the chapel choir and probably came for singing or organ lessons that he was giving at the time. Before long they were going to concerts and dances together, going boating on the river in the reaches above Hampton Court, and going to Old Stortfordian social occasions. She came to one of the huge Christmas parties the Donnisons used to hold in the Craigside

Hydro at Llandudno — taking more than thirty friends and relations with them who were brought to Euston station in a specially hired horse bus, and then to North Wales by train in a "double saloon coach" reserved for the party.

Edith was striking rather than beautiful; lively, romantic and — in the old-fashioned sense — gay. At this stage of her life she was living for much of her time in Germany. Three years after their first meeting Frank spent more than he could really afford going to meet her there, in order to propose to her. They went on a long walk from Schwalbach to Hohenstein, which they never quite reached. She accepted him; and their homes, when they eventually got married, were called "Hohenstein". Edith came to stay briefly with the Donnisons in London. Next year there was another shared German holiday (chaperoned of course) and in 1892 Frank moved out from his family's home to rent a house in Highgate at 18 Southwood Lane where he hoped they would set up together. But, despite much pleading, he could not persuade her to marry him till 1894. Why the delay?

Edith was born in 1866 in Barnsbury Grove, Islington. On her birth certificate she was called Edith Moore and the birth was registered by a Miss Lucy Moore who described herself as Edith's mother. No father was mentioned. When Frank met her she was called Edith Phipps, and always told the world that this was her parents' name. Both, she said, had died when she was very young. Her mother may have married a Mr.Phipps, but she seems to have been brought up by a couple called Mr. and Mrs. Fincham, and later to have lived for some years in a "home for little girls" in Finsbury Park — whether as a "little girl" or as a member of staff is not clear: both, perhaps, at different times? At some point, her letters record, she ran away — from this home perhaps? None of the people who cared for her had much education; but the biggest influence in her life was a man called John Sykes — a solicitor with an office in Grays Inn. He took her out occasionally, accompanied her to the continent for holidays, and left her there at various times to study music, French and German, and Italian painting.

He described her in his will as his "adopted daughter" and she called him her guardian – or, more privately, 'Papa", although no legal adoption has been traced. Her visits to various parts of Europe show there was money behind her – as did a spell in South Africa where she was sent for rest and sunshine when it was feared that she had tuberculosis. Whether Sykes was her father or acting for him we cannot tell. One or the other, I guess.

Edith was certainly devoted to this shadowy figure and insisted that she and Frank must have his permission before they could be married. But Sykes made it clear that he expected her to marry someone of higher social status than Frank, and for a long time refused even to meet him. When at last Sykes' resistance softened, Edith refused to marry – *and* refused to break off the engagement. "It seems" said Vernon later, "that she wanted romantic love untarnished by sex." Finally, for reasons Sykes and the young couple seem to have clearly understood but never revealed to anyone else, the wedding *had* to be in Germany – or, failing that, in some other foreign country. And the German authorities made difficulties because the name on her passport differed from the one on her birth certificate. Finally, the marriage was performed by the British Consul at Baden-Baden in 1894 – seven years after they first met – and they came back to set up home together in Southwood Lane. Even then, said Vernon "I think it is clear that the sexual act was denied my father, except on the very rarest occasions. My sister and I were clearly birthday presents to him, our birthdays being on the same date five years apart, and 274 days after his birthday. I have often wondered whether they ever enjoyed the sexual act on any other occasions."

Edith, to her dying day, told romantic tales about her origins. She had aristocratic forbears she hinted; coming from France...Germany...Scotland. The stories kept changing. Perhaps some of them were true? Her social aspirations for her children were limitless. Vernon was to be an ambassador; Yseult, her daughter, was to marry someone very important. She was appalled when she chose to marry an Australian friend of

Vernon's — Ken Bailey, who later became a law professor, then his country's Solicitor General, High Commissioner to Canada, and eventually a Knight. To Edith he remained a colonial. "That *terrible* country", I remember her saying. "*How* Yseult has aged in the past twenty years!" As an old lady, when I knew her best, her snobbery was still monumental. Winston Churchill, she was convinced, had turned Communist. Living by then on a pittance, she insisted that she only needed a raw carrot and a little brown bread each day. Once, when the baker's boy came on his bike to deliver her loaf at the garden gate, she returned spitting with anger. She had given him her order for next week and he had pedalled off, cheerfully calling "Right-O!" (Not "Yes, madam".) "*I* can't understand why the working classes are so rude to us these days" she said. "*We* speak to them just as we did fifty years ago." A Lady Bracknell of the lower middle class, Oscar Wilde would have loved her.

In 1900, when Vernon was two, the Donnisons moved up the hill into a larger house at 6 Holly Terrace, in Highgate. It was to be his home for the next twenty years. He remembered it later as "an unusual one: my father a middle class non-conformist Christian, brought up in a conventional home. My mother educated sufficiently to have ideas but not sufficiently to approach them critically. She fell a victim to everything that was 'progressive', however ill-assorted: pre-Raphaelite painting, William Morris furnishings, 'rational' dress, abandoning the hour-glass corsets that she, like other women, had previously worn in favour of 'greenery-yallery' clothes from Liberty, vegetarianism, the music of Wagner, Votes for Women, coeducation… A romantic, but also a determined social climber, she had no real religion but attended church because it was customary to do so — and Church rather than chapel because the congregation was socially superior." Her children's names breathed these Germanophile, romantic aspirations: Yseult and Frank Siegfried Vernon.

"So much of this", Vernon later came to understand, reflected the fact that "she had no parents or home to grow up with; she was brought up in a lower class world but gained occasional glimpses of a grander, more spacious one through her guardian, enabling her to imagine what life could be like at higher social levels. Yet, if she was in some ways ill-equipped for life, she was gifted with exceptional energy and drive. If a job needed doing, it would be done – perhaps not in the most efficient way, but long before one had thought possible. My father took all these fads and crazes with resignation – sometimes even with conviction. When her chatter became too exhausting he withdrew to his piano."

When his father died Frank had to take over "the business" as the shop was called. He worked hard but was not very good at it. Keeping it going was a constant worry to him. Those worries must have been increased by the kind of household Edith expected to assemble around her. Vernon again: "I had a French nurse and spoke her language before I spoke English: the first step, I suspect, on my way to becoming an Ambassador." (It may also suggest that his mother did not talk to him a lot.) "The next step was a German governess"; a succession of German governesses, in fact; one of whom – Elly Wehrbein, nineteen years old when she joined the Donnisons – became a lifelong friend to whom he attributed his "liking for, and proficiency in, the German language, his liking for things German, and many other good things beside."

Like Ruth, Vernon seems to have relied heavily for affection on women hired to teach and care for him. Like Isabel Singer, his mother's upbringing had left her ill-equipped to give the steady, loving support that every family needs at its heart. Vernon never showed to me the kind of anger that Ruth felt towards her mother. He just said, rather coolly, "We choose our friends. Our relatives are chosen for us."

The extensive circle of Donnison aunts, uncles and cousins seems to have been kept at bay most of the time – particularly those who spoke with cockney accents. But one encounter should be recorded. Uncle John's lady, Anne, turned up in 1908 with her son Teddy. He and Vernon, both aged ten, were sent off to play while the grown-ups took tea. Vernon later recalled Teddy's mother as being Indian – indeed, wearing a sari. But the figure he remembered may have been an Indian ayah or nurse? Anne took English names for herself and her children. They soon returned to India, and – for 25 years – Vernon forgot all about them.

Meanwhile, despite a certain hollowness at its centre, this family had a lot of fun. There was music in the house every day. Vernon said "my parents were very fond of dancing, particularly the old fashioned waltz. From time to time they had small dances in our drawing room, my father playing the piano much of the time but occasionally calling to be relieved so that he could have a dance with my mother. Later, when I was reaching twenty, there were informal Saturday night dances for me and my sister and our young friends. When we had finished there would be biscuits and fruit squash. There was no alcohol and it was all very unsophisticated, although we wore our dinner jackets." They also had great holidays, going several times a year by train to a cottage they rented on the east coast, and often visiting Germany in the summer.

Eventually, "the time approached for me to go to my next school. The custom of the period ruled out a state school, and indeed the education provided by many of them would have virtually excluded the possibility of going to a university – greatly reducing employment opportunities thereafter. Bedales would have been a 'progressive' place to go, and was indeed considered; but my mother's snobbery overruled this. She was determined that I should go to a well known public school. What led her to pick Marlborough I do not know. My father felt that all this was flying rather too high, and rather too expensively, but my mother got her way – as she generally did." There was nothing sexist about her choice: five years later Yseult was sent to the equally prestigious girls' boarding school to which Ruth had gone.

MARLBOROUGH

"I had been sent to a good school for the wrong reason, and was there put on the classical side, again for the wrong reason" – snobbish reasons.

Vernon was a diffident boy who had occasionally been bullied at his primary school. He had never been away from home before and was at first very homesick. But even in his first term he showed courage for a thirteen-year-old. Asked, with all his class, to write an essay about his previous school, he wrote a forceful account of the value of teaching boys and girls together. His form master was so impressed that he was given a "copy" – a special distinction which meant taking his work to the headmaster who asked him to copy it out in a book kept for such occasions.

Classics were harder. His progressive primary school had not taken Latin or Greek seriously, and, although he came top or near it in every other subject including French and German, the ancient languages defeated him – which was painful, for he was well aware that, if you wanted to be among the best in this kind of school, it was in classics that you had to win your spurs. Weak though his Latin and Greek were, the culture they imparted must have got through to him. Central to it were the ideas of Socrates and Plato, most vividly conveyed in *The Republic*, Plato's prescription for the good society.

Democracies, Plato believed, were plagued by conflict and eventually fell under the heel of criminal tyrants. His ideal republic would offer something better: a society led by a small elite of philosophers – the "Guardians" – selected, mainly from the children of other Guardians, for their "philosophic disposition, high spirits, speed, and strength", who would be trained for their role over many years. They would feed in communal messes, own no property, and have no home or family ties. "Women and children are to be held in common among the Guardians".[5] Indeed, children should not even know who their parents were – a thought which may have served as a preparation for the early and prolonged separations endured by the children of Britain's imperial officials.

Next in rank came the "auxiliaries" – the soldiers, policemen and executive officers who worked under the command of the guardians. Thirdly, there were to be merchants, farmers and artisans – the only people permitted to accumulate wealth. The labourers and slaves beneath them did not merit serious attention.

These ideas were not only of academic interest. In India the British had found a society already divided along these lines by cast – awaiting only the arrival of the Guardians supplied by the Indian Civil service.

Plato's was to be a pretty tight-lipped society. "Magnificent myths" (described as "noble lies" in some translations) would be created about the origins of the state and to mark ceremonies of birth and death. But not art: "The work of the painter and of all other representative artists [is] far removed from the truth" [4] and "the only poetry that should be allowed… is hymns to the gods and paeans in praise of good men; once you go beyond that and admit the sweet lyric or epic muse, pleasure and pain become your rulers instead of law and … rational principles…"[5]

Hitler and Stalin came close to creating a world much like this, but the British Empire had similar features. This was no accident, for the public schools, which trained men for imperial service, were in many ways a microcosm of *The Republic*. No democracy there; but great respect for those who had "high spirits, speed and strength" – and a good classical education. The boys slept in long dormitories, fed in communal messes, and were separated from women and family. Marlborough's "magnificent myths" were reflected in the names of eminent old Marlburians, inscribed in gothic gold letters on a purple background, which covered the walls of the great chapel attended by the boys each morning. These names commemorated soldiers, diplomats, colonial administrators and other senior officials – Guardians of the empire – together with a few politicians, and even fewer artists, musicians and business men: the "merchants and artisans" whose sons were presumably expected to go to schools like Bishop's Stortford.

Vernon's performance in classics – described in one of his school reports as "chaotic" – eventually got him reclassified as a history specialist working in a small form of six to eight boys under Pat O'Regan, a teacher who specialised in ancient history. Indeed, Vernon recalled, he had designed his house on the model of a Roman villa and "would demonstrate the working of a Roman *ballista* by shooting lumps of sugar from a model of this weapon at his wife's best crockery. I was probably the least quick-witted of this group (Beverly Nichols was one of them) and O'Regan soon made me feel this. A scholar of Balliol himself, his final condemnation of me was that I had 'a Cambridge brain'." (For historians, that meant a brain better equipped to assemble piles of facts than to speculate about their meanings.) "He gave me a lasting sense – probably well-deserved – of mental inferiority."

Ralph Gidney, Vernon's house master and another classical scholar who "exuded integrity", thought better of him than his form master, making him head of house. Later, after Vernon had left the school, they became life-long friends.

I have dwelt on the influence of the Greeks, but the Romans played a much bigger part in the myth of empire imparted to Vernon who would have learnt (as I did at the same school, a quarter of a century later) that a British history worth recording began with them – the great civilisers; keepers of the peace, and builders of towns, roads, baths and drains. Other subjects in the curriculum, through the works of Shakespeare, Kipling, Housman and many more, reinforced this story. Like Vernon, we were taught that the Irish, poor things, never benefited from Roman discipline; but nothing was said about the Celtic civilisation the Romans destroyed. Nor were we taught that the Roman empire was amassed by an army, hungry for land to reward its officers, for recruits to fill its ranks, for loot and for tribute; or that their campaigns slaughtered thousands of men, women and children – 80,000 in one sweep through northern Britain. It was not pointed out that the Romans only gained a secure grip on lowland

England, and even there (unlike Gaul where their influence ran deeper) the towns had always to be walled. Nor did anyone tell us that, although their rule lasted for 400 years, they left little to us at the end of the day but words in our language, some ruins, some genes, and Christianity – which was not their invention. (The British legacy to the Burmese was equally thin.) The Latin that Vernon and I laboured over did not include Tacitus' description of Roman imperialism:

Auferre, trucidare, rapere, falsis nominibus imperium atque ubi solitudinem faciunt pacem apellant.

Looting, killing and raping – by twisting their words they call it "empire"; and wherever they have created a wilderness, they call it "peace".[6]

Once the natives had been subdued, the Romans ran their empire as they ran their army: by recruiting and training the natives to do it for them, and rewarding those who loyally served them. This was the model adopted by the British.

The First World War began a month after Vernon's sixteenth birthday. The senior prefect in the last peace-time term was killed in action before the next term began, and thereafter the dreadful casualty lists mounted month by month. "Everyone said it could not be a long war because of the destructive powers of modern armaments. No one had foreseen the ghastly stalemate of trench warfare produced by their very deadliness. As one's senior, and then not so senior, contemporaries left to join the fighting services, one came face to face with the fact that one's turn was approaching."

The school's Officer Training Corps, previously regarded as a bit of a joke, was soon taken very seriously. Hating the dreary routine of square-bashing parades, Vernon joined the Signal Section and became the sergeant in charge of it. In 1915 he volunteered to spend part of his summer holiday training signallers for the 20th London Regiment, then in camp at Tadworth in Surrey. "Each of sixteen platoons was required to detail one man to join my Section. They consisted of a number of expert signallers – Post

Office telegraphists and such — and the rest were the platoon duds conveniently unloaded onto me. I did what I could with them, although it probably did me more good than them."

His school days were drawing to a close. What had they given him? He concluded later that the teaching was rarely inspiring. It offered too little encouragement to think for himself. He learnt to live in an orderly, disciplined community and to give some leadership. "I enjoyed and gained much from my games, including such self-confidence and ability to deal with personal relations as I have acquired". He got no music or art, but gained a love for "the sweep and solitude of open country — the strongest heritage that Marlborough gave me." A lonely inheritance but a Guardian's training.

"I was not very successful in making friends — indeed I have none left from my contemporaries there; partly because so many were killed in the war. Friendship was a lesson that I did not learn until Oxford." This slightly chilling conclusion was, I suspect, due as much to Marlborough's capacity to respond to him as to his own to cope with them. To describe himself as not so "quick-witted" as Beverly Nichols says more about social poise than ability. This rather shy boy, who learnt to mask his feelings and only came fully alive on the rugger and hockey fields or in the solitude of the Marlborough Downs, must have seemed a bit odd to the average Marlburian.

Coming from a family that had to struggle to pay his fees, he was embarrassed when his parents visited the school, which they did twice a term — more often than most. "I felt ashamed of my embarrassment. They dressed strangely and behaved unconventionally. I knew that some boys laughed at them. On these occasions I felt that they were definitely lower middle rather than middle class."

THE ARMY

Because Vernon wrote so well about his time in the Army I have constructed this section almost entirely from his own words.

"I did not know what I wanted to do in life, but I was perfectly clear that I did not want to be a soldier. I was not a pacifist and, if I had been, it would have required greater moral courage than I was endowed with to stand out against the pressures of public opinion at that time. I was not courageous, and I dreaded physical pain and death. But I looked big and mature and, walking down Tottenham Court Road during the holidays, I was given a white feather by a woman. I was too young to know what to say.

"So why did I get myself into the Grenadier Guards – classic 'storm troops'? The distinguished uniform of an elite corps, the flair of the Household troops, snobbishness acquired from my mother – all probably played a part. More important, I think, was a sense that if you enter any profession you aim to join the best. But it would not have occurred to me to aspire to these heights had I not discovered that Christopher Nash, a friend from my primary school who had gone on to Bedales, had joined the Grenadiers. Would it be possible to do this, I asked him, without a private income? Not in peace time; but I was assured that in war this would be no barrier. It did not occur to me that Chris, as the son of Prime Minister Asquith's Secretary, was better equipped than me for the circle we would be entering.

"I was accepted as a Second Lieutenant on 1 January 1917 and began my training at Chelsea Barracks – close to the haunts of London high society, which enabled officers to live at home and come to work each day on foot or by cab. Highgate was a good deal further off, but near enough for me to stay with my parents, which was cheaper than living in barracks. It was also a concession to my diffidence and shyness which was probably a mistake. I would have done better to get used to communal living in an army mess – although nothing was likely to change my lifelong distaste for clubs, pubs and the social life. We did 'square bashing', and were instructed about hand grenades, Lewis guns and gas. Every six weeks we did 24 hours of guard duty at Buckingham Palace or St. James's Palace, and once I commanded the small guard that was sent to the Bank of England.

"I found myself in a world hitherto unknown to me. Most of my brother officers were Etonians and rich; many bearing names already famous or soon to become so. I remember a good-looking, witty, gallant young officer with an M.C. – Harold Macmillan. There were Osbert and Sacheverel Sitwell, the former flabby, grey and grumbling, the latter tall, grey and gangling but more cheerful. Our Commanding Officer was Lord Francis Scott, pale and limping from a severe wound – later to become the spokesman of Kenya's aristocratic settlers. Lord Edward Hay was a harsh martinet in charge of young officers learning their drill. Stuart Montagu, later to become Lord Swaythling, joined on the same day as I did and asked me whether he should sign himself into the register as 'The Honourable'. There was also a charming young Virginian who had been an American Rhodes Scholar at Magdalen College and felt it was his duty to join, although his country was not yet at war – Bill Fleet, who paid with his life for this generous gesture. Later, in France, my commanding officer was, for a while, Lord Lascelles who was to marry the Princess Royal; and I glimpsed the Prince of Wales – later Edward the Eighth – visiting from Guards Division Headquarters. I was interested in this world, but too shy and too undistinguished to get drawn deeply into it.

"By July I was off to France with six hundred men and their officers, marching to Waterloo Station, then by train and ferry, and another march of five miles on cobbles behind a solitary piper of the Scots Guards to a camp commanded by Captain Boyd Rochfort, V.C., who, in private life, between drinking whisky, trained the King's race horses. There I was put through a gas chamber with a mask on, and allocated a servant – slightly to my embarrassment. Then we moved on closer to the front, where I joined the third of four battalions. The first three were regular battalions and the Guards were proud of the fact that they had only added one more battalion – unlike other regiments which had been enormously expanded, with all the watering down of standards that involved." Most of the men, however, were new to the Army because casualties during the war were well over 100 per cent of the original numbers in the Brigade.

"In due course we were moved up to hold a sector of the front line, near Langemarck, recently gained at terrible cost in the abortive Passchendaele offensive of 1917. There we entered the rotational routine of five days in the front line, five days in support, five days in reserve, and then back to the front line. One night, as we were picking our way in single file along duck boards that wound between shell holes and pools of muddy water, German shells burst around us. It was my first experience of close shell fire and I instinctively dived for a shell hole, but a sergeant close behind me said 'Steady Sir: The men are watching you' – and I kept going, grateful always to him, and to the Metropolitan Police in which he served in civil life.

"Another day, in bright sunlight, I and my runner were lying prone in our platoon headquarters which was a shattered German pill-box – one side blown away – and I had to take my tin hat off, placing it on the ground beside me; there wasn't room even to sit up. German shells came over, a 'whizz-bang' exploding just outside, and when the dust settled I saw a jagged hole in my helmet.

"I remember, too, Stephen Phillimore, Chaplain to the Battalion, who preached in such an exaggerated, upper class, parsonical accent that no-one could understand him, wandering coolly in the open along our front line trenches, handing out drink and cigarettes from his pockets to the men: a gallant man who had won the M.C. – universally loved and respected in the Battalion." (Many years later, Vernon took me and my sister to visit "The Honourable and Venerable Stephen Phillimore" – making it clear to us that this old man was to be treated with respect.)

"Pulled out of the line for rest and training, we were inspected one day by Douglas Haig and some French Generals. I remember my platoon sergeant's warning shout: 'There's umpteen blue coats and brass hats and gawd knows what a-comin' along... and take that smile off yer face, that man!' Every night our drums and fifes played retreat, marching and countermarching up and down the main street of the village in which we were billeted with all the smartness and precision they would have given to mounting guard outside Buckingham Palace. So the Grenadiers had played retreat in similar villages throughout the 'cockpit of Europe' – a hundred years before under Wellington, two hundred years before under Marlborough.

"Then we were marching southwards, with no idea where we were going. It was to take part in the Cambrai battle where tanks were first used in yet another abortive attempt to break through the trenches into open warfare. As usual, before the attack, the number of officers in each Company was reduced to three – a precaution forced on us by the terribly high rate of casualties, to ensure there was a framework on which to rebuild the Battalions afterwards. I recall being furious and miserable because I was sent back to join the Battalion Transport Officer with his horses when they discovered we had one officer too many. I was later brought forward again to help extricate the mauled remains of the battalion. Of the twelve officers who had led their men into battle only three were not dead or wounded.

"Through much of the winter we were holding a section of the line near Arras – a cold, grey, miserable period. Then, in the middle of March 1918, still in the front line, I developed a sore throat and a desperate feeling of weakness. I remember walking from one fire bay to the next on my rounds, and having to sit down after each to recover sufficient strength to walk on. Our Medical Officer diagnosed diphtheria and I was ordered back to hospital – walking some way, and then I dimly recall a bumpy night ride on a stretcher in an ambulance, a field hospital, an ambulance train, and then another hospital where I spent three weeks. Although I was recovering, they said my heart had been affected and I must go back to England for some leave followed by light duty.

"The beauty of the English country under April sunlight was mixed with recollections of the world to which I would soon be returning and guilt that I was not there already. Seeing Ruth was a happy accident. I remember her as a serious girl with whom I talked about books and some of my experiences of war. She said she would write, and indeed she did, sending me food, a muffler she had knitted and a marvellous book – Fielding Hall's *The Soul of a People* about Burma. Neither of us at that stage had thought we would be going there.

"A few days later I rejoined my Battalion in France – before Cambrai again. Most of the young officers I had served with had been killed. We moved into our jumping off positions, lying out in the open with the town burning, its towers outlined against an orange sky. Near dawn the advance began. There was the great noise of our barrage. Suddenly we realised that nothing was coming back at us. As daylight came and our guns stopped firing we walked, unopposed, out of the ploughed-up zone of trenches into almost undamaged country. I remember my surprise at seeing houses still standing. At this moment the cavalry came through, looking like something out of a picture, to fan out and exploit the breach in the line – their harness and accoutrements jingling. It must have been one of the last occasions when mounted troops went into action in Europe.

"The Germans were retreating, but they were far too good soldiers to break up. Sporadic stands and sharp counter-attacks slowed our advance. On one of these occasions I was required to lead a patrol under cover of night across a stream and into a village to find whether the enemy were still there. We searched one or two houses and found no-one, but then, when we got into the village street, there was the flash of rifles and the crack of bullets striking sparks off walls and cobbles. One of our patrol was hit and fell. Having discovered the enemy was there, my orders were to get my men out. This we did, without further loss but in some disorder. For many years after, my failure to bring our casualty back with us lay heavily on my conscience. The Regimental history records that I led this patrol 'with gallantry'. That was not what it felt like. But for me this was the end of the war."

Vernon was sent back to take a signals course while his Battalion continued in pursuit of the Germans – one of their officers being killed on the last day of fighting before the Armistice was signed. He then went on another course to equip him to become the Battalion Education Officer who would keep the men occupied while they awaited their release from the Army. The course took place at Oxford. While there, he went to visit the President of Corpus Christi College and noted that he was duly impressed by a Grenadier's uniform. By the beginning of the summer term, after a spell of duty at the Tower of London, he was out – and off to become a student at this College.

"We all came home from the war full of the feeling that we had learnt great lessons from the experience. Looking back, I am not so sure. I did not need to be taught that I was not endowed with great courage and did not want to be a soldier. I learned something of the *panache* that makes the Guards what they are and carries them through daunting situations. I learned to distrust all staff officers and much of the higher command; learned the value of comradeship and perky, cockney humour in times of trouble; and learned that it is not essential to have eight hours in bed every night. I learnt, too, about the virtues that make a man, and – above all – that these are not confined to any one class. We also came out of the Army determined there should never again be a war".

OXFORD

Starting at Oxford, Vernon "remembered lying alone in a punt in the New Cut of the River Cherwell, the sky a golden sunset glow, the water still and luminous with the fading light, a line of poplars tall and black against the sky, and feeling a deep thankful-ness flow through me – that I was alive, that I was in this meltingly lovely place, above all that life held a future again. This heaven-sent summer term brought a reprieve from early death, release into a wider world of the mind and spirit, an opportunity to read, to learn, and make good friends." He was twenty; entering a College which at first had only 49 students – building up later to a full strength of no more than 80 – men just back from the war, drawn from all the services and most of their ranks. The novels and films that portray the Oxford of the inter-war years present a picture of languorous, gilded youths, moving with elegant wit from party to party. Vernon's Oxford was the real thing.

"I did not take my work very seriously" he said, explaining that he read history for the practical reason that it offered him the best chance of satisfying the examiners and getting a job. His tutor, Mowat, seemed interested in him: a Balliol man like O'Regan at Marlborough, but he never dismissed him for having a "Cambridge brain". He gained a second class degree, which made him very happy because he had never aspired to anything more. "I remember with particular pleasure the look of relieved surprise on Mowat's face when he congratulated me."

It was the games that really lit up Vernon's life. He played virtually all of them, and played them well: hockey (for the University for two seasons), rugger and cricket for his College, and occasionally tennis and soccer too; and, rather accidentally, he took up rowing, helping his college eight to do outstandingly well.

Vernon's father had said he could pay him £50 a term, which just covered his fees and College bills. He also had an ex-serviceman's grant of slightly more, and some £200 saved up from his time in the Army which he hoped to hold in reserve. This meant he had to be very careful. The only University club he joined was the Musical Union which enabled him to go every week with good friends to concerts. Sometimes his father joined them. Later, he "fell to the flattery of being elected to that exclusive, athletic club, Vincents, where almost everyone was a blue." But, in general, "We led much simpler, less sophisticated lives than have since become the fashion. I don't think any of us ever thought of having alcohol in our rooms – certainly none of my close friends did. Cocoa or tea were the extent of our conviviality of an evening. Even the great Leo Price, invited to play rugger and hockey for England on the same Saturday, flew no higher than cocoa made by some special formula of his own with 'condenny' – condensed milk."

"The greatest thing that happened to me at Corpus was that I seemed to have learnt how to make friends. I liked many people and had the feeling that many liked me, and I kept in touch with my five closest friends for the rest of our joint lives." One was Ken Bailey, an Australian Rhodes Scholar, who married Vernon's sister. Girls, too, played an important part in his life, for he went dancing whenever he could; but Ruth was the one he was becoming increasingly interested in. She went to Newnham College, Cambridge, during his second year, and came over for dances, rowing races and similar occasions from time to time. All his friends accepted her warmly – which was more than some of his closest relatives did.

Britain, despite the mixture of races in its vast empire, was at that time an almost entirely white country. But while Vernon was at Oxford his parents took in a young Tibetan, Riksin Dorje Ringang, as a paying guest. He was one of four Tibetan boys brought to England by the India Office to give them an English education – starting at Rugby. "Payment received from the India Office for Ringang was a help at a time when the family finances were going through a lean time. That the paying guest was a rather exotic oriental tickled the romantic side of my mother, and somehow made the whole business of taking in a P.G. socially more acceptable. 'Rixie', as we called him, was an attractive young man and we became very good friends. I have little doubt that this early friendship with an oriental had its effect in laying the foundations for the many Burmese friendships which were to mean so much to me later. After leaving Rugby, Ringang trained as an electrical engineer, still making his home with us." He returned eventually to Tibet, and became an official in charge of a hydro-electric power station, a civil servant, a magistrate, and official interpreter to the Cabinet – and, in the stories told by Vernon's mother, a Tibetan Prince.

As the end of his time at Oxford approached, Vernon had to find a job. He did not want to go into the kind of stressful small business that his father ran, and big business was at that time recruiting few graduates. Wanting to do something challenging and of real value to the community, he looked to government service of some kind – overseas if possible. As in the days when he was choosing a regiment, he bid for the most prestigious, trying first for the Diplomatic Service. They turned him down. The Sudan Political Service did likewise: they only accepted Oxford and Cambridge "blues", and, although Vernon had played hockey for Oxford through two seasons, he had been dropped towards the end of each year, just before the match with Cambridge. So he tried for the Indian Civil Service and was invited for an interview. There he was led on to talk about the desirability of political reforms – which, however, should be "gradual" – which seemed to be the expected answer. But "I was dismissed without feeling that any personal contact had been made. Then, just before I got out of the room, one of my interviewers said 'I see that you have played a lot of games; do you still keep that up?'. When I replied that I had been rowing in the final of the Thames Cup at Henley on the previous Saturday I was immediately called back for a warm and lively discussion of the race which some of my inter- viewers had clearly been watching. We seemed to part good friends, and when the results came out I was well up in the top half of more than twenty candidates selected for service in India and Burma". He chose Burma.

Plato would not have found these selection methods surpris- ing. We may laugh today at the emphasis they placed on athletic achievement. But, in Vernon's day, the best athletes expected to excel in several different sports, and still find time to become good doctors, classical scholars, administrators – or whatever else they wanted to be. They had not dwindled into professionals, training full-time for just one sport, as top class athletes have to be today.

That was in August 1921. It meant that Vernon had a job. Although he had to stay in Oxford for one more year to learn Burmese, Indian History and Anglo-Indian Law, he was already to be paid £300 for the year and could ask a girl if she would even- tually marry him. It was October before he felt sufficiently confident of his choice to ask Ruth, and she accepted just before returning to Cambridge. "Her parents objected, partly because I was not a Jew, but mainly because I was not their choice, and asked us not to publish our engagement – at least for a while." Vernon's mother was pretty unhappy too, for similar reasons, saying with disappointment, "I had thought it would be Nancy" (a family friend he kept in touch with for the rest of his life.) But his father seemed happy with his choice.

Next summer, as the time drew near for his departure, Ruth and Vernon agreed that she should complete her Natural Sciences degree in the following year while he learnt his job and got the hang of a new way of life. They hoped she would be able to join him in two years' time if, by then, they could afford to marry.

"We were always being told by Ruth's parents and their friends that we would not be able to live on my pay. This was thrown at us so often that at last Ruth asked her father 'On what income do you think it would be possible to marry?' After some thought he said, 'Well, my dear, I would not want to try on less than £3000'. My pay, on arrival in Burma, would be under £500 a year – which seemed like wealth to me. But I realised it must look different to a very successful stockbroker."

After Vernon's departure for Burma, Ruth's Uncle Charlie was mobilised to dissuade his headstrong niece from throwing herself away in that country. She was also invited to lunch by Mr. Lewisohn, a Jew who was head of the Indian Civil Service in Burma, then on leave. Over lunch in his home the big guns were brought to bear – but to no effect.

I will draw this part of their story to a close on a happier note. Vernon, as I have said, enjoyed dancing; and the really great occasions for this were the Commemoration Balls held by different colleges in a rotating sequence towards the end of each summer term. They began at about 6pm and continued, with music, food and drink, until about 6.30 am – which meant they were expensive occasions. Vernon went with Ruth in 1920, 1921 and 1922, sharing the costs between them. In 1921 he outraged the Corpus rowing coach because he was supposed to be at Henley in the final days of training for the races. He defied the rules, danced all night, and Ken Bailey picked him up at 6.30 am to carry him to Henley in the sidecar of his motor bike, just in time to take his place in the boat. Ruth came later by train to watch the races and Corpus, as I have said, reached the finals , there to be defeated by a Norwegian crew.

Vernon recalled: "I was embarrassed at Commem Balls by my parents who, though we thought them old enough to know better, were still very fond of dancing, loved the sparkle of these events, and could not well be left out. My father, ignorant of the niceties of fashion – and with a mind above such things – tended to wear a black tie when he should have worn a white tie, and once succeeded in getting himself mistaken for a waiter. However, such small things could not spoil our enjoyment of these occasions which linger still in my memory as the very essence of romance."

CONCLUSION

Why did the Empire pick Vernon? It was unlikely to recruit many of the young Etonians – his brother officers in the Grenadiers. If they did not have to manage their families' estates they could find a comfortable billet somewhere in the City of London. And anyway, after the holocaust on the Western Front, there would never be enough of them to administer this vast enterprise. So the Empire had to attract young men who wanted to escape from families, neighbourhoods and job prospects that were cramped or boring, by offering them work and a status that were more exciting, more prestigious and better paid. It looked particularly to those coming from schools and universities that trained them for imperial service – a training concerned as much with physical fitness, endurance, leadership and comradeship as with intellectual distinction: a Guardian's training.

Vernon, fired by his mother's ambitions for him, went to a school, a regiment and a university that provided exactly this kind of training. His intellectual abilities were never as modest as he claimed. He was in fact an all-rounder, learning several modern languages – later including Burmese – and showing considerable ability in all the other subjects he tackled, apart from Latin and Greek. He knew a lot about music, he later wrote five books of history which are still consulted by students of his subjects, and anyone who has read this chapter knows that he wrote well. He said he was not courageous, but it is those who know their fears and confront them who act with the greatest gallantry. However, it was as an all-round athlete and a soldier that he learnt to break through the glass ceiling of class distinctions that have so often held down Britain's working and lower middle classes. His selection interview for entry to the I.C.S. was a classic example of these selection procedures.

If this was why the Empire picked him, why did he pick the Empire? He could have found a job – safer, as secure and as well paid – in business, in school-mastering, in the home civil service and in many other occupations he did not trouble to explore. It may be because I am my father's son that the answer to that question seems obvious to me.

Although, with the clearer vision that hindsight affords, we can now see that Britain was exhausted – ruined – by the first world war, and that the people of India and in British colonies around the world were beginning to stir themselves to throw off the imperial yoke, she seemed during these years to be at the height of her powers. She held the greatest empire – covering one-fifth of the world's land surface and one-quarter of the world's population – she had the greatest navy and had played a central part in winning the greatest war that the world had ever seen. The old conviction, born of two hundred years' experience, that Britain tended to lose the first battles in a conflict but always won in the end, had proved yet again to be true.

For a young man who wanted to do something adventurous, to test his talent and endurance to the limit, to work with people who were the best in their field, to achieve something that would make a difference to the world – and perhaps to get away from a pretty stifling family – the Empire was a natural choice. There were many others like him. Among Oxford graduates at this time, those with the highest qualifications went – in rank order – to the Diplomatic Service, the Indian Civil Service and, only thirdly, the Treasury. The low priority given to – and sought by – Britain's manufacturing and trading enterprises was another warning of the clouds gathering on the distant horizon.

One of the many questions candidates had to answer on their application forms for entry to the I.C.S. asked them if they had any relatives who lived in India or Burma. Vernon answered "No". He had forgotten all about his cousin Ted.

NOTES

1   This Chapter relies mainly on the memoir written by Vernon.
    For the part of the story that deals with his parents' early lives he
    makes extensive use of several bound volumes of letters written by
    his father to his mother during the long years of their engagement.

2   I take most of my account from Plato, *The Republic*, trans.
    Desmond Lee, Penguin second ed. 1974.

3   Plato, page 246.

4   Plato, page 433.

5   Plato, page 437.

6   My rewrite of the myth relies heavily on Norman Davies,
    The Isles. A History, Macmillan 1999. The quotation from
    Tacitus appears on page 111.

III

HOW THE BRITISH CAME TO BURMA

How did the British come to be in Burma? (It's now called Myanmar.) What was the country like? And how did the Burmese feel about their conquerors?

I shall rely heavily on books by Vernon[1] and a dozen other authors, British, Burmese and American, to answer these questions. It is the Burma of the early 1920s and its history to that point that I shall be writing about, leaving later stages of the story for later chapters, and I shall use the names for Burma and neighbouring countries that Vernon and Ruth used. I describe the whole collection of peoples who live in this country as "Burmese", and the dominant group among them as "Burmans". Slightly confusingly, the language of Burmans is also "Burmese".

THE LAND AND THE PEOPLE

Viewed from Britain, Burma stands on the far side of India. It is wedged between the Bay of Bengal and the Andaman Sea which run north and south along its thousand-mile western coastline, and a great question mark of jungle-covered mountain ridges curling up from its north-western border with India, round its northern and down its eastern borders, first with China, then briefly with Laos, and finally with Siam. (See the map on page 66.) Lying between major powers behind these formidable natural frontiers, this has always been a buffer state. Burma had a brief imperialist fling when it attacked Siam in the 1550s, and then again between 1740 and 1820 when its armies spilled out into

Siam and India, and even defeated the Chinese. But through most of its history the country has remained isolated from its larger neighbours, sometimes leaning towards India, where its Buddhist religion originated, sometimes towards China, as in more recent years.

The Burmans themselves arrived in this part of the world in the ninth century and generally dominated most of it until the British came, apart from a period between 1287 and 1539 when the country was overrun by Shans – closely related to the Siamese.[2] The Shans' homeland is now on a high plateau on the north-eastern side of Burma. As in other buffer zones between great powers, the dominant group share their country with many others who have their own languages, religions and cultures: Mons, Karens, Chins and Kachins are some of the other minorities. About two-fifths of the country is high, often jungle-clad, and sparsely populated. In these highlands the people of neighbouring villages may have different origins and speak different languages.

Burma is about 1,200 miles long from its northern tip bordering China to its southern tip bordering Malaya, and 500 miles wide – about three times the size of Britain. Until the British built roads and railways, the main lines of communication ran along three great rivers running southwards from the highlands to the sea: the Irrawaddy, which is the longest and most navigable of them, the Sittang and the Salween. Most of the people have always lived in the plains these rivers flow through when they emerge from the hills. Upper Burma – the northern half of this mainly flat land – is hot, and for much of the year dry, with an average of 30 inches of rain each year. When the British came, this area – several weeks journey from the sea – was the main centre of population and power. Lower Burma runs down to a great steamy delta around the many mouths of the Irrawaddy where the rainfall averages 100 inches a year. That leaves two coastal strips – Arakan, facing the Bay of Bengal to the north west, and Tenasserim, stretching down to the southern tip of Burma –

BURMA (MYANMAR)

N

0   150km

INDIA

CHINA

BANGLADESH

Hkakabo Razi

Kachin Hills

Kachin

Yunnan

Kohima

Saramati

Myitkyina

Imphal

Chindwin

Ui

Tamu

Indaw

Sagaing

Myitha

Shwebo

Chittagong

Chin Hills

Chindwin

Mandalay

Maymyo *(Pyin U Lwin)*

Salween

Chin

Mt. Victoria ▲

Pakokku

Kyaukse

Shan

Bay of Bengal

Pagan *(Bagan)*

Meiktila

Thazi

Taunggyi

Yenangyaung

Kalaw

Yaunghwe

Akyab *(Sittwe)*

Magwe *(Magway)*

LAOS

Arakan

Magwe

Irrawaddy

Pyinmana

Kasah

Toungoo

Pegu

Sittang

Tenasserim

Karenni

Tharrawaddy *(Tharawady)*

Pegu *(Bago)*

Bassein *(Pathein)*

Thaton

Rangoon *(Yangon)*

Moulmein *(Mawlamyine)*

THAILAND

Indian Ocean

Gulf of Martaban

Mouth of the Irrawaddy

Tenasserim

Mergui *(Myeik)*

Main Map

Gulf of Thailand

which have a massive rainfall of 200 inches a year.[3] Thanks to plentiful rain and the rich soil deposited by its great rivers, Burma is very fertile, producing, in peaceful times, rice, teak, natural rubber, palm oil, silk, and a marvellous range of fruit and vegetables. It also has great mineral wealth – oil, tin, silver, rubies and other precious stones – and once had craftsmen capable of turning these into many useful and beautiful things. But, before the arrival of the British, trade was on a small scale, consisting mainly of rice, fish and salt brought up the rivers by boat from Lower Burma to be exchanged for cooking oil and cotton from Upper Burma; together with more local exchanges of vegetables, clothing, copper pots, pottery and knives. There was virtually no trade with other countries, and even the Kings of Burma and their courtiers knew little about the world beyond their borders.

The Burmans are the dominant people in the long, lowland core of their country, although many of the minority groups also live in these plains. This is a land of villages, each with its Headman supported by a committee of local worthies. Until the British came there was no large town. Buddhism, mixed to varying degrees with animist superstitions, has long played a central part in the lives of Burmans. Every village had its little monastery where saffron-robed monks educated the children, and offered counsel and some political leadership, living on donations of food that local people put in their begging bowls each day. Every boy – and more recently girls too – spent a period, ranging from a few days to many months, as a novice in the monastery.

Buddhism is not a religion in the Christian or Islamic sense but a way of life. The monks do some preaching, but mainly they perform rituals, offer advice if asked for it, and teach the children to read and write, to do simple arithmetic and to memorise Buddhist texts. It has been calculated that, long before the British came, "the proportion of people who could read and write was...far higher in Burma than in England"[4]. In this respect the Burmans were far ahead of Indians.

The more perceptive of the Europeans gained great affection

and respect for the Burmese. Vernon spoke for many of his countrymen when he wrote of their "warm outgoing hospitality",
their "sense of humour and... salutary sense of the ridiculous",
their "open and healthy attitude in matters of sex and all bodily
functions", and their "deep charity, [arising from] a keen consciousness of the indivisibility of human kind"; concluding that
"Christians of the West need to feel humility in the face of the
love and charity of the East generally and [particularly]... the
Buddhists of Burma." [5]

The minority peoples were mainly pantheistic animists and
mostly illiterate. They were more likely to accept the Western
invaders, to serve in their army and to adopt their religion, partly
for the good reason that, by pacifying the country, the British protected them from the dominant Burmans.

To many Western scholars, this seemed to be one of the most
equal societies in the world, without extremes of wealth or poverty, no big landowners, no feudal system and no clearly marked
social classes. All agreed that women had a status, self-confidence
and freedom very similar to those of the men. They owned property and traded in their own right. Divorce was easy and common.
Women were sometimes Headmen of their villages. Even their
clothing – a skirt and short tunic – was very similar to that of the
men.

This egalitarian story was roughly true during the years after
the British conquest. But the picture it conveyed was the outcome
of a succession of social changes, beginning with the reign, from
1853 to 1878, of the reforming King Mindon, who gravely weakened the aristocracy of his day in his attempt to create a modern,
centralised, bureaucratic state. His uncompleted revolution, coupled with damaging changes in the terms of trade arising from
the Great Depression of the 1870s, led to civil wars, growing
chaos, and finally to the British conquest of 1885. Coming from
India, the British tried at first to rule indirectly through local aris-
tocrats and gentry. This policy worked well enough among the
hill tribes whose chieftains could be treated like miniature ver-

sions of the Indian princes. But in the plains, among the Burmans, there were few effective leaders left – and some of those few were leading resistance to the invaders. So the British were compelled to create a new system, based on village Headmen and civil service administrators, which completed the destruction of the old ruling classes. Since those who had lost power were men, the women gained a greater share in it; but they were still much less literate than the men and played little part in political affairs. In later years this history was little known, even to the Burmese; partly because the British, when they entered Mandalay, burnt down the royal library – accumulated over centuries from countries all around – and stole many of Burma's most precious relics. Burmese nationalists of the 1930s and 1940s had to reinvent their country's identity and traditions.[6]

Although Burma's income in cash per head was much lower than India's, the more equal distribution of that income meant there was much less poverty in Burma than in India. The way of life might be simple, but land was fertile and plentiful, and famine – a constant threat in India – was virtually unknown.

The Burmese have often been described as "happy-go-lucky" people; capable of hard work in a crisis and for a cause they believe in, but unwilling to suffer the daily grind of unremitting labour demanded of coolies, factory workers and plantation workers. They were sometimes called the "Irish of Asia". This phrase may tell us more about British attitudes to the Irish than about the Burmese, but there were indeed some common features of the two societies at this time. At the core of each were peasant farmers whose work demanded massive effort at some seasons of the year, followed by slack periods when they could recover strength and hold what the Burmese call a *pwe* – which is a bit like a ceilidh, but with more professional drama and less audience participation. The strong sense of community in both societies was reinforced by a shared faith, and the need to rely on the help of neighbours for major tasks – to build a house or barn, to make a road or irrigate paddy fields.

All agree that, after King Mindon, Burmese central government was, by Western standards, appalling: tyrannical, corrupt, and often cruel. The Mons, who lived mainly in Lower Burma, had joined forces with the Burmans during the sixteenth century to rule the country from Pegu, not far from the coast. But in 1635 this alliance broke up and the Burmans, under a new King, moved their capital to Ava, 400 miles from the sea in Upper Burma, where the country was drier and less fever-ridden. Later it was transferred to Amarapura and then to Mandalay. These moves isolated the Burmese, reinforcing their conviction "that their palace was the centre of the universe, that building pagodas, collecting daughters from vassals and raiding their neighbours for white elephants and slaves was the essence of Kingcraft"[7]. The Siamese, who built their capital on the coast at Bangkok, were more aware of the changing world beyond their borders and coped better with it.

The power of the Burmese King, surrounded by his courtiers and family, was in theory absolute. He appointed regional governors who bought their offices and were expected, in return, to raise revenue for him while keeping as much as they could for themselves. They were changed frequently as rivals offered to pay more for the job. There was no rule of succession to decide how power should be transferred when Kings died. Since they might have a hundred or more wives and even more children, their "families" were not clearly defined. Kings nominated crown princes, but if their nominees lacked popularity or power, fighting would break out within the palace as soon as the old man had drawn his last breath, and the winning branch would slaughter the losers – men, women and children – in large numbers. Buddhist doctrines of non-violence were cast aside when power was at stake. This practice continued till the last years of the regime.

What Western observers often failed to grasp was that, in Burma, central government and the state were not as important as Europeans assumed they should be. The King's power was limited by the monks who wielded a good deal of authority over him.

Travel was exceedingly difficult, and most of his people probably saw neither him nor any member of his court in the course of their lives. When the British arrived, the main authority the people would have been aware of was their own village Headman. His post, if he did the job reasonably well, was hereditary. Most of the cultivated and settled land was privately owned – disputes about it being arbitrated by the local community. Justice was administered by local judges whose task was to reach a compromise that the parties concerned would be prepared to accept. Having neither police force nor prisons, they had no power to enforce decisions. Education was provided by the local monks who were fed and supported by the village. It was a very sophisticated system.

Another thing the West often failed to grasp was that the Burmans and their neighbours had no concept of a territory defined by national boundaries. A capital and a centre of power – that they understood. In good times the authority of the regime based in that centre might extend a long way; in bad times it did not reach far beyond the city walls. It was the British who eventually staked out a boundary through the jungles and mountains to keep out the Chinese, the Siamese and the French, and thus invented what we know as Burma – or Myanmar. That boundary encircled many power centres whose rulers lived at peace with their neighbours because that was part of the contract imposed on them by the British. If the British were ever to depart, power would again be up for grabs.

Meanwhile, Burma's villagers, as Vernon noted, were very difficult to oppress. People built their own houses and could take them down again in a day, load the timbers, their goods and children onto a bullock cart, and find another site within their empty, fertile land; or, if necessary, take to the jungle where they could survive and harass their oppressors. Their attitude to authority was asserted in a well-known Burmese proverb: "Fire, water, foes, robbers, rulers – these are the five great evils."[8]

ENTER THE BRITISH

The first European known to have set foot in Burma was Nicolo di Conti, a Venetian merchant who arrived in 1435. More Venetians followed, along with Portuguese adventurers and missionaries who already had a base in Goa. They possessed firearms and had no scruples about using them. From 1635 a new and more orderly phase began as the Dutch, British and French East India Companies took over from the freebooters.

The British, in every sense, came to Burma from India. That fact shaped the manner of their coming and the way they behaved while they were there, and finally played a part in their going. Britain's conquest was a gradual process taking about sixty-five years – a lifetime. A similar lifetime later, their rule came to an end. I will tell the story very briefly, taking it to the early 1920s, when Vernon and Ruth arrived, by which time the period of Britain's rule over the whole country was already more than half over.

The opening battles that led eventually to the British conquest of India were fought in the middle of the eighteenth century against local potentates and the French; mainly with Indian troops operating under British officers in alliance with other local potentates. It took another hundred years for Britain to gain mastery of the whole sub-continent through a succession of small wars – still using the East India Company, founded in the reign of Elizabeth I, as the instrument of its power until it was finally discredited by the disaster of the Indian Mutiny that broke out in 1857. Loosely accountable to the British Government, the Company was a trading enterprise, not interested in imperial philosophies or grand strategies. Plato's *Republic* was not on the bedside tables of its officials, and they had no master plan for the conquest of India. Their job was to develop a secure and expanding base for profitable business. Nevertheless this century of expansion imprinted clearly understood doctrines in British minds.

Britain could, and did, impose its rule over vast tracts of other people's lands — operating through an amazingly sparse sprinkling of its own officials and soldiers — provided the Royal Navy commanded the oceans of the world, preventing interference by other powers; provided the British continued to recruit and train loyal soldiers and junior officials from the people of conquered lands; provided sufficient taxes could be raised from them to pay for the whole enterprise; and provided the Empire's forward momentum was maintained and every setback and insult convincingly avenged. Britain's rule, once firmly established, was generally less violent and arbitrary than the regimes it displaced, but to keep their magic working the imperialists had to be constantly prepared to enlarge — never to surrender — their territory, and to kill people when necessary.

The conquest of Burma was a logical consequence of these principles — and the country was lost again as they unravelled. Burmese Kings were so ignorant of the strength and intentions of their new neighbours in India that they repeatedly provoked them in ways that were likely to lead to war. Early in the nineteenth century they sent armies into Arakan and across the Chittagong border into India. The British, anxious to protect India, to keep French influence out of neighbouring countries, and to open up an overland trade route to China, attacked them in 1824. It took two years, and the deaths of 15,000 British and Indian soldiers, to achieve a victory which compelled the Burmese to cede Arakan, Assam and Tenasserim. The British thereby took over most of Burma's coastline and made the Indian Ocean safer for their ships.

In 1852, after the successful completion of a war against the Sikhs which freed troops for a new adventure, a series of Burmese provocations, culminating in trumped-up charges of murder brought against two sea captains, emboldened the British to invade again. They eventually took over Rangoon, Pegu and the whole of Lower Burma, thus linking Arakan and Tenasserim and completing the annexation of the country's coastline. (The map on page 66 shows where these places are.)

After each of these wars the population in the annexed territory grew fast. People living in the area around Pegu doubled in numbers between 1852 and 1862. Similar increases took place in Arakan and Tenasserim. Three-quarters of this growth was ascribed to migration from independent Burma; the rest to rising birth rates and falling death rates. Conditions were better on the British side of the border. The British were happy enough with this inflow because they needed workers to expand the cultivation of rice to keep famine at bay in India, the navy needed Burmese teak for its ships, and the opening of the Suez canal in 1869 made a reverse flow of exports from Britain profitable too.

The third Burmese war began in 1885 when it appeared to the British that the Burmese were negotiating with the French, based in Indo-China, for trading concessions, arms and a military alliance. The Burmese King was young and weak, and the court was dominated by his ferocious mother. British military technology had by now outstripped their enemy's. They came up the river in boats and after nineteen days, and with the loss of only four men, brought Burmese independence to an end.

THE NEW REGIME

The British at first regarded Burma as another backward province on the fringe of India. They had been appalled by the barbarism of the Burmese court, and had learnt most of what they knew about the country from the frontier regions they had occupied since 1824. These were fairly primitive, and they attracted migrants with bad stories to tell about Burmese rule. British expectations seemed to be confirmed by their easy conquest of the rest of the country. They foresaw no difficulty in setting up an administration much like the one they had fashioned in India. The scale of this task did not seem daunting: Burma had fewer people, a smaller economy, and needed fewer officials than several of the Provinces of India. The British would create a secular regime – for they had little understanding of Buddhism and the role of the monks – in which Western ideas of law and order, education and industrial enterprise would in time take root.

Things were not to be so simple. Once it dawned on Burmese villagers that the invaders intended to stay, they mounted a resolute and courageous resistance which continued in guerrilla fashion when larger groups of armed men had been defeated. Despite their inexperienced leadership, primitive weapons and equipment, it took an army of 30,000 men some five years to pacify the country with much killing and burning before it was done.[8] By 1890 the British had secured the lowlands and were pushing soldiers and negotiators out into the wild hill country, staking out some 2,000 miles of frontier, and negotiating treaties with tribal chieftains which offered them protection in return for tribute and a promise not to attack their neighbours or to have any dealings with the Chinese, the Siamese or the French.[10]

Once pacification had been completed, some 25 years of fairly orderly progress followed – at least in matters that the British, viewing the country from India, regarded as progress.

In the more accessible parts of the country the key figure was the local Deputy Commissioner, responsible for justice, policing, taxation and general administration for an area about the size of an English county. In the early 1920s these men were still nearly all British, but that was soon to change. In their daily work they relied heavily on the help of village Headmen, and spent a lot of their time touring their district on foot and on horseback, and getting to know its villages. In the hills, most of the administration was left to local chieftains, working with Government Advisors at their elbows.

At the centre of government, in Rangoon, the Governor, first appointed in 1862, was in 1897 given a Legislative Council – appointed by officials, not elected. The Governor himself was a senior official of the Indian Civil Service, brought in from India and accountable to Delhi. The Indians, who had played a major part in the First World War and who had to be kept peaceable while it lasted, were offered real constitutional advances under the Government of India Act of 1919. The Burmese were at first excluded from these, and that provoked protests which won them an elected Parliament and local government in 1923. That is for a later chapter.

One of the reasons why the British came to Burma was to grow the rice that would keep India's growing population fed. The cultivation of rice increased dramatically and gained the country its largest export earnings, followed by those for oil, metals and teak. There was also a large increase in imports – particularly of textiles, machinery, coal and steel – but also a handsome trade surplus. After an abortive attempt to develop schools run by the monks, the British turned to Christian missionaries to provide what they felt to be a more effective education, and in 1920 they amalgamated several colleges to form the University of Rangoon.

Thus much conventional progress had been made by the time Vernon and Ruth arrived. They were to be inducted into an imperial culture, shaped in India over more than a century, that was still at its peak. Their own country was master of the greatest empire the world had ever seen, the Royal Navy dominated the oceans of the world, and the grand fleet of the only rival to challenge them in living memory lay at the bottom of Scapa Flow – scuttled there after the German surrender. It was no wonder that able young men from Oxford and Cambridge aspired above all to enter their country's diplomatic service and the Indian Civil Service. The tasks facing this couple would be formidable, but they could tackle them with the backing of a supremely successful imperial tradition. The killing and burning required to establish British rule in Burma were over; civil servants had taken over leadership from the soldiers, and more constructive work lay ahead.

CLOUDS ON THE HORIZON

Beneath the majesty of this tradition we can, with hindsight, see that pressures were already building up that would ultimately blow imperial rule away. The First World War had devastated Britain's financial reserves. With so many of its ablest young men going off to run an empire, it was not surprising that German and American science and industry were overtaking Britain's. Many of Burma's future troubles were a direct result of British policy. Regarding the country as an outlying province of India, they were bringing in large numbers of Indians – particularly to Rangoon, the country's political capital and its only big city. These were the sweepers and the coolies, doing badly-paid, back-breaking work that Burmans found too boring and degrading to touch. It was men from India, along with hardy tribesmen brought down from the hills, who provided most of the soldiers in Burma. Despite – or perhaps because of – their resolute guerrilla warfare against British forces, a myth grew up among Europeans that "you can never make a soldier of a Burman." Meanwhile the regime also needed more and more clerks, minor officials and servants, and it was again to the Indians that the British turned for much of this labour. They knew English ways and were more likely than the Burmese to have learnt the English language. Soon India was providing money-lenders, doctors, lawyers, accountants and business men too.

As the paddy fields spread further and further across Lower Burma, the cultivators needed loans to buy seed and tools, and to keep themselves going when times were bad. In the old days, wealthy Burmans had provided these loans. Now Indian money lenders moved in to provide them, and began to acquire a growing amount of the land through foreclosures on farmers unable to pay off their debts. Meanwhile many small craftsmen found they could not compete with the cheap, factory-made goods shipped in from India and Britain. Enterprises collapsed and skills were lost – as they had been when Britain had gone through her own industrial revolution many years before.

This all seemed natural enough to British officials viewing Burma from India. Population grew, tax revenues and exports flourished. Nobody paused at this time to note that living standards among Burmese people were not advancing – may, indeed, have been falling[11] – or that taxation here was higher than it was in India[12], or that, for the first time in Burma, unemployment was emerging as a problem. What they did notice was a growth in violent lawlessness and banditry – "dacoity" as it was called. This was tiresome, but it had, so far, no coherent political direction.

Meanwhile Burmese culture was not suppressed; it was sidelined. To handle the new ideas and concepts required by modern industry and government you needed the English language: Burmese was inadequate for this purpose. Although a University had been founded, some years passed before it offered any courses in Burmese language, history or culture . Very few of its graduates went overseas. Business and banking, outside the bigger European firms, were increasingly in the hands of Indians and a few Chinese. Meanwhile the monks, who had been the main bearers of Burma's traditions and the main teachers of her people, found themselves brushed aside. Not surprisingly, some of them were eventually to become leaders of revolt.

Despite the violence involved in the pacification of Burma, relations between the ethnic groups in the early years of British rule had often been good. But the British were at their best with country people; they found the new generation of urban, educated, young people harder to make friends with. When men had to work together in small communities where the few Europeans depended on native people for everything they needed, they soon learnt to respect each other. But by the early post-war years some larger towns had grown up with white populations big enough to form their own clubs and create a social life of their own – a life from which other people were excluded.

The growing numbers of white women coming to Burma also exerted an influence. Vernon was later to write: "British women on the whole exercised a divisive influence… In the early stages, when the country was considered too unsettled and unhealthy for European women, many men lived with Burmese women in what might be a marriage under Burmese law but no marriage under British law. These unions…, happy or not, … did establish a certain contact between the races, which had its advantages as well as its disadvantages. When conditions became more settled, more Englishwomen came …[and] they tended to keep Burmans at arms length. Few spoke Burmese… They did not have the advantage, enjoyed by the men, of working with Burmans and so getting to know and like them. There was a far greater social reluctance to meet Burmans, springing from – what? Distrust of the unknown? Consciousness of colour? Fear that in some way advantage would be taken of them? An instinctive feeling that they would in some way be tainted by meeting Burmese women with whom English men had been 'living in sin'? Knowledge that here was a shadowy, unknown world where you might suddenly find yourself meeting the sons or daughters of your husband?" [15]

Gradually the Burmese were having their country stolen from them. "What we gave Burma" wrote another retired official of the Indian Civil Service, "was not a government but an administration. Political direction, so far as there was any, came from the Indian government, with the British Parliament in the dim background. It was a curiously impersonal system." [14] The Indian migrations, he said, were a "disaster". "They constituted an acute problem, and it was our doing." We brought in "…starveling hordes… useless to the good employer, …only… depressing the labour market and spreading disease." In time, the Indians also "…monopolised the professions, legal, medical, accountancy, engineering, as no Burman was qualified." [15] Thus investment, production and exports might all continue to grow without bringing any benefit to the Burmese. Rising profits would be used to pay more taxes to the government, more interest and dividends to British and Indian investors, and to hire more foreigners to come and live among the Burmese and run their country. A third official, reflecting on these patterns, wrote "In the long run it came to this, that nearly all the rich people in the country were foreigners and that the Burmese, from being poor in a poor country, had become the poor in a rich one." [16]

There were, by 1922, only sporadic, ill-organised responses to all this from the Burmese. The most sustained of them sprang from Buddhist movements. Some took conventional political forms, demanding, for example, that the Burmese be given the same rights that were being conceded to the Indians. Others were more symbolic, like the demand that visitors to pagodas and temples should follow local custom and remove their shoes at the gate, where signs went up, saying "No footwearing". "How easy it is" commented Vernon, "to embarrass any government, but particularly a government which is unwilling or unable to apply the full logic of force."[17]

Force could no longer be applied without questions being asked. In Britain, the growing strength of Parliamentary government and the liberal press had made "the full logic of force" increasingly unacceptable. Poison gas and indiscriminate aerial bombing were tolerated for many years more in Afghanistan and other wild places where liberal journalists were rare visitors. (That's where "Bomber Harris" of the Second World War first learnt the skills that led ultimately to the destruction of Dresden and Hamburg.) But, in 1919, when General Dyer, a gallant and successful soldier, ordered his Gurkha and Sikh infantrymen to fire on a crowd of nationalist demonstrators in Amritsar, killing 379 of them and wounding about 1,500 more, he was promptly brought before a Committee of Inquiry and disgraced, despite the fact that large numbers of the British in India and at home – including the Conservative *Morning Post* newspaper – thought he had "saved India"[18].

In 1905, news that the Japanese had destroyed the Russian fleet – despatched to the Sea of Japan from the Baltic – had sent a wild surmise around the subject peoples of the imperial powers. The West was not invincible. But by 1920 fifteen more years had passed without any major challenge to its empires – except from other empires. How much longer would the imperial magic work?

A robust little five year old boy was growing up near Mount Popa, a sacred mountain in Upper Burma. His grandfather had been a village Headman who died fighting the British during the "pacification" years. When his time came to learn how to fight the imperialists it would be to the Japanese that he would turn. Aung San was to become the first prime minister of an effectively independent Burma[19].

NOTES

1   F.S.V.Donnison, *Burma*, Ernest Benn, London, 1970, and
     Public Administration in Burma, London, Royal Institute of
     International Affairs, 1953.

2   G.E.Harvey, *British Rule in Burma 1824-1942*, London,
     Faber & Faber, 1946, page 100.

3   The country is well described in Vernon's book, *Burma*, and by
     G.E.Harvey in *British Rule in Burma 1824-1942*, London,
     Faber & Faber, 1946. For a movingly affectionate account of Burma
     shortly after its conquest see H. Fielding, *The Soul of a People*,
     London, Macmillan, 1898

4   J.S.Furnivall, *An Introduction to the Political Economy of Burma*,
     Rangoon, Burma Book Club, 1931; page x.

5   Donnison, 1970; page 38.

6   Thant Myint-U, in *The Making of Modern Burma*, Cambridge,
     Cambridge University Press, 2001, provides the best account of
     Burma's history during the nineteenth century.

7   D.G.E.Hall, *Burma*, London, ...1950, page 66.

8   Donnison, 1970; page 73.

9   See Dorothy Woodman, *The Making of Burma*, London, Cresset Press, 1962; p.350.

10 For vivid accounts of these frontier expeditions, see G.E.Mitton (ed.), *Scott of the Shan Hills*, London, John Murray, 1936, and Andrew Marshall, *The Trouser People*, London, Viking, 2002.

11 J.S.Furnivall, Foreword to J.Russell Andrews, *Burmese Economic Life*, Stanford, Stanford University Press, 1948.

12 Furnivall, *op. cit.*

13 Donnison, 1970; page 96.

14 G.E.Harvey, *British Rule in Burma 1824-1942*, 1946; page 30.

15 Harvey, 1946; pages 69, 72 and 71.

16 Maurice Collis, *Trials in Burma*, London, Faber & Faber, 1938. New edition, 1945.

17 Donnison, 1970; page 105.

18 Lawrence James, *Raj. The Making and Unmaking of British India*, London, Little, Brown, 1997, page 472 et seq.

19 Aung San Suu Kyi, *Freedom from Fear and Other Writings*, Harmondsworth, Penguin Books, 1992, chapter I.

IV

FINDING THEIR FEET

To find himself, at the age of 24, responsible for the day-to-day government of a quarter of a million people whose difficult languages he had only begun to grapple with must have been a testing experience for Vernon. As for Ruth, a young Londoner, to set up her first home in this far country must have been equally daunting. In this chapter I tell how they found their feet in Burma and started to learn about its people and the equally strange European society they had joined. I rely mainly on the memoir they wrote more than forty years later and, unless I say otherwise, this is the source of my quotations. Some of its chapters were written by Vernon, some by Ruth, and I will do my best to make clear which of them is speaking.

INTRODUCTION

After a course at Oxford of several months, learning a little about the law, the history and the language of the Burmese, Vernon set off at the end of November 1922 from Birkenhead in the MV "Oxfordshire", a Bibby Line ship bound for Rangoon. Ruth had come from Cambridge to share his last evening in his parents' home and to say goodbye. They had set for themselves a two-year separation, in deference to her family and their friends who insisted that, on his pay, they could not afford to get married sooner.

Vernon was one of five young recruits to the Burma section of the Indian Civil Service who travelled out together: four from Oxford, and one from Cambridge – the latter already known to him because they had been at Marlborough together. All were to become friends for many years to come. They made good resolutions to work hard on their Burmese, but Vernon only recalled learning that the instruction given at Cambridge must have been even worse than that given at Oxford. Most of them had never been in any ship larger than a cross-channel ferry, and they were soon immersed in the delights of their first long sea voyage, with deck games, dances, the arrival of another crowd of passengers who boarded at Marseilles – the smart way to travel out – going ashore at Port Said to buy topees at Simon Arzt's shop ... while every day the sun grew warmer.

Then, at Colombo, they met the Orient for the first time. "I can still remember the overwhelming smell as we drew into the harbour, compounded of spices, frangipani and other blossoms, ordure and dust. It weighed heavily on one." Vernon was to come to Colombo from the West many times more, but said he "was never able to recapture the real physical shock of that first contact with the scented East."

It was Christmas time as they approached Rangoon. Jim Lindop, one of the group who had served with the Army in India during the war, had been their mentor on the voyage – preventing them from buying the wrong kind of topee, and now warning that there would be no-one to meet them because Europeans would all be away in Christmas camps. He had under-estimated the brotherhood they were entering. As the ship tied up, four of the men received notes from hosts preparing to welcome them, and Vernon was met by "a charming and vivacious lady in her mid-thirties" who invited him to stay with her and her husband. They were Harry and Dora Reynolds, and in their home Vernon found "a taut, athletic atmosphere, mental and physical" which reminded him of his Marlborough house master, Ralph Gidney. They "could not have been kinder and more helpful" – taking him to the Golf Club, the Gymkhana Club and the Pegu Club (the centres of white society), helping him to buy tropical clothes and essential stores, and offering much useful advice. They found him a servant: Maung San Hla, who had at one time worked for them as a water-carrier. The "Maung" is Burmese for "Mister" and Vernon henceforth calls him San Hla.

"Before we set off to up-country stations we were required to attend before the Chief Secretary [head of the civil service in Burma] who, in some embarrassment (because two of the men were already married) delivered to us his set piece on the undesirability of our taking up with Burmese women".

A few days later Vernon and San Hla caught a night train to Mandalay, and then another, next morning, for Shwebo where Vernon was to work as a trainee for the next six months. "And now" he wrote, "the adventure really began".

Vernon lived in temporary lodgings in various government buildings, receiving little help from a distant and "aseptic" Deputy Commissioner and his wife who were soon posted elsewhere. (The "D.C.s" were the key figures in Britain's administration: the senior officials in each District, responsible for coping with all that happened there – which included training new recruits.) San Hla clearly did not speak Oxford Burmese, but they did their best to get on together. After a few days, a telegram arrived and Vernon read it to him with a sinking heart. It said "Wife died come sharp". But "He merely grinned, and continued in my service – and later in Ruth's too – until his death many years after." He had prepared this escape route for himself in case Vernon proved an uncongenial master.

Shwebo was in Upper Burma, about 400 miles north of Rangoon. The Europeans there were all government officials or their wives: the Deputy Commissioner, the District Superintendent of Police, a Superintending Engineer and two Executive engineers (one for roads and buildings, one for canals), a Forest Officer, a Sessions Judge and one or two Military Police Officers. They were older than Vernon, and most of them were married. The Medical Officer (known as the Civil Surgeon – as opposed to the Military one) was Indian, the Superintendent of Land Records and his wife were Anglo-Burmese, and the Public

Prosecutor was Indian. All, except the last of these, lived in Government houses within what was called "the Civil Station". This was Shwebo "society". All were members of the Club where they could be found most evenings, playing tennis or bridge and having a drink – joined occasionally by one or two Anglican missionary ladies who were working in the district. More junior officials, Burmese or Indian, were not members of the Club and "one's relations with them were strictly official, not social. Still less did one know anything of 'non-officials', few if any of whom spoke English – or played tennis or bridge". A strange world; but, as a new recruit, "one accepted things as they were and tried to make the best of them."

Work, however, was different. It called for constant communication with Burmans and Indians. For some weeks Vernon was attached to the Superintendent of Land Records, touring with him, learning about the procedures for assessing and collecting revenue from land, and hence about the cultivators, the life of the villages, and how to get around the country. Then he went out with the Assistant Settlement Officer to help him revise the basic economic information which provided a basis for tax collection. For a month he was in charge of the Treasury – the Government bank into which all revenues flowed and from which bullion was transferred to the places where it was needed. He had to try one case in court and was so ignorant of court procedures that he did not know that forms would have to be filled in or where they were to be found. His Burmese clerk, being equally new to the job, was no help to him, but a Burmese magistrate came to their rescue, and eventually a fine of one rupee was imposed (about one shilling and fourpence at the time).

The next D.C. came from one of the most remote Districts of the country. He was an attractive, friendly man who invited Vernon to come to his house in the evenings for talk and a drink. But it soon became clear that the drink was taking charge, and one day the Civil Surgeon found the D.C. sitting in helpless tears before a pile of papers in his office. He was sent on sick leave and succeeded by a Burman – which was still unusual at this time. U Pein was "a man of experience and ability", but "reluctant to order a European around. I got the feeling that he was wanting me to tell him what I ought to do; and I had no idea what I should be doing.

"Perhaps it wasn't anybody's fault that I received no proper training. But it was undoubtedly a fact."

This apprenticeship drew to a close in the hottest and most exhausting part of the year. Then the Reynolds, who had first welcomed him in Rangoon, invited Vernon and one of his young colleagues to spend ten days with them in Maymyo. This was a hill station, where the weather was blissfully cool. They had tea on the lawn out of a silver teapot, with strawberries and cream. "We picnicked, bathed, played tennis and golf, danced, and hugely enjoyed the company of Europeans we had not been meeting every night for many weeks in the Club". It was a delicious interlude in a sort of imaginary England – particularly for one who "had not yet questioned, or fully recognised, the self-protective barriers that the English erected around themselves in Burma."

"THE WORK WILL COME AT YOU"

Vernon was soon back in the heat and then called to Mandalay to take examinations on the things he had been learning about. Having done pretty well in these, he was posted to be Sub-Divisional Officer (or S.D.O.) at Kyonpyaw in the Bassein District, 400 miles to the south in the Irrawaddy Delta. (The map on page 66 shows where all these places are.) He chose to travel there slowly – not by rail but on one of the Irrawaddy Flotilla Company's great, flat mailboats: 300 feet long and drawing only four feet six inches of water, with two large barges lashed to each side and a big paddle wheel at the stern. "These boats were travelling villages and markets – a marvellous cross-section of Burmese life. The rains had broken, the country was green, a fresh breeze blew from the south-west and the river was rising, giving us broad views over the banks on either side. Kyonpyaw, when we got there, was flat as the Fens, with paddy being planted in the flooded fields and vast skies arching overhead."

Vernon was taking over as S.D.O. from a Burman – U Pe. "I suddenly had an awful anxiety that I wouldn't know where to start work and I asked him how I would find what needed to be done. 'Don't worry', he replied with a smile. 'The work will come at you faster than you can deal with it.'"

There were 250,000 people in the Subdivision and no European except Vernon. Its 1,800,000 square miles were divided into three Townships, each headed by Burmese Township Officers. Neither they nor Vernon had proper offices. He worked from an abandoned police station – a square, brick, fortified building with no windows; only loopholes. He had a staff of three clerks and several messengers who worked on the lower floor where there was still a wooden cage, built for the safe-keeping of prisoners. Vernon's office was on the upper floor, which was also windowless, but with panels under the eaves that could be propped open with a stick to let some light and air in. This room could only be entered across a drawbridge linking it to a tower of steps, built a few feet clear of the building.

Vernon had to supervise the tax collections made by Township Officers and Village Headmen, to try criminal cases, to arbitrate on boundary disputes between land owners, to issue licenses for firearms, and do many other things. But his main task, to which he devoted nearly half his time, was to tour his Subdivision, mainly on foot, visiting Township Officers and Headmen, getting to know them and their communities, checking their work and keeping track of everything that went on in his territory.

There was no government house for the S.D.O., so Vernon bought a small mat and thatch house built by one of his predecessors on the edge of the town. It cost him 800 rupees – about £50 at the time. Since the Government provided an allowance of 50 rupees a month for S.D.Os for whom there was no house, this was a good investment, bringing him a return of 75 per cent per annum.

He recruited a cook to help San Hla, so meals improved.

The low priority given by the Indian Civil Service to the buildings in which its younger officials lived and worked is not surprising. Touring was their main task. Comfortable and spacious offices and homes might distract them from that.

The monsoon which had begun shortly before Vernon's arrival was working up to its climax. The Ngawun River, a tributary of the Irrawaddy which ran through the Kyonpyaw Subdivision, began to rise in a threatening way. Vernon worked — and drove other people to work — day and night to plug the leaks which kept appearing in the river embankment that ran high above low-lying villages. "I remember how angry I got with people who wouldn't work, thinking it was *their* homes and property we were trying to save. It was then that I learned how to stop a leak by building a miniature dam around it to equalise the pressure on each side of the threatened gap. Just when we thought we had won the battle the embankment gave way a mile or more up stream. Soon there was a gap several hundred yards wide with a solid surge of water pouring through it. Hundreds of square miles disappeared under the flood." Many villages and the roads between them were submerged. Kyonpyaw itself survived but the waters came very close to Vernon's house. A few people were drowned and a lot of food stocks were destroyed.

"Trying to discover the extent of the disaster, I made a journey along the railway on an inspection trolley pushed by two railway coolies. They ran barefoot, one on each line, pushing the trolley till it gained speed and then jumping aboard to recover their breath till our speed slackened. The roads had all disappeared, but the railway ran along an embankment, and although the water had risen to the top of it the rails were still showing. Between them there was a seething, writhing mass of snakes, driven up from their usual haunts as they tried to escape the flood. I felt nervous for the barefoot runners, but they came to no harm."

Relief funds were set up, senior officials and volunteers from the big firms came to help, temporary housing was erected, and, as soon as the waters subsided, work began to repair the river embankment. The strategy was to bring in rice and give people work to do that would enable them to earn money with which they could buy it, feed their families and rebuild their lives. Gradually things returned to normal.

Vernon later said that these demanding months of work laid the foundations for his "conviction that colour bears no relation to the worth of a man. This may seem blindingly obvious now, but it wasn't then." One of the men who helped him to lay this foundation was Fred Wemyss, his Anglo-Burmese Subdivisional Police Officer. Born and brought up in Burma, in a family of twelve brothers and sisters, Fred had gone to England to train as an engineering apprentice. He served in the British Army in France where he was badly wounded, and returned after the war to Burma. Finding no congenial work there, he got a licence to shoot elephants and disappeared into the jungle, reappearing from time to time to sell tusks to the ivory dealers. After a year living this way he got a job in the police. Vernon's friendship with him lasted to the end of their lives.

Gaining confidence in this, his first proper job, Vernon was now the owner of a house and saving nearly half his pay. He had even acquired a dog. So he began writing to Ruth about getting her to join him after one year instead of two. Letters took three weeks from London to Rangoon, and then a few days longer to reach Kyonpyaw, so the discussion proceeded slowly. Finally, in August 1923, he sent a cable firmly inviting her to come. She was on holiday in Switzerland at the time and returned on tenterhooks to know what he had decided. Isabel, her mother, had received and read the cable but had made no attempt to forward it. "Was there a cable for me?" Ruth asked. "Oh yes – I think there was one somewhere" she replied. Eventually Vernon's message was reluctantly produced.

It was a little while after this that Vernon found that Fred Wemyss' fiancee was also coming out to marry him, and travelling on the same boat as Ruth. There was just time for both men to write to their women and warn them that they would be close neighbours in Kyonpyaw and must on no account fall out. The men travelled to Rangoon together when the S.S. Pegu was due, and Fred – ever resourceful – persuaded one of the pilots whom he knew to get them 40 miles down river to the pilot brig that was anchored out at sea. They slept on deck in their clothes till warned at 4 am.that the Pegu was approaching.

"We got into the cutter to be rowed across a bouncing sea in the dark. The Pegu's side was black and very tall. Somewhere above there were floodlights by which I could see a rope ladder. I managed to grab it and scramble up. And there on deck was Ruth."

MAKING A HOME

Here Ruth takes over the story for a while and it is from her that I shall be quoting – first about their home and household; next about their work, the country and its people; and then about the European society they were entering.

She described, towards the end of my first chapter, her arrival in Burma, their wedding before the Registrar in the home of Rangoon friends, their journey to Bassein, headquarters of the District to which they were going, and then their nine-day journey by houseboat along the river to Kyonpyaw. Tying up there, they walked through the small town to Vernon's house. It stood in a compound edged by a low fence, with flowering plants growing in square, white-painted kerosene tins leading up to it. The house, standing on the legs of its wooden frame, was covered with bamboo matting and thatched with grass. There was nothing on the ground beneath it but a store room. A creeper grew up one leg of the house and in through the gap left under the eaves at the top of the matting wall to flower, in season, over the dining table. A narrow wooden stair led to the upper floor which had several rooms, of which the largest were the dining room, a sitting area and a bedroom. There were also spare rooms, an office and another store room. Thickly woven cotton rugs lay on the wooden floors – fawn in colour with broad, light-blue borders. Pictures – Ruth had brought a few – could be hung on the matting walls by pushing a slice of bamboo through them to make a hook. There was no electricity or running water, and no windows – just matting panels, hinged at their upper edges, which could be propped open with sticks to let more air through the house.

Behind the bedroom were two bathrooms – one for each of them – reached by a back staircase from the ground. Water was carried up each day by the sweeper from the well dug in the compound to serve the whole household. He carried it in heavy "Pegu jars", two foot six inches high, which were left standing in the bathrooms. Ruth and Vernon washed in tin baths placed on a concrete patch of their bathroom floors, filling them from the jars with dippers hung on the walls. Each also had a wash stand with brightly painted basins and jugs they had bought in Rangoon for hand washing and shaving. Spent water was tipped through a hole in the concrete floor onto the ground below where it quickly dried in the heat. The sweeper also carried down the enamel pans from commodes or "thunder boxes" standing in each bathroom, emptying their contents into the deep latrines provided for the rest of the household at the edge of the compound. After a rinsing with Jeyes' fluid they were returned to their places.

Vernon had got the Bassein jail to make furniture for the house: two beds (the nights were much too hot to share one), dining table, wardrobe, chest of drawers, a desk and chairs – all in solid teak. In the centre of their large bedroom stood a ten-foot square cube of mosquito netting, hung from wires, that surrounded both beds. This was raised each morning and lowered at night. Light for the main rooms was provided by hissing "Storm King" lamps, fuelled by petrol under pressure that produced a bright, white light and rather too much heat. For bathrooms, the kitchen, and walking outdoors in the dark they used ordinary oil lamps or candles.

Drinking water, drawn from the well, was filtered, boiled and left to cool each day. They had no refrigerator, but things could be kept cool by wrapping them in damp straw and placing them in a basket hung under the house. Sometimes, when they felt extravagant, they sent to the town for ice from the soda water factory.

Ruth always remembered this as one of the happiest and most charming homes they ever had. That was made possible by the household they assembled around them. The servants lived in small matting houses built along the back of the compound. The kitchen, too, was a separate building standing at the back of the house.

Ruth recalled that Vernon told her he had heard that wives coming to join Englishmen in Burma nearly always began by making a clean sweep of the servants and hiring a new lot, but "he was well pleased with San Hla and hoped I would not want to get rid of him."I very soon learnt, not only to respect but to have great affection and trust for this old-fashioned Burman with his thick knot of long curly hair and his rare smile. Our trust was not misplaced. He was very firmly in charge of the rest of the servants. An Indian cook ruled in the kitchen and went early each morning to buy fresh meat, vegetables, fruit and eggs in the bazaar. A younger Burmese girl did housemaid's work, looked after Vernon's clothes, helped to wait at table and came on tour with us – leaving San Hla in charge of the house while we were away. The Indian sweeper swept floors, carried water and kept the compound tidy. Soon after I arrived, San Hla suggested to Vernon that as there was now a 'thakinma' in the house it might be a good thing if his wife came from Mandalay to join him so that there would be another woman in the compound. Ma Than joined us and we greeted one another shyly."

Vernon asked Ruth to take over the running of this household. That meant ordering stores every three months from a big shop in Rangoon: tinned butter, tinned milk, coffee, tea, cocoa, marmalade and jam, dried fruit, tinned meat, drinks and cleaning materials. She checked these orders when the packing cases arrived, and locked them in the two store rooms, for which she kept the keys.

"We paid our servants at the end of each month, and in these early days always sat together at a table on which each man's money was put in a little pile to be given to him when he came up for it. We wanted to suggest that we were jointly responsible for them and that they could look on us as one. In time, because Vernon had often to be away, I was frequently in charge alone and took over the monthly payment too.

"Vernon paid me a monthly house-keeping cheque and I kept careful accounts under separate headings so that I could spot and investigate any sudden or unusual rise in particular items. This applied particularly to the cook's bazaar bills. I was of course aware that the level of these depended more on Vernon's seniority in the service than on actual expenditure, but one had to accept the custom of the country as long as the results were not too outrageous. There came a time, in our next posting, when our cook appeared to have collected about him a very large and hungry family from India whom we were feeding. I asked San Hla to find us a new cook."

They settled into a disciplined routine, starting with fruit and a cup of tea soon after six in the morning, followed – before it got too hot – by Vernon going out to "inspect" work going on nearby. Ruth would often accompany him. Then he would return for a shave and a cold bath and they would have a large, late breakfast. After that, he would go to his office and Ruth would be left to fill the day till 4 pm. as best she could. At first there was a lot of work to be done repairing Vernon's clothes after a year's ravages from the heat and the battering they had been given by the 'dhobi'" – the laundryman who worked by beating them on a rock by the river.

After that she had more time for herself. "I had never before had time that was not earmarked for some duty – work for an examination, mending or washing my clothes, practising the piano ... – so I had never known what it was like just to sit down and read a book for sheer enjoyment. I took out all the fine, leather-bound volumes of Jane Austen which one of my Cambridge tutors had given me as a wedding present and found them fascinating. I took them with me on tour too."

Vernon's Subdivision consisted of miles of flat paddy fields, laced with rivers and waterways. There was a railway linking Kyonpyaw to Bassein, the headquarters of the District, 40 miles away. Touring meant setting out "by road or river, or both; taking our camp furniture, bedding rolls and other essentials, with the cook and second boy, a clerk from Vernon's office and lots of papers and maps." The best way of getting to their starting point was often by boat, using the public launches filled with Burmese passengers. "They always seemed to wear their best clothes when travelling and we delighted in their bright silk skirts, usually crimson or vivid pink, worn by men and women alike." The women wore their long hair, shining with coconut oil, coiled in elaborate shapes like miniature top hats, and "ornamented with jewelled pins or sweet-scented flowers. Men, too, often wore their hair long, knotted jauntily slightly to one side and held with a bright silk scarf whose ends hung behind one ear".

These tours really began on foot which was the only way to meet the people, to see what was going on – and now to assess the damage done by the floods . Accompanied by a clerk, the local Headman and one or two of his minions, Vernon and Ruth would visit villages, talk with their people, inspect fields and crops, check township records, and later receive callers at the "dak" bungalow where they usually stayed for the night. These bungalows were provided by the government for officials on the move. There, at the end of the day, people with events to report and complaints to make would come to see Vernon. "It was not possible to achieve the necessary confidence for these things to be put into words until the trivialities had been exchanged and the polite formalities complied with. A good officer had to have plenty of time and endless patience to understand the 'feel' of his charge."

"Sometimes, after a morning's tramp over fields, we would be invited to rest in a Headman's house. The family would gather round, taking a special interest in me because few European women had visited these parts. They would ask my age and how many children I had; then touch my clothes, purr with approval and ask how much this or that had cost. I was usually wearing a khaki cotton shirt and breeches, a khaki topee and canvas boots — not nearly as charmingly dressed as our hostesses in their bright longyis (skirts) and dainty white muslin jackets."

The main occupation of these people was growing rice, but there were also potters, and makers of beatiful silk sunshades stretched over laquered bamboo spokes. Ruth was invited to try her hand at some of these crafts.

"Each village had its grove of coconut palms and whenever we paused to rest someone would shin up a tall trunk, select a ripe nut and bring it down for us. Chopping off one end of it with a hatchet or 'dah' (a knife), he would cut a small hole in the shell and pour out for us a deliciously cool, delicately flavoured drink. It might be clear or milky, still or prickley, depending on the ripeness of the nut, but always a marvellous thirst quencher.

"I soon learnt how easy and natural Burmese people were to live with at close quarters. On one occasion, when I had fallen out to answer a call of nature, I was attracted by the sweet scent of wild jasmine. I went over to gather a few sprays, and found myself beset by a swarm of large red ants which swarmed out of the flowers, down my shirt and up my sleeves, biting ferociously, and there was nothing I could do but strip as fast as possible to get rid of the vicious insects. I received only sympathy."

Ruth worked hard to learn Burmese. But a language that uses three tones is very different from European ways of speaking and this made it difficult. San Hla was not helpful; perhaps because he felt safer with a mistress who could not speak the language. A local school master came to give her lessons, but he was too polite to correct her mistakes. It was not until her son was born and Ma Than, San Hla's wife who spoke no English, came to work with her that she made real progress. But that comes later.

They took Vernon's dog with them on tour. As they walked

with him through a village one day, a local dog rushed out from
beneath a house and ran by, grazing him with its teeth. Some days
later he began to show nervous symptoms and, travelling home on
the launch, he snapped at other travellers crowded around them
on the deck. Ruth had to stroke him continually to keep him calm.
"On arrival at Kyonpyaw we took him straight to the Civil
Surgeon who suspected rabies. He offered to keep him under
observation, and by the time we returned, two hours later, he was
snapping in the air, his jaws dripping with saliva, and could not
recognise us. He was rabid and had to be destroyed. We examined
ourselves. We had played so often with this young dog and his
teeth had left many marks on our hands and arms. So we had to go
to Rangoon immediately to have anti-rabid injections for a fortnight – 14 of them – at the Pasteur Institute there."

RUTH AMONG THE MEMSAHIBS

The only dreary experiences in this happy time were the occasional visits they had to make to their headquarters in Bassein where
Vernon had to report from time to time. Fred Wemyss, his chief of
police, often came too with his wife Maud whom Ruth had got to
know on the way out. Wives were expected to accompany their
husbands on these visits and to make formal calls on senior officials' ladies. Vernon and Ruth would usually stay as guests of the
Commissioner and his wife – Ruth abandoning her touring
clothes for the formal day and evening dresses sent out with her
from home. Their seniors had come from Edwardian England
before the war, and many of them knew little of the changes that
had taken place at "home"since then. George Orwell, writing his
novel "*Burmese Days*" at this time, recorded the way in which
such people had sat out the war – always saying they had "stuck
by their jobs", never "stuck *to*" them.

Although cosmetics, other than face powder, were never worn
– Queen Victoria had banned them from royal palaces, and that
tradition persisted – many Europeans wore evening dress every

night for dinner, and if guests were present this was *de rigeur*. This habit was not so absurd as it now seems. After a day's hard work, most people played tennis, squash or some other game in the short period of daylight that was left. In that climate, exercise meant sweat; so when they got home they needed long drinks and baths. Dripping tennis clothes went straight to the dhobi, and it was then no greater effort to put on evening dress than any other kind of clothing.

"I was entirely unprepared", Ruth recalled, "for these formal gatherings, and did not know that, since I was a bride, and senior to Maud by reason of Vernon's service, I would be treated as the guest of honour and expected to decide the moment when all present would rise to say goodnight and go home. I would be seated beside our host, who seemed quite an elderly gentleman to me. Having no small talk and knowing nothing of the gossip of Bassein, I found conversation desperately difficult. Meanwhile I could see Vernon and Fred engaged in lively chat at the foot of the table. After an appalling long evening at the home of the Deputy Superintendent of Police it dawned on me that I was expected to bring proceedings to a close. We stumbled away amidst looks of exhaustion, frustration or relief all around us. Maud, who knew more about this world, helped to educate me in my social duties; but, for years after, my bowels would turn to water at the prospect of such occasions." In their next posting, even worse was to come .

Vernon received orders to move after a few months. It was the hottest part of the year. Before leaving Kyonpyaw, he was determined to complete the inspection of a large area of paddy fields, much of which had been devastated by the floods, leaving the land fallow or with a thin crop because it was too late to plant the rice by the time the waters had subsided. Since everyone had applied for remission of their tax, Vernon, as Subdivisional Officer, had to check every claim. "There was not enough time to complete this work" Ruth recalled. "So we divided the territory between us and I took over a share of it. Each day we would go out early together, taking with us the maps that recorded ownership and soil classification for every field, and agreeing a place to meet at the end of the day. Vernon sent his head clerk, who spoke a little English, with me. We each had our picnic food, and I would take a break about midday. I and the clerk would be invited into a Burmese house; a rickety deck-chair would be brought for me and a long draft of coconut water offered. Then we were out again into the glare and heat to complete our work before meeting Vernon at our agreed spot. I could not understand all the reasons for their claims put forward in Burmese by the farmers, but a reasonable judgement could usually be made by seeing whether there was a crop on the land or not.

"I had a dry skin and, in the past, despite playing lots of games with great vigour, I had never been conscious of sweating. Indeed, my mother regarded sweating as pretty low-class and disgusting – not something we did. One blazing afternoon I was returning to meet Vernon after a long day in the open fields. 'Whatever is that?' I asked him, pointing to drops of water on my forearms. How he laughed! My body had learned a valuable lesson.

"We had made our first home together in the little matting house which was really ours, rarely seeing other Europeans and getting close to the life of the country. Promotion, we knew, would alter all that. We were very sad to be leaving Kyonpyaw."

THE OILFIELDS

Yenangyaung, where they were going, was 250 miles north, on the banks of the Irrawaddy in hot, dry, Upper Burma. The name is an old one, pronounced "Yenan Chaung" which means "the evil-smelling stream". The smell was oil. Twenty-five per cent of the oil produced in the British Empire came from this oilfield and others nearby.

Vernon was to be "Warden of the Oilfields" – a charmingly academic title for the official whose main job was to collect revenue from the oil companies and ensure they kept to the rules laid down by the Government. In technical matters he worked with a small Advisory Committee of three men from the companies and was responsible directly to the Development Commissioner in Rangoon. For general administration, which included supervision of the police, collection of income tax, registering births, marriages and deaths, and much else, he was responsible to the usual hierarchy of Deputy Commissioner and Commissioner. This was a different world from Kyonpyaw. There was no touring in the job; only occasional visits to other oilfields and to sites where the companies were prospecting for oil. The senior administrators in the area were mainly British, the senior oilmen mainly American. Most of the manual workers were Indians, and several large Indian villages had grown up on the fringes of the town to house them. Burmans, apart from a few clerks, were rarely to be seen.

Vernon and Ruth set off for Yenangyaung by road and then travelled for several days on one of the flat-bottomed mail boats, steaming up the Irrawaddy. "We were cabin passengers" wrote Ruth, "but there were much larger numbers of deck passengers – families camping there with their children and their belongings. All our household was with us, together with our possessions packed in crates and baskets, the piano we had bought in Rangoon, and our cats. Meals were served by Indian stewards in a small saloon. The crew were mostly lascars – Muslims from Chittagong – one of whom would always be in the bows with lead and line, singing out the depths as we glided through shallows and sandbanks.

"At night", she recalled, "the boat would tie up at some village landing place. People would come aboard to offer local produce for sale and to buy things that passengers had brought from further south. In the shallows close by, mothers would be giving small children their baths. Then, as the sun dipped below the horizon, they would go back to their village, a child by the hand and a big pot of water balanced on a piece of cloth wound round the hair knot on their heads. The air was full of laughter, and the smells of evening fires and meals cooking".

Approaching Yenangyaung, they could see dry cliffs and a

Vernon and Ruth

ridge beyond, some six hundred feet high, which seemed to be clothed with a dead forest: not trees, they realised, but wooden oil derricks − only then being superseded by slimmer steel ones. Major Ewing, whom Vernon was succeeding, was waiting on the jetty for them with his wife and the old Ford car which they had agreed to buy from him, together with Maung Kyin, its driver, whom they would also be inheriting. The Ewings were going back south next day on the same mailboat. Vernon and Ruth saw them off next morning. Returning to the car, they found it had a puncture and Maung Kyin had to change a wheel before they could set off.

Successive Wardens had lived in the same house, rented from an Indian gentleman. Because the Government had refused to increase the rent he had declined to do any repairs, and the Ewings had been equally neglectful. Ruth recalled her shock as she entered their new home. "I thought I had never seen so filthy a place and could scarcely believe that educated Europeans − and a woman at that − could have lived in it. The ground floor was brick-built with concrete floors. The upper floor was made of wood. There was dust and rubbish all over the place. Even the drawers and cupboards − for the house was supposed to be 'furnished' − were filthy. Where once there had been flower beds outside the windows the ground was littered with crown corks. We made an expedition to the shops, returning with brooms, soap, scrubbing brushes, cloths and disinfectant. The next few days being a holiday when Vernon's office would be closed, he and I and the rest of our household all got down to scrubbing and cleaning the place from top to bottom. After that, we unpacked our few possessions, I made some curtains for the windows, and we felt we could call this a home.

"The old Ford, of which we were the fourth owners, was a mystery to us. We had never driven or owned a car, so we were completely in the hands of Maung Kyin. It seemed to devour spark plugs and other small parts. Maung Kyin grew fat and was unfailingly good tempered − as he had every reason to be. In time,

Vernon began to understand the internal combustion engine and our repair bills came under better control".

Once she had got the house in order, Ruth became restive. Sewing was difficult in the heat, with fingers sticky and needles rusting; she could not read for the whole day; and a good teacher of Burmese was hard to find. "So Vernon offered to take me on in his office as a part-time clerk – unpaid. But he insisted that I must work regular hours so that he could rely on me. For a time, therefore, I spent the mornings there, opened his letters and drafted replies for those I could deal with. He also gave me interesting reports to read."

Social life in the European community was painfully formal. At the top of the pecking order were the managers of the three biggest oil companies who had huge houses and gardens, with hordes of Indian servants. Newcomers to this community – mainly young bachelors – were expected to make the rounds of the European houses, placing their cards in "calling boxes" which stood at their doors: two cards to be left by men – one for the resident husband and one for his wife – and one card for women – for the resident wife only. These calls had to be made during the brief hour between the end of work and sunset, so men had to change into a suit with collar and tie, and forego their only oppportunity for exercise that day. No social contact was made: the cards were dropped in the box and collected later by a servant who handed them to his mistress on a silver salver.

"Since they appeared to have no interest in the country from which they derived their fat incomes" Ruth acidly wrote, "social intercourse with these people was halting at best. I was still a 'bride', so had to take precedence over all the senior ladies on formal occasions. Their long dinner parties were tedious beyond words and I longed to join Vernon at the foot of the table where he was making friends with other young men. Those newly recruited to the Burmah Oil Company – the B.O.C. – were debarred by company rules from getting married for their first five-year term of service. Some of them had been at Oxford and Cambridge since the war; some were interested in Burma and its people and came with us on holiday expeditions into the country; sharing in our ribald sense of humour about self-important ladies.

"We never had a calling box, but we kept open house and made a host of friends. They often came for breakfast on Sunday mornings (eaten at ten o'clock, and large as a Sunday lunch back home) or for supper in the evenings and to listen to our gramophone" – or, Vernon added, "to listen to Ruth playing the piano". This became their informal, hospitable life style throughout their time in Burma.

"The Burma climate" Ruth continued, "had split Vernon's old, wooden flute, so we put together a number of wedding present cheques to make £25 which enabled his father to choose a xylonite flute for him from Rudall Carte in London. I played the metal-framed, tropical, upright piano we had bought when I first arrived in Rangoon and Vernon resumed playing his flute with me. Fortunately as it turned out, I was never a fluent music reader because I was able to memorise tunes so quickly. Any pianist in Yenangyaung who could read well was constantly in demand for popular songs and dance music."

Outside their homes, social life for white people was confined mainly to a few clubs. "Most of the British belonged to the Yenangyaung Club where we played tennis in the dry season, and golf in the rains when the small course turned green overnight. I disappointed Vernon, who was a beautiful dancer, by giving up dancing – deterred by the heat, the sticky hands of my partners, and the awful dance music.

"Occasionally we visited the American Club which was full of oil drillers and their wives. They came to Burma partly for high salaries and partly to escape prohibition. In the poker room, players sat all through the night, topees pushed to the back of their heads, and the corners of their tables loaded with huge wodges of notes, revolvers, and constantly refilled glasses of drink. I have seen American wives so drunk that they ended by pouring liquor down their chins instead of their throats. Rex West, an expert player whom we knew, made a steady income there by going one night a week, playing till midnight, going home for a few hours sleep, and rejoining the table before dawn to sweep the board when other players were too drunk to know what they were doing.

"Another of our friends was Father Foliere, a French priest who had come to Burma as a young man. Falling desperately ill after a few years, he was sent back to his family in France to die. But there his health rallied, and he returned to Burma to work among his flock of illiterate Tamil coolies. He lived in a small, wooden house on a stipend that was little more than any of them earned – striding about the oilfield in his topee and long habit. We immediately sensed his natural goodness and warmth, and would often invite him to Sunday breakfast. We did our best to give him a good meal, knowing that he would be living for the rest of the week on vegetable curry and rice."

The Burmese had been digging oil wells long before the British came on the scene. For each they had to gain permission from a hereditary corporation of 24 men, originally set up by the Burmese Kings, which had continued unchanged under the British. Burmese wells were three or four hundred feet deep at the most, dug by a man who climbed down on a rope. Since there would be no oxygen for him at that depth – only oil fumes – the man at the bottom of the well wore a helmet made of a kerosene tin with a small, glass window in front of his eyes. This helmet was attached to a rough shirt that was tied to his body at the waist and wrists. Air was sent down to him from a primitive pump on the surface through a long tube. Only close relatives who depended on his earnings were allowed to work the handle of this pump. They also hauled to the surface the kerosene tins he filled with the oil that he collected at the bottom of his well.

Western wells were drilled to 3,000 feet and more, where they operated in different strata and did not interfere with the native wells. But concessions for them had to be negotiated with the same 24-man corporation, and were subject to the rule, originally designed for native operators, that each well must be at least 60 feet from its nearest neighbour. This was far too close for a modern well that would suck oil out from a much larger area, but it enabled the companies to compete with each other by drilling day and night to get down to oil-bearing strata ahead of their neighbours in the field. Arrangements of this kind led to disputes which had to be arbitrated with the help of Vernon's Advisory Committee, consisting of the three American Field Superintendents of the biggest companies. He recalled them clearly: "Emrick from the B.O.C. was the most sophisticated – tall, urbane and a good mixer – Fowler, a more homely man, short and fat; and Whaley, who looked like Abraham Lincoln – tall, thin and gloomy. What they made of a young limey, less than two years out of university, I can only guess. It was perhaps better that I should not know the negotiations, the alignments and realignments that took place behind my back."

Collecting the royalties due from these companies posed other problems. The big boys were straight enough, but there were two small Indian companies owned by the same man who had linked their tanks with a pipe through which oil could be pumped to ensure that any tank being assessed for tax purposes would be nearly empty.

Income tax was introduced in Burma during Vernon's time at Yenangyaung and he had the job of collecting it. Printed notices calling for a return of income were devised, each beginning with the words "Dear Sir/Madam". Sending one to Miss Glencross, the formidable lady who was matron of the B.O.C. Hospital, Vernon's clerk felt neither mode of address would be quite right, so he crossed out both and wrote "Dear Maiden". Vernon was also the Marriage Registrar for Christians, but marriages proved rare – and disappointing. His first brought together "gold-toothed Minnie", a well-known Anglo-Burmese lady, and an American driller who already had six children. They all went on leave to the States where he was killed in a car crash. His second marriage joined "Susie", a Burmese lady, and a young Glasgow engineer. Three months later they came back asking for a divorce. The first strike of coolies took place during Vernon's time and there were some spectacular fires – wooden oil derricks are very easy to ignite. A million-gallon oil tank went ablaze at night. "In the dark you could see the level of the oil, red hot through the translucent walls of the tank".

In this kind of work, Vernon was responsible to his Deputy Commissioner: first, an able if unlikeable man who at least taught him a lot about accuracy, thoroughness and exact thinking; and then a man who had been a Lieutenant-Colonel in the Indian Army, "an ineffective gas-bag, disloyal to his Commissioner, for whom I gained no respect." But the Commissioner, Derick Grant, based about forty miles away in Magwe, became a good friend for them both. On their visits they were always invited to stay with the Grants in the large, cool, white-washed house provided for a Commissioner. If Vernon was at work before breakfast, Grant would take Ruth out walking, "explaining the crops, land revenue, river transport and anything else that occurred to him" she recalled. "We had no such talk in Yenangyaung and I was grateful to him for treating me like a sensible woman. Most Europeans in Burma treated women as playthings – certainly as people incapable of understanding anything serious."

Grant perhaps had reason for enjoying Ruth's company. Mrs. Grant, Ruth said later, "was an ambitious woman with a quick mind, who resented having to leave two school-age children in England and live in this rather isolated part of Upper Burma. She made her husband's life a misery – and embarrassed their guests – with constant complaint and ridicule, at the bridge table, at tennis and when he was driving their car. He never replied to her taunts, but the atmosphere was not a happy one." Perhaps Ruth was witnessing the stresses of separation imposed on families by life in Burma – stresses her own family would encounter in due course.

Vernon had done well in all the examinations young recruits to the I.C.S. were expected to take, apart from one in the Burmese language which he still had to pass at an acceptable level. This would be difficult in Yenangyaung where scarcely anyone spoke

Burmese, but he did his best to prepare for it. When the time came to take the test he was approaching the point at which those who failed would be deprived of their normal increments in salary. The examination was taken by a number of young officials from various departments of government and supervised by an Anglo-Burmese excise officer. "As the first paper began, this gentleman walked among the candidates, ostensibly to check that all was going well, but in fact to slip sheets of paper with translations and answers onto their desks as he passed." This so disgusted Vernon that he walked out without completing the examination – later taking it successfully in his next posting, by which time he was losing increments in salary.

A SON IS BORN

For Ruth, the most exciting times they had were the holidays that enabled them to escape from hot, smelly, messy Yenangyaung for a few days; always going to the wildest and remotest places they could reach, starting in the car, and then walking – travelling light, without servants. They were a couple who could not view a landscape without yearning to get to the furthest ridge, the highest mountain, in sight. Ruth gives marvellous accounts of these journeys and the people they met – some of whom had never seen a white woman before.

There were monks who fed and sheltered them, and villagers who insisted they ride on their bullock carts because it "was not proper for them to be walking". There was the old lady in a one-room hut, high in the Chin hills, who was puzzled by the colour of Ruth's skin and wanted to know if she was white all over. "I rolled my sleeve up to the shoulder and took off one boot and stocking. She examined my foot, feeling the sole with her hands, and said 'Have you come all that way on that soft thing?' No-one wore shoes in the Chin villages, so their feet were as horny as the soles of my boots." There was Captain Terndrup, of the Irrawaddy Flotilla Company, who had been navigating the upper reaches of the river before the British took over in 1885 – ferrying Burmese soldiers to the far north to fight the Chinese. (They sat on his decks among jars of gunpowder, smoking cheroots.) He took Ruth round Mandalay, the old capital of Burma, telling her how he had guided the British troops in for their conquest and told their officers where the women were housed so that they could prevent rape and pillage. There was Colonel Biggwither, a Deputy Commissioner whom they met at the top of a mountain. He was a notoriously choleric man, but charming to them (he took them to see snake charmers working with their cobras) – known to the Burmese as "the Tiger D.C." on account of his wife's habit of accompanying him on tour with a pet tiger in tow. There was also the time when Ruth went on her own to visit Fred and Maud Wemyss, now at Lashio in the far north, and came back by rail and steamer with a terrier pup who crawled into her bed each night for comfort. She called her "Patsy".

When the cold weather arrived, friends from Oxford days came to stay with them. They included Ken Bailey, the Australian who was to marry Vernon's sister, Yseult. These visits gave opportunities for more explorations.

Vernon's father retired at this time and the family moved out of London to a house at Blewbury, in the Berkshire countryside. His mother's letters mentioned that he had not been well, then that they were going "to take a course of the waters" in Germany. From there came a cable to say that he was very ill, followed by another to say he was dead.

"This first death in the family was a great sorrow" wrote Ruth. "We had both been deeply attached to this warm-hearted, kind and patient man. I told San Hla the news we had received and later that evening, as we sat together silently, trying to grasp the reality of it, San Hla came quietly in, bringing note paper and a pen to set on the table before Vernon, and saying how sorry he was. He understood our needs and feelings very well."

In June, 1925, Ruth realised she was pregnant – her baby conceived, I suspect, when they were out in high and wild mountains, two months earlier. She was overjoyed. "The future suddenly seemed to stretch out indefinitely before me". Feeling very well, she went on playing tennis and walking with Vernon, but gave up working in his office. He seems to have been a good deal cooler, "accepting the prospect with his usual patience" she noted — patience which must have been tried even further by his mother-in-law's and his mother's reactions. Isabel Singer, who had for 18 months been pestering them for this news, announced that she would be coming out to join them. His own mother expressed "her indignation that now, not only early marriage but father-hood too would prevent him from rising to the highest levels in the service."

The monsoon had come, bringing cooler weather, and Ruth got down to making baby clothes. Her mother sent a pile of baby things from the Singers' bottom drawers and cupboards — quite unusable in a hot country, so Ruth got the "dirzee" (the tailor) to copy a few of them in light materials.

Europeans usually acquired a nanny for their babies, but Burmese nannies were rarely to be found and the Donnisons did not want an Indian "ayah" in what they felt was a Burmese household. So they found a well-recommended Christian Karen whose employers were returning to England. She spoke in rather bad American English, learned in the Baptist Mission School, but seemed attractive, cheerful and clean; so they took her on.

Isabel Singer arrived at Christmas time, dressed, to Ruth's horror, in the new fashions they had only seen in magazines: short skirts, pale pink stockings, white shoes, her beautiful silky hair cut very short… They had taken a great deal of trouble to make her welcome but she sat for a long time, bolt upright, with her hat on, before gradually relaxing. (Perhaps she knew her close-cropped hair would be a shock?) When bed-time came, she insisted on pushing her bed out of the room they had prepared for her to stand it alongside their beds on the open verandah; so next day, to get some privacy, they had to move their own back into their room.

Mrs. McCallum, who had been so helpful to Ruth on the boat out, was now in the Shan States – the high country to the east – where her husband was Commissioner. She had spotted Isabel Singer's name in the passenger lists, guessed she must be Ruth's mother, and invited her to visit them. These highlands are breathtakingly beautiful, so Ruth and Vernon gratefully sent her off with one of their servants for a couple of weeks and she returned when the baby was due.

Labour pains began on January 16th, faded out, and resumed two days later. Ruth recalled that they called in "the big, kindly, Anglo-Burmese midwife who regaled them all with the usual midwives' horror stories. But I was not perturbed. After all – I was a healthy young woman with a healthy young husband..." But by 19 January it was clear that things were not going well. A message was sent for the doctor. He was out of town, so Dr. Svensson, his partner – unknown to them – came instead.

"I cannot remember much of that day; I was getting exhausted from lack of sleep and the constant contractions. Eventually there was Dr. Svensson's kindly face above me; a murmured consultation, a smell of anaesthetics... then nothing. Vernon, I learnt later, had been sent to the B.O.C.hospital for a large container of boiled water" (to get him out of the way, I suspect).

"Next I heard a sound of sharp slapping, followed by the cry of an infant. 'Is the baby all right?' 'Yes, a beautiful boy'. ...we had a son." Which was what she had passionately hoped for. He would be named David, after her beloved father.

"They told me later that he did not breathe for twenty minutes after the forceps delivery, and their slaps eventually revived him. There was a faint bruise on his forehead, but the skin was unbroken and he was soon looking beautiful.

"Patsy, our dog, wanted to stay by me, so, to prevent her getting under people's feet, I had asked them to tie her to the bannisters outside our room. When the baby had been washed and dressed and brought to me she was released and came running. I held the baby over the side of the bed and said 'Look Patsy, it's a

Vernon, Ruth and infant David

Vernon and David

puppy'. She put her paws up and gently licked the top of David's head in welcome. From then on, she was always on guard beside the pram outdoors, or lying near him indoors".

Ruth had been through a rough time that left her exhausted and in pain for some days; but she managed to breast-feed the baby. Her mother, who had borne six and raised four of them, took complete charge – even arranging that he be circumcised when he was a week old, without consulting either of his parents. She went home to England when he was a month old and Ruth was back on her feet. Dr. Svensson warned her that she should not have another baby for five years.

Ruth's first visitors were half a dozen bachelor friends from the B.O.C. who were delighted to see her and welcome the baby. Not a single woman came. Although she had obviously been pregnant – a young woman having her first baby 8,000 miles from home – only one of the white women in Yenangyaung had even referred to it: the wife of a Glasgow engineer who used a prim, Edwardian euphemism, saying "I hear you are in an interesting condition".

WHY WERE THEY SO AWFUL?

A dozen years later, David realised that, apart from a small number of lifelong women friends – Margaret Godfrey (previously Hope) and Annis Gillie, both in England, were the two most important – his mother's European friends were nearly all men. As I have learnt more about her earlier experiences, first in her childhood and then in Burma, I think I understand better why that was so. What was it that made these white women of Yenangyaung so awful? Ruth and Vernon were entitled to feel alienated from them and their whole society. But this is not only the Donnisons' story; it is about these women too. So we should try to understand them.

The British brought to their empire, intact, all the snobberies and conflicts of their own complex society – or rather, a version of them drawn from memories of the "home" they had left many years before. After only two years absence, Ruth was already shocked by the fashions her mother brought from London. Most of the women around her would have had ideas and expectations that came from Britain as it had been before the cataclysmic war that had changed everything in Europe – but very little in Burma.

The story goes still further back. Many British people had always come to their empire because they could not attain the status – or find the man – they had hoped for at home. Once there, many of them found they were capable of things they could never have achieved if they had remained confined in Britain's socially oppressive little world. Even Clive, the great eighteenth century conqueror of India, had been sent out to be a clerk in the East India Company because he was not likely to "make it" at home. It is not surprising, therefore, that many of these people cared a lot about status – were connoisseurs of its nuances – and the women, who had so little else to do, cared most of all.

A dozen years earlier, Leonard Woolf, then a young colonial administrator in Ceylon, was observing the same things. "White society in India and Ceylon, as you can see in Kipling's stories, was always suburban. ...the social structure and relations between Europeans rested on the same kind of snobbery, pretentiousness and false pretensions as they did in Putney or Peckham." [1] (I think "suburban", for him, meant anti-intellectual, lower middle class, and often anti-semitic.)"Intelligence and the intellectual" he continues, "produced the same feeling of uneasiness, suspicion and dislike among the white population of Jaffna (the remote northern outpost to which he had been sent) as... in nearly all strata or pockets of English society." [2] He says the class system in Ceylon placed the civil servants at the top, army officers followed by planters in the middle, and businessmen on the fourth rung. (Plato would have approved.)"There was in the last three classes an embryonic feeling against the first. The civil servant was socially in many ways top dog..." – as became only too clear when he met white matrons looking for "potential sons-in-law". [3]

Race relations, too, were shaped by the social sensitivities that England had bred into these people. Other nations write novels about sex and power. The English novel, since Jane Austen, has been mainly about class. They wrote poems about class — Betjeman's and Auden's are full of it. They even wrote hymns about it. When he went to school, young David found himself singing about "The rich man in his castle, the poor man at his gate; *God* made them high or lowly and ordered their estate." So when the English came to Burma and found themselves surrounded by people of many colours they felt obliged to place them all on the rungs of the mental ladder of status they had brought with them from Putney or Peckham. And the Indians, if not the Burmese, would have understood that very well.

There were other, cross-cutting suspicions dividing the men who *did* things from those who advised, administered and controlled: between the engineers, drillers and ships' captains on the one hand, and the managers, public and private, on the other. In his novella, *"Heart of Darkness"*, written some years earlier than Woolf's experiences, Joseph Conrad vividly described the feelings of his first-person narrator, Marlow — engineer and ship's captain — for the wealthy invaders of the Congo. Marlow desperately needs rivets to repair his ship which is stranded far up the river. No-one bothers to send them, and "instead of rivets there came an invasion, an infliction, a visitation" of men wearing "tanned shoes", bringing with them "the loot of innumerable outfit shops and provision stores..."[4]

Just how nasty this suburban world could seem to the intellectuals who hated it most was at this time being vividly described in another part of Burma by George Orwell. In his novel, *"Burmese Days"*[5], every character is exploitative, every relationship corrupted — essentially by imperialism. White people see the country as a backwater of India, talk about it *as* "India", and maintain their power there through a brutal intervening layer of mainly Indian soldiers and policemen. Even the climate, the insects and the vegetation are hateful. Vernon read the book when it was pub-

116

lished in the 1930s and commented only that "it did not seem like that at the time".

Which poses the question, Why was it so different for *him*? Not because he was sheltered from these social tensions. Yenangyaung, one of the few industrial towns in Burma, must have brewed a specially virulent mix of them. The top business people were far richer than the top civil servants. The drillers and engineers — the "doers" — were better able than either to cope with crises such as burning derricks and oil tanks. So Vernon and Ruth, athletic Oxford and Cambridge graduates with a talent for languages and music — but taking no pleasure in social drinking and refusing to play for dances at the club — must have seemed odd fish, both to the engineers' wives and to the kind of memsahib described by Orwell as nagging her servants for twenty years without ever learning a word of their language. Although Vernon was young, as an I.C.S. official coming from Marlborough, Oxford and the Grenadier Guards, he would have been socially fireproof. But his young Jewish wife must have made many in this suburban society uneasy: a girl with a science degree who worked in her husband's office and went out into the wilds with him. This was a time when many English people (including, she discovered, their doctor, who should have delivered her baby) still believed that women ought not to have higher education, or a profession more prestigious than teaching or nursing — and they should give that up as soon as they got married.

Babies must have added yet another ingredient to this brew of tensions. White women generally believed that Yenangyaung, like other hotter parts of the empire, was not a place where you could have children. So they either remained childless — with who knows what stressful forms of birth control — or they sent their children "home" at an early age for other women to look after, or they went home with them and left their men to seek comfort in other beds. So a young woman having a baby must have provoked envy and disapproval among many in this community.

We should remember too that most married, middle class

English women of that time were deprived of higher education and forbidden to work. In Burma they could not even cook or clean the house. That stunted their minds, their wisdom and human sympathies as surely as the binding of feet stunted the physique of genteel Chinese ladies. Writing about her life in Europe and America at about the same time, Peggy Guggenheim, another independent, intelligent, Jewish woman – creator of great galleries of modern art – said "I don't like women very much, and usually prefer to be with homosexuals if not with men. Women are so boring."[6] All of which may make the memsahibs' behaviour a little easier to understand – if no more attractive.

MA THAN

For a while after David was born, Ruth found that "every strange sound – the crowing of a cock down in the village below, or the rats rustling in our roof – seemed to threaten the baby. Which must have been exceedingly trying for Vernon who wanted me to come out with him now and then." So she nerved herself to go out to dinner, leaving the sleeping child in the care of his nanny. "Returning before 11, we were met by San Hla who asked me to come upstairs with him. I was puzzled, but followed him to our nanny's bed where he pulled back the sheet. There was nothing under it but a rolled bundle she had placed to make it look as if she was sleeping there, while she herself had gone out. So that was the end of a Karen nanny."

For some days Ruth took complete charge of the baby. "Then I asked San Hla if his wife, Ma Than, would like to come and work in the house as the child's nurse. He said that she had never worked for Europeans and knew nothing about babies because they had none themselves. Nor, as I knew, did she speak any English. I said that all I wanted was that she should do as I asked her. I would show her how to do things. I would be responsible for the child at night so that she could continue to sleep with him in their quarters, and she would have time off whenever he did, so that she could still prepare his food. Thus Ma Than came to be David's nurse. I do not know how old she was: it never occurred to me to ask her. But she must have been over 40, which to my 26 years seemed quite a venerable age.

"Ma Than had an instinct for handling babies. I taught her our ways of bathing and changing, and how to wash and thoroughly rinse clothes and napkins. In return, she taught me so much — about her language, and about Burmese customs and superstitions, which I encouraged her to follow, provided they did not conflict with our ideas of hygeine or comfort. It was unlucky, for instance, to cut hair or nails on a Friday or if the child felt unwell. So we would wait for a more auspicious time. Ma Than's own cure for feeling unwell was to smoke a cheroot. She usually carried one tucked into the well-oiled knot of hair on top of her head. Out of doors, resting by the pram or feeling tired on a hot day, she would light it and take a few puffs — then put it back for later use. The scent was delicious, Ma Than was refreshed, and the smoke helped to keep flies and other insects away from the baby.

"The Burmese use a mixture of powdered bark called thanaka, worked into a fine cream with powdered sandalwood and water, to anoint their faces, arms, hands and feet — partly to make their beautiful coppery skin whiter, and partly for its cooling effect in hot weather. Ma Than brought thanaka for David's heat rash and I soon learned to put as few clothes on him as possible. I am afraid the elaborate baby clothes my mother brought, full of tucks and lace, passed down from my sisters, were never used.

"As the hot weather came upon us, our house became like an oven all day. After dark, lying out on our open verandah under the stars, a soft breeze brought some freshness; but by morning our clothes were hot to the touch and newspapers crackled in our hands as if they had been held before a fire. David's skin was covered in prickly heat — an irritant rash — and I became increasingly exhausted."

Vernon was soon to be moved to a new post in the Shan States — in the high country to the east where it would be cooler. Reluctantly, for she did not want to leave him, yet with relief, for she was feeling so weak, Ruth went to Maymyo, the hill station to which Vernon had been invited by the Reynolds, where Government officials could rent rooms for holidays. She would spend a few weeks there in a two-room flat until Vernon could join them for a few days before they went on to take up his new post.

Ruth took Ma Than and the baby with her, along with Kasim, their "second boy", and the usual pile of baggage required by European families travelling in a country without hotels or Western shops: bed rolls, towels and clothing; food, crockery, cooking pots and cutlery; the baby's bedding, pram and bath... They had to be completely self-supporting.

The journey began restfully, with two days steaming slowly up the Irawaddy in one of the Flotilla Company's paddle boats to Mandalay, along with the usual crowd of deck passengers. At the Mandalay jetty, as Ruth was wondering if she could cope with all the decisions needed to get her party three miles through the heat to the railway station, Ma Than brought a bright and friendly man to her who said " If you will give me the money for your train tickets, I will go to the station to reserve seats for you and get your luggage on to the train. You can stay here where it is cool and come by car to the station just in time to catch the train. In this way, you and the child will be saved much exhaustion and heat." "Who are you?" Ruth asked. "I am Ma Than's younger brother" he said.

"These people", she wrote, "had come, unasked, to take care of me. Some hours later he returned with a taxi to take us to the station where all was ready — seats reserved and luggage stowed. He disappeared almost before I could properly thank him.

"Vernon told me later that San Hla had asked him if all had gone well for us, and when he said what wonderful help I had been given by Ma Than's brother he said 'Oh yes. I sent a telegram to him to tell him of the Thakinma's journey, and with instructions to help her.'

"The train climbed very slowly, pausing at the end of each short section to reverse equally slowly up the next through a deep, green forest that cast cool shadows. I had not brought food with me, and as the afternoon wore on I began to feel utterly exhausted. A fellow passenger – an elderly Colonel Rich – spotted that I was wilting and offered me tea that he was making on a travelling stove on the floor of the carriage. Never had tea been more welcome. As some strength returned, I managed to nurse the baby, and then get my party out of the train and up to our flat on the upper floor of a two-storey block. There was basic furniture for us, and electric light – the first I had had for years. There was no-one else in the flats and I knew no-one in Maymyo. We began unpacking our stuff – towels, soap and the baby's things first.

"Then it grew very dark outside. There was a flash of lightening and a deafening crash of thunder. Rain came down in sheets; and a whirlwind hit the building. The lights went out and I could hear a window battering loose against its frame. Water began to splash down on us from the ceiling. Paddling around in it, I managed to dig a towel out, bundle the baby in it, drag a bed to the driest place I could find and place him on it. Then I saw Ma Than's glowing cheroot and realised how frightened she must be to have lit it indoors with me. We put our kit in the safest places we could find in the dark, then sat side by side to wait for the storm to pass. While she drew on her cheroot, we held hands to comfort one another, and all heaven roared outside.

"The cyclone lasted two hours, and it was only next day that we could see the extent of the damage it caused. Trees were down, taking electricity cables with them; tiles were ripped off roofs, and windows had been torn out. But the baby slept undisturbed throughout the night. Soon we were moved to another flat on the ground floor where we spent the rest of our holiday."

Here, in a world where there were families from the I.C.S., the Forestry and Education Departments and other public services, Ruth at last found friends among women of her own age who shared her interests. Some of them had young children, too. Enid Dawkins, wife of a Forest Officer, toured with her husband for half the year, taking their children with them on elephants and ponies, living in tents, yet maintaining a regular routine of lessons and play. She spoke Burmese and knew a lot about the lore and customs of the people; she had good advice to offer about how to protect the family from malaria, and she was a talented photographer and water colour painter. For Ruth, who had for months been surrounded by women who told her that she would never again be able to go on tour and would soon have to send her child home, all this was a great encouragement and the beginning of a lasting friendship.

A young I.C.S. wife, walking one day with Ruth, pointed out two formidable ladies, wives of senior members of the Education Service which was responsible for schools in Burma – Mrs. Snow and Mrs. Bulkeley. They had been students at Somerville, Oxford's most scholarly college for women, and were now spending the hot weather in Maymyo with their children. "Walking behind them", Ruth recalled, "I recognised the old blue-stocking gait and style, so often seen in my Cambridge days, but never before in Burma. I was too shy to approach them, but the sight of them gave me comfort." Eight years later, one of them was to give David comfort too.

Ruth's other delight during these weeks was to talk in the evenings with Ma Than who would come in and sit on the rug at her feet, helping her to learn Burmese. "I persuaded her to correct my pronunciation. By listening carefully and matching her lips when she spoke, I began to acquire a colloquial command of the language at last. Quite unaccustomed to European ways, she showed great interest in all my belongings. Burmese people use combs to groom their hair and hold it in place, but a brush was quite new to her. She handled the things on my dressing table one by one, and I did my best to explain what each was for. I told her I would show her everything I had and explain each thing to her, if she would ask me. I only would not like it if she examined my things when I was not there. We each kept to our agreement and a deep trust grew up between us."

KING MAKER

Up to this point in my story I have been drawing on the chapters of a memoir written alternately by Ruth and Vernon some forty years after the events they describe. At this stage of the story Ruth, losing her battle with cancer, was unable to write any more. Unless attributed to someone else, my quotations now come from Vernon. In Yenangyaung he had been waiting for his successor, Denis Phelips, who was reluctant to leave a remote place where he was very happy for the bright lights of a town. When he eventually showed up, Vernon was able to join Ruth in Maymyo for a few days before they went on to Taunggyi, headquarters of the Shan States. (The name means "the big hill". There's a great crag overhanging the town.)

Like his predecessors in Yenangyaung, Vernon passed on his car, with its driver Maung Kyin, to his successor. He bought a second-hand, two-seater "Overland" to replace it. To get to Maymyo and Ruth, he had to drive for a day to Meiktila — the first seventy miles on rough and mountainous tracks — and there put the car on a train to Mandalay, for there was no motorable road for the next stage of his journey. Then he drove another forty miles up a very steep road with hairpin bends all the way. I recall Mrs. Snow, the blue-stocking lady glimpsed by Ruth, saying that she used to come down this road on a bicycle, dragging a log behind her to act as a brake. Still uncertain about his ability to drive the car, Vernon brought Maung Kyin with him as far as Meiktila, saying goodbye as he got on the train. It was to be nineteen years before they met again: Vernon would then be in uniform and driving a jeep at the first Irrawaddy crossing during the reconquest of Burma.

After a few days more in Maymyo the whole household moved to Taunggyi. This was a much more demanding journey, partly by rail, partly on rough, unsealed roads, climbing more than 4,000 feet. The servants went ahead. Vernon and Ruth stayed a night on the way at the Kalaw Hotel; one of only two or three in the whole of Burma. It grew cooler as they climbed, "Suddenly we smelled the pine trees. It was like adding gin to the tonic." Before they got to Taunggyi they had to replace a split tyre, cross rivers by ferry and top up a blown radiator from nearby streams. Before setting out, "Ma Than said to San Hla, her husband, that she was afraid to go into this remote, mountainous country. 'Do not fear' he replied. 'The Thakin and the Thakinma will look after us.' But in many ways" added Vernon "it was they who looked after *us*."

On the Shan plateau they were in high, sparsely populated, green country, laced with crystal-clear streams. Ridges and peaks rose thousands of feet higher, with lakes lying between them. There was no snow, but all the rest of nature's paint box seemed to have been thrown into the picture.

One-third of the people in Burma are not Burmans. The Shans, who are the largest of the minority groups, resemble the Siamese (or Thais) in language and appearance: indeed, "Shan" and "Siam" are the same word. They occupy Burma's eastern plateau which reaches out to mountainous borders with China, Laos and Siam. When the British took over the plains of Upper Burma in 1886 they set up there the system of direct administration originally developed for India and already operating in Lower Burma. But the Shans lived in some thirty small kingdoms, each with its own chief — sawbwas, myosas… they went under various titles. These kingdoms were robustly independent, joining together for the first time in a Shan federation only four years earlier. The Burmans had claimed to rule all this territory and collect tribute from its chiefs — and in a good year they got somewhere near to doing so. The British claimed to have succeeded to these powers, but in practice they allowed the chiefs to manage their own small kingdoms, provided they made a contribution to the revenues of Burma, and did not attack each other, form alliances with foreign powers or behave in ways that would outrage their overlords. In return the British ensured that no-one attacked them. Although the Rangoon government was gradually shaping these kingdoms into greater uniformity — in the way bureaucracies do — there was still a lot of independence, variety and scope for creative improvisation among them.

Before the arrival of the British, local rulers were sometimes brutal – George Scott's expeditions, towards the end of the nineteenth century, encountered much mayhem and murder, and met one who tried out new guns by firing them at his own people[7]. But these men had to be pretty effective, politically and militarily, to stay in the saddle. The pacification imposed since then had brought many benefits, but it meant that chieftains could degenerate for years before they were replaced. This was the source of some of the more difficult problems Vernon had to deal with.

Vernon, now 28, had to do several jobs in this posting. He was office assistant to the Commissioner and Superintendent (two posts had been combined under the same man) who supervised the whole plateau; he was Assistant Superintendent of one of the kingdoms – Yaunghwe – and for, considerable periods, Assistant Superintendent of the Central Subdivision which included no less than nine kingdoms, ranging from one the size of an English county to one the size of a parish. Jim McCallum, his Commissioner, was a marvellous man to work for: "a Scot of lively and liberal imagination, a Socialist in politics, a great reader of H.G.Wells and the New Statesman – always prepared to delegate in a way that was very flattering to a young man. It was his wife who had befriended Ruth on her voyage out."

This work required Vernon to travel to fascinating places, often beginning in slim, dug-out canoes, rowed down the lakes by men who stood on one leg in the stern, wrapping their other leg around a long oar and leaning forward on it to drive the boat through the water. (Difficult, but efficient when you know how to do it.) Then he would walk through country that started at 3,000 feet and rose in places for another 4,000 feet.

The eccentrics and black sheep of European and mixed origin who took refuge in Burma often found their way to this hill country – there working with, and marrying, the hill people. Vernon's memoir vividly describes them, and often takes their story forward to their later lives in Britain or Burma – his recollections reflecting his loyalty to these friends and theirs to him.

A story with a typical aftermath dealt with "the Hsatung Sawbwa in the Central Subdivision. He was a tall Shan — unusual in itself — with a magnificent physique who looked every inch a ruler. Where so many of these men had grown degenerate, one had to admire him. But he was hot-tempered and sometimes high-handed. There were dark rumours of beatings and worse. The rule of law, which we were trying to extend, was difficult for this fine old despot to understand. He had been warned that he must mend his ways. Then I received a report that an Indian had been imprisoned and done to death by the Sawbwa in the course of some private feud. Murder we could not condone, so I set off with a clerk and a messenger to tell him that he must leave his kingdom at once and go to Thaton in Lower Burma. He had relatives there who would care for him. It was with some anxiety, coupled with feelings of real distress, that I communicated these orders to an upstanding man, but he accepted them and prepared to go. He was succeeded by his son, whose son and daughter came, 35 years later, to stay with us when she needed to convalesce after hospital treatment in England."

There was also "the Yaunghwe Sawbwa who, at 78, was the oldest and probably the most influential of these Chiefs. As a boy he had been brought up in the Mandalay court of the Burmese Kings, which made him the accepted authority on court customs and ceremonial. The British had given him a knighthood and he had all the dignity and charm of an aristocrat. I grew to feel a warm liking for him.

"Sir Saw Maung had for many years been building for himself a grand, two-storied, stone palace on the lines of the palace in Mandalay. Meanwhile, he lived in a temporary palace perched on bamboo poles, with matting walls and corrugated iron on the roof, to which further rooms and outbuildings were added from time to time like some crazy rabbit warren. It creaked and shook as you walked through it.

"The Sawbwa had twenty wives but no heir of his body. He

had adopted a worthless debauchee as Thadawgyi or Crown Prince. But the British had always insisted that their approval be obtained before an heir was recognised, and they had never conceded this to the Thadawgyi. The Sawbwa was long past exercising any effective control over his officials or his personal entourage. He was being defrauded of state and personal revenues, and every kind of abuse was rife. Money was being poured into the construction of the new palace without the slightest result.

"On one occasion I demanded to see the cash in the Treasury. This, I knew, would be a grave social solecism, which became even clearer when I was told that this would be quite impossible because all the cash was in a tin trunk under the bed of the chief wife – and she was asleep. I said I was perfectly prepared to wait till she awoke, and after a long period of acute embarrassment I was allowed into the bedroom to find, of course, there was very little in the trunk.

"After I had been some six months in office the Government decided the Sawbwa must be compelled to appoint not an Advisor (we had tried that before) but an Administrator, to whom he would have to delegate control over his officials and the administration of his State. I visited the Sawbwa in person to deliver this ultimatum, keenly aware how unpopular I must be, and sorry to have to handle the old man so harshly. I had with me a list of persons the Government would be prepared to accept as Administrators – mainly retired officials of the police or civil service. To my amazement, he turned to me and said, 'If I have to have an Administrator, I would like you.' I had to say that I did not know how the Governor would respond to this proposal, but I would convey his wishes. When it filtered up to him, Sir Harcourt Butler, who was then Governor of Burma, said Sir Saw Maung should be allowed to have the man of his choice. I took the news to the old man who was delighted and set in hand the grand, ceremonial induction to my new duties.

"This ceremony went ahead under a great, coloured canopy

Vernon made Administrator: Vernon standing behind the Sawbwa,
Ruth and Mrs McCallum at the Sawbwa's right hand; Vernon's
mother, Edith, on the Sawbwa's left

before his household and officials, the monks, the Headmen of villages, the local European officials and their wives. My appointment was read out in Shan, Burmese and English, and inscribed on a scroll that was placed in a small bag of red and gold brocade which was given to me." (The picture opposite was taken at about this time, showing Sir Saw Maung, seated in the centre, along with Ruth and Vernon, local Europeans and Vernon's mother, who was visiting them at the time.)

"That very night", after Vernon's installation as Administrator, "Sir Saw Maung fell seriously ill. This was alarming as well as tragic, for it would inevitably generate rumours that he had been poisoned by me or my people. The doctor from the American Baptist Mission, called in as soon as he fell ill, warned us that he would not last long. I feared that his death would be followed by an outbreak of looting and possibly murder. That, too, was an old royal custom. I knew there was a standing order in Taunggyi, our headquarters twenty miles away, that when news of the Sawbwa's death came a platoon of Military Police – all of them Indians – would be despatched to Yaunghwe.

"Through the night, as death drew near, I gathered together three of the most trustworthy of the old man's relatives and officials, explained what I feared, and asked for their help. We assembled the keys of all safes and chests, placed our seals upon the locks – a purely symbolic gesture, but it might help – and stationed armed guards at key points. I was determined to control the situation by our own efforts if possible. This would establish relations of trust with the best local officials and their people.

"When the old man died there were violent and confused scenes of grief. Several of his wives threw themselves at my feet and implored my help as their only protector. My three stalwarts were quietly establishing their hold on the palace. Telegraphing news of the Sawbwa's death to Taunggyi, I added a pressing request that the Military Police stay away. But early in the morning the Indian troops arrived. I was furious and ordered them out of town to camp under some trees beyond the wall. The

Commissioner arrived later in the day and decided I had better take full control of the State until a new Sawbwa was appointed. My first request was that the Military Police be sent back to Taunggyi. I remained in charge for eight or nine months.

"The next tasks were to re-establish administrative order, and to settle the Sawbwa's debts, official and personal, selling for this purpose much of his jewellery – great rubies and diamonds, mostly unmounted – along with other property. Above all, I had to choose a successor.

"There were many claimants to the throne. The Thadawgyi was first among them, supporting his claim with three reasons: 'I do not drink, I do not smoke opium, I do not spoil other people's daughters.' I thought it improbable that he could substantiate any of these claims. It was easy to reject some candidates but very hard to decide between the three best – all fairly close relatives of the late Sawbwa. In the end it was Saw Shwe Thaik whom I recommended and who was appointed. As a soldier in the Burma Rifles during the war, he had walked alone through the jungles along the whole Chinese border, gathering intelligence.He also had a good deal of administrative experience.

"His first duty was to arrange a state funeral for Sir Saw Maung whose embalmed body had been lying in state all this time. Sir Harcourt Butler attended, made a little speech paying tribute to him, then turned to me and said 'Translate that please'. I passed my examination in Burmese at about this time, but did not have a fluent command of the flowery language required. Haltingly, I spoke a few words – thanking God that Sir Harcourt knew no Burmese. But the smile on the face of the Chief Secretary – head of the civil service in Burma – made it clear that he did.

"The new Sawbwa's wife, daughter of a Minister in Sir Saw Maung's court, spoke no English and little Burmese, and knew nothing of the ways of the Europeans she would have to entertain. But she was intelligent, and of a sweet, gentle disposition. So Ruth invited her to come and stay with us. We ate Shan food for half the week and European food for the other half. I learned to play Shan chess. (When I pointed out that the rules seemed to permit her to make moves that had been denied to me, her laughter was unabashed.) Her two boys – a little older than David but much the same size – played with him and their mothers grew closer as they shared the problems and pleasures of childhood. (The accompanying photograph shows David, aged two, and Sao Hseng Pa aged four.) This was the first of many encounters with Burmese and Shan people who shared our home. For many years thereafter we kept in touch with Saw Shwe Thaik and his children – one of whom came to study in England. Our contacts grew more difficult when he became the first President of an independent Burma, and impossible when he was imprisoned in 1962 by General Ne Win. He died in jail, but we were able to see another of his sons who eventually escaped to England." (And I have had the help of one of his daughters, now living in England, when writing this story.)

The friendly, easy working relationships of this time were lost when Jim McCallum was succeeded by a new Commissioner, although Vernon loyally commented that the new man's tighter control and reluctance to delegate made him in many ways "sounder" – at least from the Government's point of view. But it was his wife, "Georgie", who really put the acid into their lives – taking them back to the memsahibs of Yenangyaung. Forty years on, Vernon still recalled some of her remarks to Ruth. "On hearing that we had been married not in church but by the Registrar, she said 'Then I suppose you don't feel properly married'; and on hearing that Ruth had been to university, she said 'I would never have spoken to you if I had known that when we first met'."

Nevertheless, Taunggyi remained in their memories as one of the happiest places of their time in Burma – for the friends they made, for its wonderful scenery and climate, and for the maturity and confidence they both gained there. Although Vernon had to deal with much bigger issues later in his career, Ruth was prouder of his handling of the Yaunghwe Sawbwa's death than of any-

Sao Hseng Pa & David (aged 4 & 2)

thing else he did in Burma. Meanwhile, her Burmese improved and she passed the special examination set for the wives of officials — a success which won her a reward of 100 rupees. She also learnt to drive, passed her test, and began to take an increasingly active part in community affairs.

COUSIN TED

Like many other families, the Singers and the Donnisons both had deviant or unlucky members who left Britain to seek new lives in the empire. Some of these people achieved things that would never have been possible for them at home. But what of their children? How did the next generation fare? Descendants of the Singer asylum seekers in Australia and New Zealand did well. But how about Ted, Vernon's cousin, and son of his uncle John who went to Bangalore and took up with Anne who had been the wife of the Chief of Police. Vernon had last seen him in London when both boys had been ten years old. Knowing that Uncle John had died in 1920, believing his children to be illegitimate, and having heard no more about them, he had not even troubled to mention them when asked, on the application form for entry to the I.C.S., whether he had any relatives in India.

It was at about this time that a packet came through the post, addressed to Vernon, which contained photographs, including some he recognised as pictures of his family, and an unsigned letter saying that he had a relative in the Insein jail, close to Rangoon. The letter and the photographs, I guess, came from Anne, who had parted from John shortly before he died. She would have sent them later to Ted's sister, Daintie, when she found work as a nurse in the hospitals of Burma so that she could keep in touch with her brother in the jail. Anne would have told her to find where Vernon was and send the packet to him.

This was very worrying for a young I.C.S. official who had not yet securely established himself in the service. The imprisoned "relative" was presumably cousin Ted or some member of his family. Why was he in jail? Would his own failure to record that he had such relatives count against him? Would the senders of the letter force themselves upon him and Ruth?– try to blackmail them perhaps?

Vernon went to Insein as soon as he could and discovered in the jail a big fellow with blue eyes and blond hair: Cousin Ted, serving a life sentence for murder. Vernon was able to talk with him and learn that he had a few more years to serve. He promised to keep in touch and visit occasionally. His next step had to be to report to the Chief Secretary that he had failed to declare this relative in his application to join the service; an anxious task. He explained all the facts and was sent a reassuring reply.

He then wrote to his mother who was appalled by the news and told him to have nothing further to do with Ted, who, she feared, would be yet another obstacle on the route to becoming Viceroy. But Ruth and he did keep in touch, and helped Ted when he was released from jail after surviving a sentence of fifteen years.

I will take Ted's story further in Chapters V, VIII and XI; but before leaving him I should briefly tell how he got to the Insein jail, piecing the tale together from things he and his family told me many years later. Vernon's uncle John had built up a business in Bangalore. He and Anne never got married but they had two children: Edward and Daintie. Anne eventually left John for another man – some say a sergeant of police, some say an army sergeant (perhaps a sergeant in the Military Police?). Ted had left school in 1916 at the age of about seventeen and tried very hard to get a commission in the Indian Army, but they would not have him. (Too poorly educated? The wrong class? Too obviously Eurasian? He could have passed as white but his accent – "chi-chi" it would have been called – would have betrayed him.) So he joined as a ranker and after a brief training was sent to fight the Turks in Mesopotamia. Vernon would at the same time have been going with the Grenadiers to France. Ted was wounded quite soon and sent back to a hospital in India. Vernon would have been going to hospital around the same time with diphtheria – both young men probably owing their lives to these interruptions in their fighting service.

When Ted had fully recovered, the war was over and he set about looking for a job – without much success. He did not like his mother's new man and became alienated from her too because she took her partner's side in family quarrels. He must have felt very lonely – stranded in a limbo between different classes, different ethnic groups and different families. He found support in a small gang of young men. Together they held up trains, robbing the passengers. Soon, three of them were involved in the murder of a guard; all were caught and the other two were hanged. Ted, said to have been the youngest and least culpable, was given a life sentence. For administrative purposes Burma was still an integral part of India at that time, but it seems a bit odd that he was sent to a jail so far from Bangalore. Ruth said there were training opportunities at Insein which were not available in Indian jails. If so, I think the training was pretty rudimentary.

The jail was a big, hot, rough place – later used by the Japanese. There were a few European prisoners there who were given a separate diet and ate at separate tables. The Superintendent had to be protected by guards when he walked through the prison; but there was a doctor – Colonel Tarrapore, a Parsi in the Indian Medical Service – who was respected by the prisoners and could walk about unguarded.

Ted had a natural mechanical skill. One day crates of machinery for making shoes arrived in the jail. This was to provide work for the prisoners. But no-one there had seen such things before, so Ted was told to get the parts out of their crates, assemble the machines, and make them work; which he did. Thereafter his job was to keep these machines going. Later, his skills enabled him to make his way in the world.

IN CONCLUSION

Vernon and Ruth were gaining confidence in their ability to play their parts in a liberal, life-enhancing imperial task. With hindsight, we can see that they were poised on the crest of one of the long waves of history. The brutalities and bloodshed of conquest were over. The British no longer had to prove they were top dogs. With only a clerk at their side, young men could walk into the palaces of formidable chieftains and evict them from power — confident that they were doing this in the cause of peace and justice, and would be obeyed. At times of crisis they could usually send the soldiers back to their barracks and act as community leaders rather than oppressors. And the soldiers, being only a platoon or two of dark-skinned men, were there for reasons that were more symbolic than military. Many of the leading figures in Burma's white society were throw-backs to a previous generation; stuffy, snobby and so unreflectingly racist that they would not have understood the meaning of the word. But there was hope for the future in a new generation of younger people who were joining their ranks: intelligent, athletic graduates who learnt the languages, travelled light and far, enjoyed the native peoples and made friends among them — Plato's Guardians in training. But the wave on which they were all poised could not be frozen motionless in this halcyon moment. And the future of Burma would not be decided in the Shan States.

NOTES

1   Leonard Woolf, *Growing. An autobiography of the years 1904-1911*, London, Hogarth Press, 1961, page 7.

2   Woolf, page 56.

3   Woolf, pages 16-17.

4   Joseph Conrad, *Heart of Darkness*, Ware, Herts; Wordsworth
    Editions, 1995. First published 1902. Page 30.

5   George Orwell, *Burmese Days*, Harmondsworth, Penguin Books,
    1944. First published in the U.S.A., 1934.

6   Peggy Guggenheim, *Out of this Century. Confessions
    of an art addict*, London, Andre Deutsch, 1979; page 200.

7   G.E.Mitton (ed.), *Scott of the Shan Hills*, London, John Murray,
    1936 – eg. page 150.

V

PARADISE WON AND LOST

Although by the early 1930s clouds were gathering on its distant horizons, the British Empire was still being ruled with unassailable confidence. People like Vernon and Ruth Donnison, recruited after the First World War to help in the task, had found their feet and were ready to take on heavier responsibilities. The coming years were to be some of the happiest in their lives. But further ahead lay many uncertainties.

More and more Burmese and Anglo-Indian (meaning mixed-race) officials were being recruited and trained to run the country, and, from 1923, real power was being transferred to Burmese politicians. The advance towards democracy was expected to be "gradual", as Vernon's own selection board had sagely agreed. Whether the British would in fact be able to control the pace of that change or the directions it would take were questions to which no-one had given much thought.

Meanwhile Vernon's generation were acquiring wives and children. In Burma, these infants must have felt that the world they were growing into was a happy and confident one. But outside Rangoon it was a world without Western schools or reliable medical services. Before long, these children would be sent "home" to what, for them, would be an entirely strange country; and their mothers would have to decide whether to abandon them or their fathers. Early consignment to boarding schools was the norm among middle class families at that time. But, in a world without cheap air travel, children of the empire would not be able to rejoin their parents for the holidays.

On the margins of these households were European bachelors and spinsters – officials, planters, teachers, governesses – hoping to find a partner in this game of happy white families; some of them wondering whether to join forces with women and men "of the country", and knowing the implications such a step would have for their status in a world ranked by race and colour. Local recruits were not given the expatriate allowances and travel expenses which provided higher incomes and opportunities for home leave for those recruited in Britain. The children of those who took Burmese or mixed-race partners were unlikely to go "home", yet would not be wholly accepted within mainstream native communities. Choosing or hoping to be chosen, many faced difficult decisions with harsh consequences. Ruth and Vernon had friends who had been ostracised by main-stream white society because they had married Burmese wives.

FIRST HOME LEAVE

The time was coming for Vernon to be promoted to take charge of a District. Before doing that he was entitled to home leave – a whole year of it, which was longer than most people got because he had served six years with no more than brief local holidays. These long leaves between long spells of work made sense in the days of slow and expensive sea journeys when no-one travelled by air; but many years spent in remote places, without newspapers, radios or long-distance telephones, made Britain seem a very long way off. One senses in their memoirs the anxieties some men had about "home" and the long journey leading to it. "What on earth will you find to *do*?" one of them asked Vernon. For him and Ruth that question was complicated by the fact that the only two houses in England they could describe as "homes" belonged to mothers they did not particularly like.

The Government eased one part of their problems. It was at about this time that they decided to pay for the leave passages of I.C.S. officials and their wives - four times in the course of their careers. Children only got one free passage each: they were not expected to come back to Burma.

Vernon and Ruth said goodbye to their servants and set off with three-year-old David on a ship from Rangoon. "We got home early in January, 1929," recalled Vernon, "travelling over-land from Marseilles. Ruth's mother was waiting at Victoria Station to meet us, wildly excited to gloat over her grandson. As we got out of the train she snatched David out of Ruth's arms and dashed off down the platform to her waiting car. David must have thought he was being kidnapped. His howls reverberated under the great glass vault of the station. They at least enabled Ruth to track her mother through the crowds to the car. He could not be comforted till we got him into the safety of our bedroom in his grandmother's house. 'I want Mother-and-Father' he said indig-nantly."

After years in a hot climate, the family needed new clothes. They were driven down to the West End in David Singer's big, fabric-covered Sunbeam car. The "Blue Bird", the Singers called it. Although it was mid-day, "there was a dense, black fog over-head, dark as the darkest night, cutting out all the light". Groping about, with help from headlamps, street lights and brightly-lit shops, they got what they needed.

Then things began to get better. Vernon had written to ask his father-in-law for advice about buying a car. "I should perhaps have foreseen the result. He replied that he proposed to give us one. He was thinking of a new Chrysler which had stolen the applause at the Motor Show. We said, if he was really thinking on this scale, could it be the more solidly dependable Buick? And so we were given a splendid, 29-horse-power Buick with a graceful, grey body, built like a great bath. The spare wheel sat in a well in one of the front wings, but David Singer thought two spares – one in each wing – would look smarter. So we had two, along with other extras. What a generous and lovely gift!"

A week or two later they set off for a skiing holiday in Switzerland with some friends, leaving the infant David with a nurse in the Singer home in Lyndhurst Road. Ruth had skied before, but Vernon was new to it. Before long he was going on long expeditions: "falling about a good deal, but not holding up the rest of the party": another athletic skill for this all-rounder. Ruth became quite ill in the train on their way home and, back in Hampstead, grew worse, with a rash, ear-ache and threatened mastoids. It was scarlet fever, which Vernon developed too. He recovered quickly, but she had a bad time. Her mother hired a nurse to look after her and wanted to send Vernon to a fever hospital, but "the nurse said fever hospitals were dreadful places and she was perfectly willing to nurse me too. I'm glad to say she won. This was not the best way to begin one's first long stay with in-laws. Ruth's father, David, unable to bear any longer the tensions generated by his impossible wife, disappeared without a word and took refuge in his club. She was furious, but we and the nurse knew where he was and he 'phoned each day for news of us."

As Ruth began to recover, Vernon took her to Bossington in Somerset to convalesce, "together with David and another, rather formidable, nanny who would look after him. 'Why do you roar in your sleep, Nanny?' David asked."

They had been under competing pressures from both grandmothers — vociferously from Isabel — to settle down with each of them for their leave. "Although there were luxuries at Lyndhurst Road that were not to be found in 'Dibleys', the much less affluent Donnison home in Blewbury, my mother offered us a friendly place surrounded by lovely country. She was willing to put her house, her garden, indeed herself, at our disposal, and to allow us to establish our own routines — playing the game as far as possible according to our rules, particularly in the treatment of David, whatever her own feelings about those rules. At Lyndhurst Road Ruth's mother could not resist every opportunity — if we were out for the day or for a week-end — to change the rules and start bringing David up as she, not as we, wanted. At Dibleys we felt safe, if sometimes grievously irritated. And so it was that Dibleys became our home in Britain."

During the summer most of the Singers were going for a long holiday in the Dolomites. So, as some thanks to Ruth's father for the car, Vernon and Ruth invited him to travel in it with them on their way to join his family in Italy – revisiting, on route, some of the French and Belgian battlefields where Vernon had fought. David was left in London with his nurse. "When we refused to let him pay for petrol my father-in-law retorted by saying 'Very well then, I shall pay for the hotels – and choose them'. There followed six splendidly hilarious days. It was not easy to keep moving because he kept wanting to stop for a 'bock' at some attractive roadside *estaminet*. Arriving late at one of the hotels he chose, we found it afflicted by a strike of waiters. Guests had to fetch their own food from the kitchens. He entered warmly into the spirit of the evening, bustling about with a napkin over his arm and giving a splendid performance as a waiter." (A Labour voter he might have been, but this little bit of strike breaking did not trouble him.) " Next day, stopping for a lengthy and luxurious lunch at a great hotel in Luxembourg, I noted a woman wearing the highest heels that I thought anyone could balance on. But he, with worldly wisdom acquired at the Stock-Exchange, said this was nothing. A day or two later we spent the night at Lindau, the island city on Lake Constance. The white steamers in the miniature harbour with its lighthouses, the glassy water, the mountains and the sunset sky seemed unreally beautiful – like a stage set.

"Two days later we were approaching the Dolomites and the rest of the family. Suddenly, for David Singer, the sun went out. Such good, happy company all the way, he reverted to being a grumbling, fussy, peevish little man."

They survived for two weeks in the bosom of Ruth's family – their best days spent walking in the mountains on their own – and then set off with relief, Isabel being horrified because they neither knew nor cared where they were going. Winding their way home through Germany, they stayed for bed and breakfast in family cottages, did a four-day walk through the mountains, and called on Elly – now married – who had cared so well for Vernon when he was a boy, teaching him to speak her language and to love so many things about her country.

Back in England, they were soon off again to visit friends, explore the countryside and escape from their families, leaving David, as usual, in the care of a nanny. "They were always convinced", Ruth's youngest sister later remarked, "that you could pay other people to look after your children."

Leo Price, one of Vernon's Oxford friends glimpsed in Chapter II, was among those whom they stayed with. Now head of his old school, Bishop's Stortford, but still unmarried, "he was a charming host, coming with us in the evening to make sure our beds were turned down and putting hot water bottles in them for fear that we might be cold after years in the tropics. He had entered into rugby football legend by scoring between the posts for England against Wales within ten seconds from the kick-off. But it was to be the last time we saw him. Before our next leave he got appendicitis, and when his doctors called for an immediate operation he insisted on finishing his term's work first – and by then it was too late. It was a tragic loss of someone with almost god-like gifts."

These were among the recollections of my parents, repeated in Vernon's memoir, that I recall when they spoke of their first home leave. They are those of an English middle class still hoping to return, after the horrors of war, to the years before 1914 – years in which increasingly affluent, tolerant and liberal societies had been created: years when the British, like the French, felt confident in their civilising, imperial mission. But this was 1929 – the year of the great Wall Street crash. Soon unemployment was rising to levels never seen before: over 20 per cent in Britain and worse in North America, Australia and most of Europe. International trade fell by 60 per cent between 1929 and 1932. International lending – Britain's most successful industry – virtually ceased, falling by more than 90 per cent between 1927 and 1933. The movement of people across national frontiers was frozen: about a million people a year had entered the United

States during the years before the war, but during the 1930s that flow fell to virtually nothing. The price of commodities imported from colonial countries fell by about two thirds – sometimes more – and the industrial nations resorted, one after another, to tariffs and other restrictions on trade to protect their own industries, thereby doing yet more damage to their colonies' exports. The only countries to maintain full employment through these terrible years were the Soviet Union and – after the Nazis took over in 1933 – Germany. The hopes for so long invested in capitalism and liberal democracy were killed; for many, Communism or Fascism seemed to be the only options for the future. Meanwhile colonial peoples – more and more of them crippled by debt, some threatened by starvation – were turning to nationalist movements. It was in 1931 that Gandhi launched his second, and most effective, mobilisation of the Indian people against the British.[1]

Although David Singer, as an established stockbroker, a member of the Stock Exchange Council and a Jew, must soon have been painfully aware that these were to be turbulent times, these threats were not discussed with his daughter and son-in-law who seemed to remain unconcerned about the economic and political weather. Neither were they much interested in the artists, musicians or films of the time. Their commitment was to each other and to Burma. Britain and Europe seemed increasingly distant places: a setting for rare but lovely holidays. Burma, too, would before long feel the impact of the worldwide disaster that was beginning to unfold.

Growing isolation from the Western world affected Ruth's relations with her family. Although her closest sisters were only four and six years younger than she was, they were of a new generation from whom she and Vernon became increasingly distanced. Eleanor would refer jokingly to "Ruth's H.M.T.", meaning her "high moral tone". She herself was doing scientific research at Berkeley in the labs of the University of California, and was already moving towards the Communist Party which she later joined. Prohibition ruled in the States, but she said that "you could always get alcohol from the Rabbi or the Vicar". Left wing politics and free love often went together. Petite and vividly attractive, Eleanor makes it clear that from the age of 24 a succession of men from various nations – and later a woman too – shared her bed. Returning home next year in a Norwegian cargo ship, she was "employed – very unofficially – to do some ship's painting till the captain decided that my bare legs hanging down the ship's side were too disturbing for the crew. Unbeknown to him, I was having a gorgeous affair with the fourth mate." When she got back to London and further research posts, she joined the National Council for Civil Liberties and was regularly in the East End, reporting on police treatment of Fascist marches – and throwing marbles under police horses.[2] Her older sister would have been shocked. Vernon too. He records that Barbara, the third Singer daughter, who came with her family to the Dolomites "became enamoured of a guide and behaved, as we thought, in an embarrassingly emotional and unrestrained way". Later, Barbara went to Berlin as a music student, living there with a young Jewish violinist whom she eventually married. They hid another young man in their small flat– an opponent of the Nazis whom they managed to conceal from the Brownshirts when they came to call.

As the time came to return to Burma, Vernon and Ruth looked for someone who would come with them "to give David lessons and share more generally in caring for him. We decided", said Vernon, "to take Lally Gwillim, who had been a friend of mine before I married. She was the younger sister of my Marlborough housemaster's wife. Some people warned us against choosing someone I had been friendly with." Difficulties between them did indeed arise, but not for this reason.

They set off for Rangoon with Lally and David – now approaching his fourth birthday – and the Buick. They had no idea where they would be posted. On arrival in Rangoon, Vernon reported to Hugh Baker, a senior official, who said he was sorry to break the news that they were being sent to Mergui, among the islands at the far southern tip of Burma. "We were delighted. We had heard what a marvellous territory this was and had no hankerings for Rangoon and the dusty, urban centres of power." Lally, however, must have been dismayed to find they were heading for a place where there would be so few single, white men.

MERGUI

San Hla, their head servant, had died while Vernon and Ruth were in England. They were moved to find that when he knew death was approaching his concern had been for them. He had sent for a friend, Maung Pe, who was working for another Englishman, and told him he must leave that job and take his place with the Donnisons. So when they got to the Wemyss' house in Rangoon, where they were to stay until another boat left for Mergui, there was Maung Pe, together with Ma Than, San Hla's widow, who was ready to resume caring for David. But their first greeting was from Patsy, their dog, who had been left with San Hla and Ma Than. Ruth gently called her name when they got to the Wemyss' house and the dog came tearing madly across the compound from the servants' quarters to welcome them.

"Maung Pe" Vernon recalled, "had been in the army – which was rare for a Burman. He was tall, good looking and had a certain military bearing and panache". Soon they were all embarked with the car and a mass of baggage on a 36-hour voyage in a cockroach-infested coaster heading south to Mergui. I will describe, first, the place, next the work, then the people of Mergui – mainly in Vernon's words – and add some memories of my own.

David recalled nothing of the England the family had left behind , and retained only brief glimpses of the voyage back to Burma: the cold wind blowing across the vibrant, moving decks of the ship, and the hot Bovril offered there to passengers at ten o'clock each morning. He didn't particularly like Bovril but, when they got to Port Said and the heat, ice cream appeared instead: his first encounter with this blissful stuff. Every morning after that he was waiting on deck for the ice cream. Somewhere in the Indian ocean they said there were whales blowing in the distance and everyone rushed to the rail. But he could not see them. Then they reached Bombay and tied up alongside a jetty amidst strange, rich smells. David came out on deck and there, following them in, was a big ship, curving past them with smoke coming from her funnel and white water curling outwards from either side of her forefoot as she carved her way through the water. An awesomely beautiful sight. It was as if *he* was that ship, sailing into consciousness under his own steam at last, and knowing henceforth who he was and where he was.

The Mergui District is the southernmost and the biggest in Burma – a strip of land with offshore islands, 250 miles long and sometimes less than 50 miles wide, lying between the Indian ocean and jungle-clad mountains along the Siamese (now Thai) border. (See the map on page 66) It was densely forested and thin- ly populated, with no railway and few roads, but lots of rivers and creeks. Most of the coastline is muddy and defended by mangrove swamps, with hundreds of islands offshore – some of them rocky, some tree-covered, some with dream-like sandy beaches, and nearly all of them uninhabited.

Until 1765 Mergui had belonged to Siam far more often than to Burma. It was Siam's port on the Indian Ocean, an important link in the trade route between China and India – shorter and safer than the long sea journey around the Malay peninsula. In the nineteenth century, as steam superseded sail, as the Malay pirates were brought under control by the Royal Navy and as Singapore developed, Mergui's importance dwindled. But it retained a character of its own, quite different from the rest of Burma.

Vernon recalled their arrival. "Islands and the shore closed in on us as we headed for the mouth of the Tenasserim River. Ahead lay a small town and our ship lined up on two landmarks: the nearest a beacon in the sea, the far one a white triangle painted on the corner of the red, shingle roof of a large, darkly oiled timber house standing on a bluff a hundred feet above the harbour. This was to be our home for the next two years.

"It was a spacious, old-fashioned, well-proportioned house with deep verandahs, standing in a large compound – not in the Civil Station of new houses laid out in a gridiron pattern on the edge of town for Government officials, but right in the centre of the old, unplanned town, next to a pagoda and monastery. The smells and sounds were often as rich as the character of the place. We looked out from it to the bazaar and main shopping street below, the harbour and its ships beyond, and an island in the background. We felt we were a part of Mergui as we never did in any other place we lived in.

"I was relieving Ralph Wilkie, a sunny, easy-going batchelor who had lived in the house with several large mongrel dogs. We found the cracks between the floor boards were full of ticks and fleas and had to spend days scraping and scrubbing with soap and water, large nails and kerosene to disinfest the place. Wilkie said the room I used as an office was pleasant except that every day, about 3pm, the sun shone through a window overhead and he had to don a topee to work at his desk. I solved the problem by moving the desk. His sweeper applied to us for a job with a testimonial from him saying 'He has swept me adequately for the past year'.

"Becoming Deputy Commissioner in charge of one's first District is an exciting landmark – like getting command of a battalion". Vernon was 31 at the time. "Although subject to the usual hierarchy of a Commissioner and the central government in Rangoon, you were the man to whom all officials and the public looked for decisions, and those decisions were in the vast majority of cases accepted. Your main responsibilities were for the general administration department, but officals in all other departments – the magistracy, police, medical, education, forests and so on – were expected to consult the D.C. and conform to his policies wherever their decisions affected the general administration of the District, and particularly the maintenance of law and order.

"In Mergui, this heady draught of power was made even more

exhilerating by the remoteness of the District. My Commissioner was 300 miles away and he was unlikely to visit me more than once a year. Central government was much further away. Their only way of reaching us was by a mail steamer, for there were no roads along the coast. This boat came once a week on Saturday morning; during the week we could only communicate by telegraph. The mail contract required the boat to wait six hours before departing for Rangoon, and this imposed a regular rhythm on the week. There were six hours of desperate work on Saturday to deal with all the mail and prepare replies before the boat left; relaxation on Sunday; then short tours out into the District during the week. I had two sub-divisional officers and four township officers under me, together with a chief of police, civil surgeon, education and forest officers and others – all Anglo-Indians, Burmans or Karens .

"At Yenangyaung my work had been entirely concerned with oil; in the Shan States with the Sawbwas – the local chieftains. Mergui was completely different and much more varied. Apart from standard tasks common to all Districts – the administration of justice and collection of revenue – I had to deal with tin miners and their mining concessions, with rubber planters and their leases, with fisheries and pearl divers (the latter Japanese), and with the Chinese who leased the right to gather edible birds' nests from caves in remote, rocky islands. This work called for extensive and splendid touring, mostly by boat for there were so few roads. I had a fleet of five launches under my control for government use. The main ones we used were the 'Mercury' and the 'Curtana' – woodburning, sea-going, steam launches which had quarters for a small crew and for Ruth, me, our cook, and sometimes David too."

Although the people of the District would mostly have been described as Burmese, they were in fact Merguians, conscious of being racially distinct and speaking a dialect that was difficult for Burmans to understand. There were also Siamese, Karens, Malays, Chinese, Indians – Muslim and Hindu – and unusually large English and Anglo-Burmese communities. Elsewhere in

Burma, Westerners were usually employed by large European firms or the Government, and had few close contacts with local people. But these were prospectors, miners, and planters, operating on a small scale and at their own risk, often in partnership with Indians and Chinese. Many had Burmese women living with them. There were also three steamships calling regularly at Mergui with European officers who brought a whiff of the outside world with them. "As a result of all this" Vernon recalled, "Mergui had a relaxed and racially egalitarian character which we had not met elsewhere – a character we greatly enjoyed. With a house in the middle of the town, not in the usual segregated civil station, we could share in this society and invite many of its people to our home." He goes on to describe some of those he remembered.

"There was Benjamin Bateson Jubb. Rumour had it that he had once been a ship's cook but deserted to try his luck mining tin. Always engaged in some slightly shady transaction, his fortunes waxed and waned. Sometimes he was broke, debts piled up and it became necessary to expel him from the club. On one of these occasions I found him, rather drunk, stalking the unsuspecting secretary around the billiard table, muttering 'There's that creeping Christ of a secretary-man'. Sometimes he was prosperous, paid off his debts and was readmitted. He had a Burmese wife and a flock of children, and managed to get them all out from under the noses of the Japanese ten years later." (I will tell that story later.)

Another couple "considered themselves socially superior to the Jubbs. Max was long and lanky, a well-educated 'gentleman' – honest but helplessly ineffectual. He always missed concessions because someone smarter had been quicker to apply for them, and then spent a lot of time telling you what wonderful concessions they would have been if dishonest competitors had not got in first. His wife, a formidable battle-axe, had been a hospital matron, and was all the more aggressive because she felt she had to fight Max's battles for him. They hated Jubb because he so often got the better of them.

"John Doupe, a good natured Australian tin miner, worked by himself in a remote part of the District where he had a Burmese woman who had made him a happy home and borne several children to him. But the poor woman was banished to the kitchen when the ex-matron visited because she would have considered it a blatant insult if John's woman had been allowed into her presence.

"There was Kinloch, a rubber planter who was the nicest of white-haired, elderly Scots with a highly respectable Burmese wife and three shatteringly beautiful daughters. There was Elsom, a little Australian tin miner with a vastly larger Russian wife – enormously voluble and totally unintelligible. There was Ahmed, the pearl trader from whom Ruth bought a necklace of seed pearls – we couldn't afford anything grander. And 'Daddy' Thomas, whom we visited when he was dying of cancer of the throat. Later I had to conduct his funeral. The ropes broke as he was being lowered into the grave and the flimsy coffin split open, whereupon one of his Anglo-Indian daughters threw herself into the grave shrieking 'Oh my Daddee, my Daddee!'

"During the monsoon season there was a Mergui football league, and I persuaded my staff to enter a team. We could just get eleven players together, provided matches were held on a Saturday when the mail boat was in port and we could get some of their officers to join us. We were moderately successful as footballers, but enormously successful in drawing the crowds who loved to watch large, clumsy, white men trying to cope with the nimble, bare-foot players of other teams."

Touring had to be done mainly by boat, anchoring overnight by uninhabited islands where Vernon and Ruth would go ashore to stretch their legs, finding only the tracks of birds and perhaps a monkey. They visited the Marble Rocks – a ring of cliffs reaching almost a thousand feet out of the sea that had to be entered at low tide when a small boat could be rowed in through a tunnel. Within the lagoon inside there was a vast cave, high above, where swallows built the edible nests which were collected by the

Chinese. The license to collect them was sold at auction in Mergui each year, along with fishery leases. From Victoria Point they crossed the river into Siam and paid a courtesy call on the Siamese provincial governor there. At the Great Western Torres, outermost of the islands, the water was so clear they could see the brilliant colours of the coral five or six fathoms beneath.

There were landward tours too, one of them calling for a four-day walk, climbing to 5,000 feet on the Siamese frontier, wading through rivers and sleeping out in the open. Their cook, Nikunja – a small Bengali, permanently lamed from an earlier injury, but marvellous at his job – came with them. "I can see him now" wrote Ruth, years later, "wading armpit-deep through rushing torrents and striding along jungle paths, his longyi girt up, a Storm King lamp, too precious to entrust to elephants or porters, swinging in one hand, and his knotted Shan bag of personal valuables hanging from his shoulder.

"I brought back from leave all sorts of nice recipes for him to try. He would write them in his own book, translating from my Burmese into Bengali. Sometimes we gave parties for eighty or more guests of many races, starting with hilarious games to break the ice and ending with a buffet supper. Nikunja would stand behind the long table to serve them the good things he had made. You could not see that he was lame then. He wore his crimson longyi, and his bright brown eyes, above a sparkling white jacket, shone with pride. I always introduced him to my guests and explained that all these delicacies were his work."

Vernon tells us about the kinds of games they organised for these parties. "All were encouraged to take part – performing tasks such as lifting peas into a pot with a pair of knitting needles, guessing the weights of things, identifying substances by their smell, and throwing playing cards into a waste paper basket. Sometimes we would conclude with musical chairs, sometimes with a treasure hunt that led couples from one clue to the next all round the house and out into the garden. Food, drink and conversation followed."

Vernon recalled the Headmen of villages they visited on their tours. One was "a lion-hearted man who had been attacked and mauled by a bear years earlier. (He was probably trying to shoot it, for he was a great hunter.) Carried down through the jungle and then put on a boat to the hospital in Mergui, he lost an arm and much of his scalp but recovered from other grievous wounds as few men would have done. When I knew him the old fire still burned, and he ruled his village tract with unfashionable, but I think in the main benevolent, despotism."

VISITORS

They had occasional visitors from the outside world. One of the first was the Governor himself, Sir Charles Innes; a white-haired, white-moustached, benign-looking gentleman. "It fell to David, just four years old, to entertain him for a while. This he did by pulling some of Ruth's anatomy books out of the shelves and proudly displaying the more intimate illustrations. After Sir Charles' departure David asked 'Whose grandfather was that?' We took him and his staff up the Tenasserim River in the 'Curtana' and gave them a splendid lunch made by Nikunja – and were horrified when he poured custard over his cheese souffle before we could stop him. He insisted that he liked it. Perhaps he did. When, later, we were invited to lunch at the Residency in Rangoon, we were served very small quantities of champagne poured over large blocks of ice.

"Our friend Donald Petch visited us in unusual circumstances. He was being chased by a man-eating woman who followed him even when he went into hospital – his health undermined by the strain. His friends rescued him and put him on a boat to convalesce with us. We took him away for a few days to a beach where he slept in a tent by the shore. I recall David, who went about quite naked like any Burmese boy, paying a visit to the tent to converse seriously with Donald for some time; then saying 'I have nothing more to say. So I will go.' Donald so wished that others would follow his example.

"The strangest visit was completely unheralded. A four-masted sailing ship dropped anchor in the harbour and its American 'sailing master' brought a group of his compatriots ashore – one of them an elderly lady who used a large ear trumpet we had to shout into. He said they were on an educational cruise, but his next question – 'What country is this?' – suggested their studies did not go very deep. While ashore they paid for everything in one-pound notes which were all brought to the Treasury for exchange into rupees. Next Saturday, when the mail boat arrived, a further flood of one-pound notes was presented for exchange; at which point we discovered that my Treasury Officer had given his customers a few annas too much for their pounds and every trader in the bazaar had wired his Rangoon agents to send all the sterling they could lay hands on by the next boat.

"The most memorable visit was that of the cruiser, *H.M.S. Effingham*, with Admiral Fullerton on board. We were invited to a party on the ship and returned the invitation; there were parties and dancing at the club where the tall, handsome, gold-braided flag lieutenant danced the whole evening with the dazzlingly lovely Peggy Kinloch. The Admiral's lady told how they had called at Istanbul on the way out and the Turks had awarded her the Order of Chastity – 5th Class. What simple jokes. And what fun to have this great warship in our harbour." Built, like much of the Royal Navy, to steam long distances, showing the flag in tropical climes, she was designed more for fuel economy and good ventilation than for battle.

PARADISE YEARS

David's memories of Mergui start with the party, held for his fourth birthday, soon after the family arrived there. This was clearly going to be a lovely world. The great, cavernous house was full of dark hiding places. In it there were two civet cats – half-wild creatures which ran from room to room and from floor to

David and Cook's son

floor along secret passageways within its wooden frame. He lay on his tummy on the verandah that reached out under the lid of a heavy roof towards the harbour – smelling the smells of the port, listening to its strange sounds and drawing ships of every kind: steam ships, and sailing ships ranging from schooners with five or more masts to native outriggers. "Aunty Lally", as he was taught to call Miss Gwillim, began to teach him to read and write, but made scant impression as a human being. For warmth and affection, when his mother was away on tour with his father, he turned to Ma Than; a loving, coppery-brown woman. Bath times, when she threw bowls of cool water over him, were a hilarious, almost erotic, rite.

There were mysteries to explore outside the house too. A great cannon, abandoned nearby during the First Burmese War when sick and wounded soldiers were sheltered in Mergui, was set up in front of the house on its heavy wooden carriage. David climbed all over it, and one marvellous festival day it was fired – shooting smoke, blazing paper and cabbage leaves over the harbour. In the evenings he could hear the screams of frogs, caught in the grass by snakes. Once a year there was a water festival at which everyone was entitled gaily to throw water over everyone else – and particularly over the rich and powerful. Then came the fire festival, with fireworks shooting into the night sky, and huge fire balloons, made of coloured paper in the shapes of pagodas, elephants and mythical beasts, floating by in the night. Out on the edge of the compound were the wooden houses of the servants, with a crowd of naked children squatting and chattering on the ground at their door steps. David would mingle shyly with them but never recovered the Burmese which had been the first language he had learned, so could not really be part of their gang.

A hundred yards up the red, gravely road from the house was Vernon's office: a simple, single-storey block with red tiles and yellowing walls. David insisted on putting a shirt on before walking up that road because the Burmese sentry standing at the office gate would come to attention with much stamping of feet, and

Lally, David and Annis

salute him by shouldering his rifle and slapping its butt as he went by – a jokey way of relieving his boredom, I guess. With a shirt on, David felt better equipped to carry off this first experience of embarrassment.

The family went further afield in the big, grey Buick. David remembered coming down a winding road under trees and rounding a bend to find five men wildly battling with staves a giant python that whirled about in mid air, dodging their blows. There were cows nearby, and a calf lying dead, crushed by the snake. Vernon made to stop the car but Aunty Lally, fearing the snake might jump in among them, shouted "Go on! Go on!". So he did, and David wondered ever after how this drama ended.

Away on tour, or at home working early and late in his office, Vernon was a distant, powerful figure. When he was away without her, Ruth would sometimes invite David into her bed for an early-morning cuddle before the day began; a four-year-old's delight that was brought to an end when he came in one morning to find that Vernon had returned – and curtly ordered him out.

For David, the high points of this time were the occasions when he went on tour with his parents in the 'Mercury' or the 'Curtana'. To look out from these boats across blue water as small islands, crowned with fronded palm trees and fringed with golden sand, went gliding by – these were experiences that remain imprinted in memory for life. Going ashore in a smaller boat one day, he allowed a much-loved soft toy to drop over the side. Before he could howl with dismay, one of the servants dived into the water to recover 'Silly Doggy' and lay cheerfully floating with him till they could turn around and pick them up.

Ruth would read to David – often from A.A. Milne's books about Christopher Robin and his animals. In the evening, when he had gone to bed, he could hear the adults reading these stories over again to each other in different, adult tones, and roaring with laughter. Every imperialist would have recognised A.A.Milne's characters. Rabbit, that tiresome, clever-stupid know-all, and Eeyore, the ever-dismal donkey, would for them have represented intellectuals and Lefties – people like George Orwell and Leonard Woolf, sharpest critics of the imperial tradition. Tigger and Roo were the boisterous but loveable natives who had to be treated kindly but firmly, raised to a civilised state and persuaded to take the 'strengthening medicine' – extract of malt – prescribed by their elders and betters. Kanga, Roo's mother, was patient, maternal, enduring... a proper memsahib. And Pooh, principal character of the stories, although he modestly believed himself to be 'a bear of little brain', was unfailingly adaptable, courageous and unflappable, coping successfully with every crisis: a splendid District Officer.

Imperial duty and dignity were not discussed, but they could never be forgotten. David recalled going ashore to call on a village whose principal citizens were lined up to receive the D.C. and his party. They must have smiled inwardly, for between them a low tide had left a broad stretch of mud which the visitors had to stumble through as they got out of their boat. When David screamed in disgust as sticky mud sucked at his shins, Vernon shushed him with a severity that made it clear he was letting down the whole British Empire.

Distant though he might be, David knew that, in a crisis, he could rely totally on his father. Occasionally Vernon would take him into the jungle to a pool which had been made by damming a stream with a stone weir. Here he would teach David to swim by walking along the weir, holding out the end of his belt with the buckle end of it looped around the child's middle. One evening the belt broke and David sank into the depths. Eyes wide open, he could see tall weeds below, rising towards him. Then there was a bump as Vernon came diving in to grab him. He was quite disappointed to be snatched from this new and fascinating world. Vernon was in subdued mood as they returned home and went straight in to report to Ruth. Later, as she put David to bed, she asked what had happened. "It was lovely" he said. "All green!"

It was next year– 1930 – that Ruth told David that she was going to have another baby. (The five-year wait prescribed by

Dr. Svensson was nearly over.) Soon she was inviting David to put a hand on her tummy and feel the baby moving. She had had a rough time producing him in Yenangyaung, and in Mergui the medical services were more rudimentary. So she went away on the boat to Moulmein, 400 miles north, where there was an American Baptist Mission Hospital. It was six weeks before she returned, which seemed a long time to David, bringing his new sister Annis with her. This infant, she said, was to be his baby as well as hers, and she explained all about the birth – inviting him to feel the soft place along the top of the baby's head where the two halves of her skull had yet to weld together.

AUNTY LALLY

To win and run Britain's vast empire there had to be a great out-flow of men from every town and village in the country. Many of them would have little chance of marrying one of their own countrywomen. Meanwhile many of their sisters, left at home, had little chance of marrying at all. Before long, the women began to follow the men in search of husbands. Already, by the early years of the nineteenth century, there was talk of the "fishing fleet" which set forth in December each year when the cool weather began in India and countries beyond. Thomas Hood wrote a bitter-sweet poem about it in 1832, called "I'm Going to Bombay". This is one of its verses.

> By Pa and Ma I'm daily told
> To marry now's my time,
> For though I'm very far from old,
> I'm rather in my prime.
> They say while we have any sun,
> We ought to make our hay –
> And India has so hot an one,
> I'm going to Bombay!

It was not surprising that Aunty Lally made scant impression on David. Although he understood nothing of this at the time, her energies were focussed elsewhere — as I came to realise when I read Vernon's memoir, written forty years later. "She was", he said, "much older than we had realised, and a devout Christian to whom conventions and appearances mattered much more than they did to us. But she was highly sexed and desperately looking for a husband before her chances of marriage slipped away. She fastened on a much younger man — a rubber planter who seemed completely lacking in moral fibre. Our impression of him appeared to be confirmed when he was brought before me for misappropriating a large amount of his Company's funds. To this charge he pleaded guilty, but refused to give any explanation for his actions. I had tried a Chinese accountant on a very similar charge not long before, and sent him to prison." The whole community, Vernon knew, would be watching to see if a European would be treated in the same way. "Since he would give me no mitigating circumstances I felt I had no choice but to pass a similar sentence. I sent him to prison for six months." (What must breakfast have been like next morning for Lally and her employers?) "The young man's refusal to offer any defence was in fact a courageous and dignified act, designed, I was convinced, to protect someone else — I have no idea whom. He was sent to the jail at Moulmein where there was accommodation for Europeans. Meanwhile Mr. Justice Dunkley in the Rangoon High Court (known to his circle as 'Wobbles Dunkley') called the case in for review, sharply castigated me for my sentence and set it aside. The young man was sent home to England soon after.

"Having lost one man, Lally turned her attentions to another equally unpromising one: a rubber planter again, untrustworthy again and much older than she was, with — it was rumoured — a wife in Malaya. We were anxious about her passionate entanglements with unsuitable people, tried to persuade her to wait awhile, come home with us and think carefully, and sought advice from her family; all to no effect. Finally, as we were preparing to go home, she dragged her new man to the altar and married him. He left that very afternoon and, to the best of my knowledge, has never been heard of since."

Poor Lally Gwillim! It must have been a lonely life; made all the bleaker by the daily presence of this self-sufficient, happily married couple, and the well loved children she feared she would never have. The other two women who came to Burma in later years to care for Annis were younger and more attractive people. Both found husbands.

BURMA AWAKES

It was at this time, in 1930, that Saya San's rebellion took place. It was put down in little more than a year; it reinforced the conviction of the British that they had an important job to do in Burma; and it led younger nationalists to pursue entirely different strategies henceforth. So it failed. But it was too important a stage in Burma's history to leave out of this story.

Their British rulers regarded the Burmans, not as a proud nation with a long history, but as a poor and generally peaceful backwater of the Indian Empire. They brought Indians into the country in huge numbers and the Burmese had increasingly to approach their white rulers through Indian intermediaries. One (Indian) magistrate has described how little he knew about his job when he first sat on the bench, and how he had to rely on his peons (Indian clerks) to tell him what to do[3]. Language played an important part in this story. The babel of tongues in the vast Indian subcontinent compelled Indians to learn English in order to communicate even with each other. Once learned, the language gave them access to jobs and – for the more educated and travelled minority – to a wider world, including its newspapers and the writings of Mill, Marx, Engels and many more. But the Burman was slow to learn English. For him, a scholarly I.C.S. official commented at this time, "the narrowing of his life may be measured by the impoverishment of his language. Formerly it was a national language… Now it is merely a language of the domestic circle and the cultivator, and the Burmans who only know Burmese know less of their own world than their fathers and no more of the modern world."[4] The Anglo-Saxons must have had a similar experience after the Norman conquest when French and Latin became the dominant languages. Meanwhile Burma's traditional moral leaders and law givers – the monks – were brushed aside, increasingly deprived of their main role as teachers of the young, and offered no other in exchange.

The British were strong on administration, policing and tax gathering, but weaker on economic development and longer-term political vision. "The Burmese", said Vernon in his own history of the country, "were deprived of self-respect and left without any symbol of national purpose."[5] The taxes levied by the British were heavy by Indian standards, and they bore mainly on land, and therefore on peasant cultivators. Yet the British took no steps to increase agricultural productivity or to extend the range of crops produced by the Burmese. They sent few Burmese students abroad – less than ten a year during the 1930s – and Burmese people were largely excluded from the management of the country's larger enterprises.[6] Local industries were increasingly put out of business by cheaper imports from India and Britain, and unemployment emerged for the first time. Historians dispute about the progress of Burmese living standards, but rice consumption per head declined, and incomes fell behind those of neighbouring people. Furnivall, an I.C.S. official who became one of the country's best historians, summed up the situation by saying that "England opened up Burma to the world but did not open up the world to Burma". "Burma has become a workshop rather than a state, and the people and the land of Burma are regarded, like the workers and the machinery in a factory, as means for the production of wealth rather than as the end for which wealth is produced."[7]

John Stuart Mill, whom we know as a great social reformer, was quite frank about this, writing that colonies "are hardly to be looked upon as countries... but more properly as outlying agricultural or manufacturing estates belonging to a larger community... the place where England finds it convenient to carry on the production of sugar, coffee and a few other tropical commodities."[8]

It was to their Buddhism that Burmans turned as they sought to resist these forces and reclaim a sense of their own identity. As early as 1897, while the brutal suppression of Burmese resistance was still going on, Buddhist societies began to appear in Moulmein, Mandalay and other towns to foster Buddhist education and social improvement[9]. In 1906, Western-educated Burmese founded the Young Men's Buddhist Association – deliberately matching the Christian Y.M.C.A. – which became a centre for nationalist political activity. This was the year after the Japanese defeat of the Russian Navy. The Burmese began insisting that visitors to pagodas and other holy places must take their shoes off as a mark of respect – which meant that liberal families like the Donnisons taught their children to do this, while those who felt their dignity could not be maintained barefoot ceased to visit pagodas[10]. In 1921 the growing number of nationalist groups tried to unite under the umbrella of a General Council of Burmese Associations, but the movement was for many years riven by internal conflicts. The building of new political movements with a programme capable of challenging the dominant regime is a long, slow task.

The destruction of Burmese political leadership and all unifying moral authority, the growing numbers of migrant workers, the spread of unemployment among the poor, and of corruption in the middle reaches of the bureaucracy – these led to growing disorder, particularly in lower Burma. But serious nationalist thought was largely confined to India. In 1917 the British still asserted there was no appetite for democracy in Burma. Their outlook is reflected in the title of an official study published that year: the "Report of the Committee Appointed to Ascertain and Advise How the Imperial Idea May be Inculcated and Fostered in Schools and Colleges in Burma"[11].

During the First World War, in which the Indians played an important part, the Secretary of State for India promised progress towards a sharing of power. Indians secured their first elected assemblies under the Government of India Act of 1919, but Burma was excluded from these advances – a signal to nationalists there that they would have to fight their own corner. The Y.M.B.A. sent delegations to London in 1919 and 1920, pressing for equal treatment, which they got in 1923. For Burma proper – excluding the hill peoples – education, forestry, public works and health powers were transferred from Delhi to Rangoon, to be administered by the country's first parliamentary government. But financial control and security remained in the hands of the Lieutenant Governor, advised by an appointed Legislative Council. The British promised to review progress in ten years time and go further if that seemed justified. In reality, they had set foot on the slippery slope that would eventually compel them to hand over power. There could be no turning back. That would mean they would have to get among the young political activists in Rangoon and engage seriously with them – which they failed to do.

Meanwhile order was unravelling. Robberies, stabbings and murders became increasingly common. In 1927 there was a small uprising in Shwebo, north of Mandalay in Upper Burma, where Vernon had served his first apprenticeship. Then, in 1930, murderous riots broke out in Rangoon between Indians and Burmese, arising from a strike of Burmese dock workers and the bringing in of Indian strike breakers. At the end of that year there was the more serious rebellion already mentioned – beginning in Tharrawaddy, about 80 miles north of Rangoon, and spreading to 12 of the country's 40 Districts before it was finally put down in March 1932. Some 9,000 prisoners were taken, mostly to be freed at once. The 350 men brought to court were those believed to be guilty of serious crimes and 78 of them were hanged. Among the government's forces 39 men were killed. This was a rural rebellion confined to Burmans – the hill people were not involved. Its leader, Saya San, was regarded by the British as a mad, superstitious monk. He persuaded his men that his charms and spells would protect them against bullets and make aeroplanes fall out of the sky.

These disturbances arose from poverty, social disintegration, religious fanaticism and conflict between ethnic groups, with no unifying political ideology to drive them. Henceforth, the younger generation of nationalists turned their backs on movements of this kind. It was in 1931 that an up-country boy with poor command of English passed into Rangoon University from a secondary school in Yenangyaung. He found other students there with militant nationalist convictions. Together they captured the Students' Union and its magazine which they used to attack university staff. When he was expelled, the students organised a strike and compelled the Government to set up a Committee of Inquiry whose report eventually compelled the Principal to resign. The young man's name was Aung San. Henceforth the strike was to become his main political weapon, the capital his main base. He and his friends sought to build an alliance of students, workers, peasants and priests that would eventually drive the British out. They started by joining a small group, formed in the aftermath of the Rangoon riots, who pointedly called themselves the "Thakins": Masters – the title with which white men expected Burmese people to address them.

It was about 1931 that radical literature, coming mainly from India, began to circulate among young nationalists. Aung San wrote – in Burmese – "We are fully prepared to follow men who are able and willing to be leaders like Mahatma Gandhi, C.R.Das, Motilal Nehru and Tilak of India; like De Valera of Ireland; or Garibaldi and Mazzini of Italy. Let anybody appear who can be like such a leader. We are waiting." [12] It was a new voice – but not one that the rulers of the Empire paid much attention to. Meanwhile the barbarity of race riots in the streets and of rural rebellions led by fanatical monks, coupled with the loyalty of the great majority of Burmese citizens who expected to be protected from such violence, reinforced their conviction that they had a continuing and important job to do.

Vernon, like all Deputy Commissioners, was warned to be specially vigilant during these turbulent months, but not a ripple from Saya San's rebellion penetrated to Mergui. Further afield, however, forces were stirring that would eventually make larger waves. In 1931 the Japanese invaded China. Soon the British, with American help, were building through the mountains the road that supplied the munitions which kept China's resistance going, and the Japanese began to calculate how that route might be cut off. Hitler's men were on the march, coming to power in 1933 with a determination to reverse the humiliation of Versailles and perhaps take over the British Empire.

HOME AGAIN

After two demanding years in Mergui Vernon became ill. The Civil Surgeon diagnosed sprue, a disease with potentially serious consequences, and sent him to hospital in Rangoon. There the diagnosis was confirmed and he was told that he must go back to Europe for a while to recover. Armed with the necessary medical certificate, he returned to Mergui to pack up and hand over. "My relief was Maurice Collis: much too senior to be posted to this District. He had fallen foul of the authorities and they were hinting that it was time for him to go – which he did, after several blissful years in Mergui, doing little or no work, but writing his marvellous historical novel, 'Siamese White', and collecting pieces of Ming porcelain. His book, *Trials in Burma* tells his side of the story about his conflicts with authority, but there was more to the tale. He said that in Mergui people from all over the District pressed forward to offer him Chinese ceramics, once his civilised tastes became known – but did not add that in return they received much coveted licences for firearms which were supposed to be very sparingly granted. However, to us personally, no-one could have been more charming than Collis." Collis, like other

Irishmen in the imperial services, brought an ironic, outsiders's vision to the scene; and – like some of them – was not much troubled by loyalties to the British Crown.

For David, just six years old, the voyage home meant more ice cream. Infants, he learnt, are strange and tough little creatures. His sister Annis, not yet two years old, was, in very rough weather, about the only passenger determined to eat a full dinner. Adults in the family had to take it in turns to go below and sit with her in the dining room. On calmer days she would play out in the sun till she became drowsy, then gently let her head drop on the deck between her outstretched legs and fall asleep. When they got to Marseilles the grey car was hoisted out of the hold and David was borne off by his parents to drive home through France, Switzerland and Germany – which can't have been much fun for Annis, going on by sea with Aunty Lally.

David was gaining a sense of the passing of time. Lying on his back on a bed in a cheap hotel, he gazed up at a crack that crawled across the ceiling. "One day", he said to his mother, "When you're dead... and father's dead... and I'm dead – this ceiling is going to fall down."

They went high into the Swiss Alps to visit Derick Grant who had been Vernon's Commissioner when he was at Yenangyaung – now retired and recovering from tuberculosis in the mountain sun. They stopped the car when they came across the first snow David had ever seen and he climbed down, filled with wonder. "Can I *jump* in it?" he asked. When Derick took them to a patisserie and invited the child to look along the shelves and choose a cake he was paralysed with indecision. Never had he seen such delights.

In Germany they called on Elly and her family. David went out to play with her children in the garden and they chattered to each other in their own languages, understanding each other perfectly. He was puzzled when his mother asked him how they had coped. Next day was Easter Sunday and they all went walking in sunlit woods – Elly's eldest son, Siegfried, going ahead with a pocketful of brightly coloured eggs which he deftly dropped in mossy places for the younger children to find. They were laid there, he insisted, by the Easter Hare — which, as a staunch rationalist, David didn't believe for a moment. Then a deer flashed across the path and Siegfried shouted "There's the Hare!" It was years before David could be convinced that rabbits and hares do not lay eggs. He had *seen* them.

In April they rejoined Annis in London where Vernon went to the School of Tropical Medicine. He would make a good recovery, they said, provided he lived gently for a while and had a high protein diet. Aunty Lally disappeared and in her place came Nan Hooper, a young woman without much education but with a warm and kindly nature. David loved her. Annis and he stayed most of the time with her at Dibleys, their Donnison grandmother's home, while their parents went visiting friends and relatives.

Although this was a house and a country that grown-ups called "home" David had no memory of it. So every day was an adventure. The sun seemed always to be shining on the big, unkempt garden with its crazy-paving pathways and shaggy lawns, and a cavernous barn beyond where they could play on wet days. Venturing out the first morning, David crept up on a beautiful butterfly, yearned to hold it, so, very gently, took off his floppy hat and dropped it on the creature — to discover that he had caught a pansy. There were roses — marvellously scented — red hot pokers, and magic lanterns like orange lamps under green leaves; the light shining so brightly through them, he was convinced they must be switched on. He would sit, transfixed by the sound of bees, and by the sheer, longing sadness rung out by the eight bells in Blewbury's church tower. There were great trees in the garden — plums, greengages, apples, a damson. He scraped his shins on their bark as he climbed their branches to pick the fruit.

The house was very old — Elizabethan they said — with steep, narrow stairs and little rooms with little windows on the top floor for children. The birds nested just above, under the roof tiles, and David would bury his head beneath the blankets when they made spooky, scuffling noises in the night. It didn't matter that there was no electric light, no refrigerator and only an outdoor earth closet which had to be emptied into a cess pit once a week. Jack the postman, who had lost one arm in the war, came every few days to pump water from the well into the tank in the roof. Lena, David's grandmother's cook, called him "Master David" and invited him into the kitchen to scrape out mixing bowls and lick the spoon, or sent him down the road with sixpence in his hand to the water cress beds where a friendly man waded out in gumboots to gather a bunch of cress for him to bring home. They would have it for tea with brown bread, butter and marmite. Gorgeous!

Further afield they explored the downs, picking big bunches of cowslips to bring home. Later they found chestnut trees and broke open the spikey green shells of their fruit to dig out the dark, silky conkers. One morning David was awakened early and taken to the edge of the village where a cinder track climbed into the downs. There, at seven o'clock, by the village's lone petrol pump (it's a big filling station now) Jack arrived with his post bag slung over his good shoulder and they walked up the track and miles across the downs to deliver mail at lonely farms. Their people welcomed the pair, offering tea to Jack and a cup of their own cows' milk to David. One of the farms had a cat that was nursing a litter of kittens among whom she had adopted a baby rabbit, suckling with the rest.

David made friends with Billy Higgs who lived at the other side of the village, and they rode bicycles together around the lanes and footpaths. Billy's father was a race horse trainer and there were stables at the back of his house with great, shining, tail-whisking creatures and rich smells. Their home seemed rather posh to David. Mrs. Higgs had filled it with more doilies, shining silver, cut glass, lace curtains and polished tables than he had ever seen before. She had been "in service" before she met the young jockey whom she married, so she knew about these things (and David's grandmother was snobby about her). But she was kind and generous, and made the most marvellous teas, with strawberry jam to put on cream-covered scones, and silver tongs to lift lumps of sugar into elegant china cups. (Many years later, David read John Betjeman's cruelly funny poem – " 'Phone for the fish knives Norman... I must have things daintily served" – and knew exactly where he had seen it all; hated him for it... but laughed.)

They went to London to visit David's Singer grandmother and the dentist: his first experience of deliberately inflicted pain. Sitting on a doorstep, just to watch the cars, taxis and buses go by and smell the interesting scent of petrol fumes was the best bit. David Singer, Isabel's husband, had died and she now had a flat in Portland Place, and a big house and garden at Penn in Buckinghamshire. Eleanor, Ruth's next sister and David's favourite aunt, would come to the flat to visit, roaring to a stop in her little red M.G. sports car. Entering, she would greet everyone, and before long would be talking to him. She would duck down behind a sofa, cushions would be thrown, there would be tickles and screams of laughter as he tried desperately to stop himself peeing his pants with excitement – till other adults intervened to calm everyone down. One fabulous day she took him through London in the M.G. – right along the Strand, with the hood down and David sitting beside her. She had a mane of curly, black hair and elegant gauntlet gloves reaching to the elbow with beautiful embroidery down the backs of them. Glamour!

In June, Vernon, still a bit frail, invited his mother-in-law to come with him and Ruth in the grey car on a holiday to Scotland. They left Annis and David behind so I tell the story in his own words. "First Isabel deemed it necessary to buy lots of new clothes for the tour. We of course were going in our old things. We agreed a date and place to meet, well in advance, and at the last moment she said she would have to leave two days later. Since that would upset all the bookings we had made we had to refuse and asked her to get the train to Edinburgh where we would pick her up. We slept in the open by Hadrian's Wall on the way north, rolled in car rugs. Isabel arrived on the sleeper, much put out, and grumbled about the hotel we had chosen. Two days later we climbed Ben Lawers and, high on a shoulder of the hill, Isabel spotted a stone, about the size of a football, which she would like to have in her rockery. Please would I carry it down for her? I refused as politely as possible. Back at the foot of the hill she found that she had left her new hat at the top. Please would I go back and fetch it? Once again I refused. We toured around the west coast in marvellous weather. As a sort of socialist she was most concerned about the poverty of the people in the crofters' cottages, and said she could not understand why they did not all get Aga stoves like the one she had. Finally, on the homeward journey, we stopped in Inverness to go shopping. She and Ruth immediately split up and I had great difficulty getting them back together for long enough to start our journey homewards."

To balance this trip, Vernon felt he had to take his own mother for a holiday and invited her to come with him to Ireland for a week or two. This was a sadder experience. They visited friends: a protestant ascendancy family living in a big house in great poverty – the plaster crumbling, brocaded curtains and curtain rails drooping off the walls – then drove on to Killarney to explore Kerry. "I remember very little, for I was always so ill at ease and unhappy with my mother, I would in some curious way switch off my senses and blot out all memories of our time together. After putting her on the boat at Rosslare I went to see an Oxford friend in Dublin and regain my composure – hoping she was regaining hers. It must have been tragic for her. "

Feeling he should do something more useful with the rest of his leave, Vernon went to work for a while in a Stepney parish for Stephen Phillimore, the gallant chaplain with whom he had served in the Guards, but felt rather shamefully that he was not much help to him. Then, after nearly a year at home, he returned with Ruth to Burma in 1933, "leaving David and Annis in the care of Nan and my mother." He says no more on that score, going on to talk about their next posting and recovering their dog Patsy. Annis was just over three years old.

THATON

Vernon and Ruth were sent to Thaton, a typical District of Lower Burma, lying north of Moulmein where Annis had been born. It had a much bigger, if less exotic, population than Mergui, most of them living in eighty miles of paddy fields that ran up the coast and along the Sittang River. The great Salween River flowed down through the middle of the District, while to the east there was a range of mountains rising to five and six thousand feet along the Siamese border, and to the north a tumbled stretch of hills which were Karen country.

Thaton was not a happy place when Vernon took over as Deputy Commissioner. His predecessor and the Superintendent of Police – almost the only white men in the public services – had quarrelled publicly in the club and were not on speaking terms. They had quarrelled with just about every other European too. Vernon managed to get on terms with the Superintendent who was, to his relief, posted elsewhere before long. As ever, he tried to see all sides of the argument. Writing years later, he said "The I.C.S. and the Police formed the 'steel frame' of the administration, upon which depended the functioning of other services, the ability of ordinary people to go about their business unmolested, and the safety of the European population. If anything had actually to be done it was the Police – recruited straight from school at the age of nineteen – who had to do it, and the Police Officer who had to carry the can. This must have made it difficult for them to bear with the more favoured conditions of service enjoyed by the I.C.S. – Oxbridge graduates, with better pay and pensions – and the occasional condescension of some of its members, and, still more, of their wives." Meanwhile the Deputy Commissioner, as the District's chief magistrate, responsible for law as well as order, would sometimes have to throw out police prosecutions that had insufficient evidence to support them.

Among the friends Ruth and Vernon made here were two brothers, products of one of the famous Scottish public schools, who had a rubber plantation. Athletic, hard drinking, and both married with children – they illustrated different responses to the dilemmas faced by European families. Jim's wife stayed with her children and never came to Burma. "We were sorry for him, but the trouble was that he was always being sorry for himself. He drank very heavily and easily became maudlin. John was a much better, tougher, type. His wife always looked so delicate, and indeed was frequently ill. But she always came to Burma with him. Perhaps she wondered what on earth would happen if she didn't." Vernon had nothing to say about what was happening to her children, left in Scotland.

One of Vernon's duties was to visit the jail that formed part of every District's headquarters, and its quarry camp by the Sittang River. His account of it may provide a glimpse of the life of his cousin Ted who spent fifteen years in the bigger Insein jail. "I always found it a distressing experience. At the quarry, gangs of convicts were employed to extract stone and break it into met-alling for roads and the railway. The sun blazed on the quarry faces. Below, some shade was provided for the stone-breakers under thatched awnings. All wore fetters to prevent escapes. They were marched to their work under armed guard, and at night they slept in long barracks with mat walls and corrugated iron roofs. A chain running the length of the barrack was passed through their fetters. It seemed barbaric. The Superintendent of the jail was a coarse-looking Anglo-Indian with a face like a boot. But the pris-oners – all convicted of violent crimes – did not look so suppressed as many others I had seen. At the time of the Burmese New Year they were allowed off work early and each of the barracks pro-duced an entertainment. I was taken round to see all the shows. They went with a swing and there was great gaiety in the air. One consisted of animal dances at which the Burmese are adept. At another there was a conjuror as good as I have seen anywhere. The last was a spirited take-off of the English-officered Indian Army."

Vernon spent three years in Thaton and made friends there among all the different groups, but the work, the tours, the visitors, the brief holidays in the mountains, were much like those I have already described in Mergui, so for the rest of this chapter I will focus on his children, left behind in England. He was to return to Thaton in desperate times, eight years later.

DAVID LEARNS TO SURVIVE

Aunty Lally's lessons had made little mark on David, so when he was sent to his first school, at the age of six and a half, he had to start from the bottom. For reasons, both academic and social I guess, he was sent not to the all-age village school but to a private school in Wallingford, six miles away. Although it was a modest and fairly genteel establishment, his first encounter with it remains a vivid memory. Brought straight into the midday break, he was suddenly engulfed in a pandemonium of running, scream-ing children: a riot, it seemed. He cowered behind a pillar in terror. But he found his feet before long and learned to cope with the lessons, although he always remained a bit of an outsider – observing the crowd from the shelter of a metaphorical pillar. (Ten years later, choosing a topic for the last essay he was to write at any school, he picked as his theme the words "I am never less lonely than when I am by myself".)

Getting to school was not so easy. He had to ride his small bicy-cle early in the morning for two miles along an empty, wind-swept road to Aston Tirrold, the next village, where he left it in the front garden of a family whose girls went to the same school. Their father drove them into Wallingford – his daughters conveying the silent contempt for small boys that only a ten-year-old girl can inflict. They stayed later at school than David, so at the end of the day he had to get on a crowded bus which dropped him, after a stuffy, sick-making journey, in their village where he recovered the bike from behind their hedge and peddled home. Which was not too bad in the autumn.

When the Donnisons set off at the end of the year, Ruth had explained gravely to David that she was sad to be leaving, but

Father had to go back to his work and she had to take care of him. They would write letters to him every week and he must write back, be a brave boy, and help Nan to take care of Annis. She would come back to see them after eighteen months and she and Father would both come home on leave after three years. Then they were gone.

The delights of Dibleys were due, not just to its sunlit garden, but to having a Mother there, and a Father who did not have to go to work. With both gone it was a different world. Nan did her best and David found shelter in her kindness. But he knew Annis was not happy, knew he should be helping to care for her, and didn't know how to do that. Dark, winter journeys to school, with an icy wind blowing across open, frosty fields and chilblains swelling painfully on his fingers, were bitter. Later in the year he became a weekly boarder, staying at the school from Monday till Friday. There would be no more bitter mornings with snooty girls. That was a relief – but no help to Annis. At school he was doing well and had made a friend. Philip, a bright boy of his own age with parents working abroad, was in the same class; they slept in the same room together and kept each other going.

In the holidays Annis and David were sometimes taken to visit their other grandmother. She lived mainly at Copse Hill – her big house in a countryside that seemed all fenced and hedged off; so different from the wild, open downland and the secret little chalk streams to be explored around Blewbury. Her house was full of beautiful, breakable things, big carpets and shiny surfaces. Outside, the garden was enormous, but made for viewing, not playing in, with clipped hedges, great flowering borders, neat lawns and hard edges. In the middle there was a terrace of rectangular concrete slabs surrounded by prickly cotoniastas, with a rectangular pond in the centre – water lilies floating on its surface with gold fish hiding beneath their leaves. One hot day, Annis and David– she small and rotund in a tight green bathing suit– were playing on the terrace. It was hot, so they got into the pool and sloshed about. Deep in a corner of it she found a shiny round thing which she pulled out to show to her brother. Then they climbed out to dry off and explore other parts of the garden. Suddenly there were screaming adults all around and gold fish flapping in the slimy bottom of an empty pool.

Their Singer grandmother had to be treated with caution; you could never be quite good enough for her. But she had a butler and house keeper – Cyril and Bertha – who were good, kind people. Isabel sometimes took the children out in her new car which she drove in a rather scary way. I can still remember her driving down roads with high hedges on either side and belting across a junction, saying "I always go as fast as I can over that cross road. It's so *dangerous.*"

David had learnt how to be – most of the time – a good boy. But at night he would lull himself to sleep with fantasies of a darker kind. Standing in a drawing room full of beautiful things – delicate antiques resting on polished sideboards and small tables – he had a small axe in his hand with which he set about smashing everything in sight – vases, chairs, windows, the lot. *Marvellous.* Then sometimes the face of a woman, middle aged or older, would appear and he would smash that too – and pull himself up with horror.

The poems he responded to later, without knowing why, often said for him things he could not say for himself. Housman for example.

> Others, I am not the first,
> Have willed more mischief than they durst.
> If in the breathless night I too
> Shiver now, 'tis nothing new.

The promised letters came from his parents, taking five weeks on their sea journey to Burma. They told stories about what they were doing, and places they were visiting that he would never go to... ending "with lots of love from" Mother or Father, and "Give Annis a kiss from me". Nan would read them aloud and help him to write back. He was aware that she was somehow sad. His grandmother treated her like a servant, making her take meals in the kitchen with Lena.

Ruth returned for a few months in the spring of 1934. She came to collect David from school at the end of term. He and Philip had come top of the class together: his first experience of academic success, and he liked it. Aged eight now, the two boys were both to go on to other schools and were sorry to say goodbye to each other.

Nan disappeared, and Ruth took the children to visit friends in Northern Ireland. It was not a carefree time. On the train to Armagh she suddenly broke down in tears; then apologised to the children, saying it was so difficult for her to manage without their father. Eight-year-old David, his sister recalls, said "But Mother, I try to do something to help you – every day". They stayed for some weeks in a boarding house in London. Ruth was sad there too: without Vernon the light seemed to have gone out of her life.

David's new school, "Oldfeld", seemed enormous, although it had only 80 pupils: a coeducational boarding school on a hill on the edge of Swanage in Dorset. This was David's first complete separation from home and family and he was desperately lonely; but cried only in private places. He was challenged repeatedly by another boy of his own size – Ian March – while others stood round watching them fight – something he had never had to do before. But he found he could get the better of Ian, and in time they became quite good friends. He could do the lessons well too; and made more friends. They did some wild things together: played innocent sexual games with each other; and took it in turns to stay awake through the night so that someone could wake the gang in the small hours. Then, in pitch darkness, these eight- and nine-year-olds would climb down a lattice that was nailed to the wall below their dormitory window, walk down into the town and roam around till the dawn came; then hurry back up the hill to climb through the prickly roses and back in through the window. When he got home at the end of term Ruth said he had suddenly grown up; and he knew why.

Oldfeld was a good, "progressive" school. Ruth and Vernon chose those things very carefully. There was a farm and market garden attached, and the children had to learn how to plant potatoes and beans and harvest them, how to make hay and set up stooks of corn. There were scout camps in the woods, where they cooked over open fires; and in the summer term the whole school was marched every morning in a long crocodile down to the beach where there were two big huts, for boys and for girls. Changing into bathing pants, they had to learn to swim; then, as soon as they could do that, to make their way out to the school raft and back.

In the entry class the children were taught by a lovely Scottish lady, Miss MacDonald, who got them to sing traditional songs while she played the piano. David loved Robert Burns ever after. Every Saturday morning, those who had been good were allowed to choose a picture postcard from a big pile of them strewn on a table. David collected pictures by Van Gogh and Rembrandt – then Degas – and put them in his locker. At the end of term Miss MacDonald stood up and said that, after many years in the school, she had to go back to Scotland and would be leaving them. Then she cried. David was grief-stricken too.

With Ma Than and Nan and Miss MacDonald lost, he didn't wholly give his heart to anyone else during the next half century. Housman would have understood.

> Give crowns and pounds and guineas
> But not your heart away;
> Give pearls away and rubies
> But keep your fancy free...
>
> [for] The heart out of the bosom
> Was never given in vain;
> Tis paid with sighs aplenty
> And sold for endless rue.

Yet, in a calf-like way, he fell deeply in love with Monica Boyer, a pretty girl with dark hair and brilliant blue eyes. (Years later, stumbling on a photograph of his mother in childhood, he realised how that image had imprinted itself on his heart.)

Maths and French were taught competently in this school, English and History very well, Art brilliantly – Latin very little and Greek not at all. Jo Hickson, who was the headmaster's sister and the art teacher, terrorised all the children in a benign way. She gave them big boards on which they pinned sheets of paper, and told them to ladle dollops of poster colour on to enamel plates which they used as palettes. Then they went outdoors to paint things they could see. "Remember the medieval monks", she would say. "They had to cover the background of their pictures with gold leaf, and that's very expensive so they could not afford much of it. That's why they had to paint things big. Make your pictures big!" She produced great school plays which got masses of children on stage, and asked the better artists (like David) to help her paint the scenery with huge brushes.

The music master was a big, clumsy man: a good musician, but somehow childish. One Saturday afternoon he invited David to come with him and Richard Harrison, a pretty lad of the same age, for a picnic on the downs above Swanage. They lay in the grass and ate marmalade sandwiches he had brought, with the scent of golden gorse all around: a happy time. But David was uneasy and refused this man's invitation to come again next week. He knew that hurt him and felt bad about that. A few weeks later, the music master disappeared, and next term they had a new one.

At the end of the summer holidays Ruth departed with Annis and Grace Harvey, a new mother's help whom she had discovered in the boarding house. She took David back to school by train, walking up the hill early in the day before other children had arrived, and saying the usual things. "Father and I will write to you every week… We'll be back home in eighteen months…" Meaningless to an eight-year-old. She said goodbye in the changing room, where David hung his coat, suddenly clasping him with passionate grief before turning to hurry back to the station. It was the only time she showed him how hard these partings must have been for her too.

The letters came each week, written in Ruth's and Vernon's elegant, flowing scripts, too small for David to read. Or was it that they made him cry and it was easier to try to forget his parents? He hid them in a growing little stack and wrote back each week about things he was doing. The children were all sat down at their desks on Sunday afternoons to write home.

Eventually these birds came home to roost. David was asked to come and see the Headmaster who had received a letter from his mother saying that she thought he was not reading their letters. He confessed, saying he *could* not read them. The Head kindly said that he or one of his staff would read them for him. Crying in front of them would be even worse, so he struggled to do better — and his parents to write more clearly.

Next holidays David went to a new family — the Snows, who lived in Halberton, a Devon village. They were, Ruth assured him, a "Burma family", so would understand what he was talking about. They had four children of their own and he was to call their mother "Aunt Una". She had been the solid, blue-stocking lady, glimpsed by Ruth on that first holiday in Maymyo — married to Dick Snow who became Director of Burma's Education Service before retiring early. Three other foster children arrived fairly soon — the McCrackens, another Burma family — and they all called her "Aunt Una". But David firmly called her "Mrs. Snow" until, twenty years later, he felt entitled to call her Una. He knew how to treat her: like a teacher for whom he would do his best. But give not your heart away.

David had another brief battle in the Snow family — with Nicho, their only son, a little older than him — before he found his place among the children. Nicho — short for Nicholas — soon became a firm friend, and together they formed a happy alliance against "the girls", his three sisters.

A year or two later, the good, local, private, day school the

Snows had been relying on to educate their three girls, closed. Unable to pay for boarding schools *and* their splendid old house, they moved to a cottage, a dozen miles away on the edge of the Blackdown Hills, which belonged to Dick's sister. I will say more about that marvellous place later.

David had learnt to survive, partly by turning away from his own family. A symbolic gesture illustrates that small revolt. His mother was determined that he should learn to play the piano. "Then you can move on to any other instrument you choose" she would say. So music lessons were paid for, and each week at school David would have one, and be given another simple piece to practice before the next was due. Being fairly bright he picked the first tunes up pretty quickly, but he had no real talent – and at the back of his head lay the sounds of piano and flute constantly to be heard in his home. His teacher grasped that something was wrong, and eventually, after another visit to the Headmaster, he was allowed to give up. He came out wagging his tail with relief. I don't think it ever occurred to Ruth and Vernon that their children might find it easier never to see them again.

IN CONCLUSION

Every empire must have a conviction about its mission that surpasses its rulers' lust for adventure and wealth, and justifies what they do – including their willingness to abandon their families, and, in the last resort, to kill those who challenge them. In Burma the British were running into rougher water than they had met since their conquest of the country, half a century earlier. But the challenges they were meeting and their successful response to them only reinforced their conviction about their mission. The young Burmans who would eventually drive them out, if known to the British at all, would still have seemed no more than a slightly ludicrous irritant.

Unlike other imperialists, the British intended to go. The crucial steps had already been taken to launch Burma on what would become the path to self government. Nationalists, so far, had only a flimsy ideology that was still being fought over by small groups competing to dominate the future. As those bidding to take over power began to look like a more serious political force, the willingness to kill in defence of empire weakened. Soldiers and policemen — dark-skinned, local recruits in the main, who would have to stay on in the country — could not readily shoot down those who would before long become their political masters.

Each family resolved the dilemmas of empire in its own way. Vernon and Ruth, who came to Burma partly as an adventurous way of making their way in the world, partly to escape from their own families, found refuge in each other and in their commitment to a country they fell in love with. Their children came third in their priorities. Proud of them though they were, and determined to see more of them some day, they thought that other people could look after them meanwhile, and told themselves that affectionate links between them could be rebuilt later.

In times of stress and conflict it is always children who are most vulnerable. Compared with millions of others at this time — Indian children starving in the famines, Chinese children in the path of the Japanese assault, Russian children perishing among the families deported by Stalin — David and his sister were a privileged pair. He was lucky to find that in stressful times the women who were paid to look after him— Ma Than, Lena, Nan, Bertha ... like Elly who had cared for Vernon, and Miss Griggs who had cared for Ruth many years before — provided a haven of kindness. Housman's "Epitaph on an Army of Mercenaries" always brought tears to his eyes — he knew not why.

> These, in the day when heaven was falling,
> The hour when earth's foundations fled,
> Followed their mercenary calling
> And took their wages and are dead.

Their shoulders held the sky suspended;
They stood, and earth's foundations stay;
What God abandoned, these defended,
And saved the sum of things for pay.

But each of these women, he learnt, will be taken from you in time. Do not give your heart away to them. Meanwhile remember that, whatever new worlds you may be thrown into, you can find friends once you have confronted those who will challenge you and fought your way into their gang. Teachers, foster parents and other adults have an important but more limited role. If they are honest, kind and fair, then the rules of the gang and the wider society they preside over are likely to be reasonably honest, kind and fair too. So their values matter a lot. (You will still have to fight your way in, but with closed fists, not knives.) Good young people, like Vernon's cousin Ted, who get into bad gangs with no humane limits to constrain them, fare much worse.

David was lucky in his teachers. Some of the best were drawn from that army of able spinsters left without any chance of marriage by the holocaust of the First World War. Others, I now recognise, were gay men who devoted much of their lives to children and young boys without ever abusing their power – apart from one musician, perhaps. I am grateful to them all.

This is all very boyish talk. For girls it may be harder to find a protective gang outside the family. And if, like my sister, your parents abandon you at a younger age, life is harder still.

NOTES

1   My data can be found in Eric Hobsbawm, *Age of Extremes: The short twentieth century*. London, Michael Joseph, 1994; Chapters 3 and 4.

2   Recollections and quotations from Eleanor Singer come from her memoir.

3   Balwant Singh *Independence and Democracy in Burma,*
     1945-1952. The Turbulent Years, Ann Arbor, Michigan,
     University of Michigan, 1993.

4   J.S.Furnivall, *An Introduction to the Political Economy*
     of Burma, Rangoon, Burma Book Club, 1931; page xiv.

5   F.S.V.Donnison, *Burma*, London, Ernest Benn, 1970, page 92.

6   Everett E. Hagen *The Economic Development of Burma*,
     Washington, D.C., National Planning Association, 1956.

7   Furnivall, 1931, pages xiv and 194.

8   John Stuart Mill, *Principles of Political Economy*,
     Toronto, Toronto University Press,1965; page 693.

9   Frank N. Trager, *Burma. From Kingdom to Republic*, London,
     Pall Mall Press, 1966; page 44.

10. Donnison, 1970; Chapter 7.

11   John F. Cady, *A History of Modern Burma*, Ithaca, New York,
     Cornell University Press, 1958; page 195 et seq.

12   Aung San Suu Kyi, *Freedom From Fear and Other Writings*,
     Harmondsworth, Penguin Books, 1992; page 128.

VI

THE GATHERING STORM

Within Burma life was becoming increasingly turbulent, and beyond its borders there were looming threats of war. The brutality of Britain's main challengers, the Germans and Japanese, united liberals and old-fashioned imperialists in a shared determination to defend the Empire and mobilise its strength for the anti-Fascist cause. But "empire" meant different things in different parts of the world.

BACK TO ENGLAND AGAIN

In 1936 Vernon and Ruth were again due for home leave. They wanted to take the opportunity their homeward journey would give them to explore other parts of the world and visit friends from Oxford days who were now scattered about in it. So Annis, aged five and a half, was sent home by the usual sea route to Liverpool with her governess, Grace Harvey, to be deposited at the Snows, with whom David stayed during his holidays from school. Ruth and Vernon would return by a longer route through Africa. They took a ship heading that way that stopped for ten days in Calcutta where they boarded a train for the hills and hired a car to drive to Darjeeling to visit friends from Vernon's time at Oxford. From there they went into the Himalayan forest on foot and on ponies for four days – camping out at night and calling at mountain-top monasteries and the palace of the Maharajah of Sikkim where their signatures in his visitors' book followed those of the Everest expedition who had passed through a few days before.

Vernon and Ruth

Rejoining their ship at Calcutta, they had a rough passage across the Indian ocean, went ashore for one clove-scented evening in Zanzibar; then sailed on to the African coast where their ship anchored off Beira and they were taken in to the harbour in a small boat. This was Portuguese territory. Vernon recalled that "although the town seemed seedy, the houses flimsy and the roads unfinished, the place had a pleasing continental atmosphere and the Portuguese had provided a park with a bandstand — light-hearted amenities that less imaginative British administrators would never have thought of."

Next day they took a train up to the Rhodesian highlands to Salisbury (now Harare) and went on to Marandellas where they stayed with Maurice Carver, another Oxford friend last seen when he had visited them in Yenangyaung. Maurice was now running a very successful preparatory school that he and a friend had set up with help from the wealthy Beit Foundation — a school for white children only. Maurice and his teachers, Vernon noted, seemed never to meet a black African other than the servants working at their school. (Later he was to work in mission schools for black children in Malawi.)

It was here that Vernon and Ruth heard of a young dentist; Keith Donnison, a half-forgotten cousin. They went to stay with him and his wife Margot at Gatooma. Keith treated Africans as well as Europeans, but at different times of the week. Vernon gained the impression that his African patients — some of whom came many miles to the surgery — were given equally good treatment at a fraction of the usual cost. Keith took Vernon and Ruth to see the big gold-processing plant nearby. It was later to incapacitate him, and doubtless thousands of others, with its poisonous arsenic fumes.

While staying with the Carvers, Vernon and Ruth received a cable from Una Snow saying that Annis had fallen off a seesaw and broken her elbow. She was being treated in the hospital in Exeter. Vernon and Ruth assumed that Mrs. Snow would cope, and pressed on with their holiday.

Writing forty years later, Vernon remembered that "through-out our time in Rhodesia we were shocked by the treatment accorded to Africans. There seemed to be no schools for them except those run by missionaries. No African could travel unless he first got a pass from his employer. When we met them on a footpath in the course of our walks they got right off the path to stand in a suitably deferential posture until we had passed. Things had never been like that in Burma, and by 1936 the right of the white man to be in Burma at all was being increasingly questioned."

They headed on southwards, riding in the cab of a mail lorry, to visit the great African ruins at Zimbabwe; then into South Africa – after a long and hostile cross-examination from an officious customs officer – to tour the Kruger National Park for several days, seeing wild beasts of every kind. From there they went by train to Pretoria, Johannesburg and Cape Town, being entertained by friends and friends of friends all the way. They were as "distressed, shamed and angered at the treatment accorded to black people" as they had been in Rhodesia.

Annis had broken her elbow only a few days after arriving at the Snows, a family quite unknown to her. It was set in the Exeter hospital but the bones came apart again at once. She was returned to the hospital where they tried again – and again failed. The doctor there offered to set the elbow by surgery which would leave her with a locked elbow for life. Una Snow, in desperation, telephoned Dr. Gillie, Ruth's old friend, and she offered to set up an appointment for her with the best man in London – Mr. Bristow. He eventually set Annis's elbow successfully. By now the poor child was so lost and battered among all the white coats that she had become quite withdrawn – no longer able to respond to anyone. Her Singer aunts and grandmother who visited her in Bristow's ward were so distressed that Isabel cabled Ruth, insisting that she and Vernon return – which eventually they did, on a Union Castle boat from Cape Town.

They arrived at the end of David's summer term and he was

brought by one of his teachers from Swanage to meet them as they got off their great ship at Southampton docks: an awesome sight on a longed-for day for a ten-year-old. They drove to the Snows' home in Devon in a car they had hired for their leave. Annis, looking pretty wan, was waiting for them.

Soon they moved to Dibleys, Vernon's mother's home in Blewbury. For David it was marvellous to be back in the cavernous, wood-panelled house with its gleaming brass and copper, its red curtains, the living room that always smelled gently of the earth that lay beneath its red-tiled floor, and the welcoming, half-wild garden outside. But best of all was to be with his parents — anywhere. At Christmas time they all went to Switzerland for five weeks and learnt to ski and skate — roughly speaking. It was the first time they had all gone together on one of these continental holidays.

As the Nazis strengthened their grip on Germany, Jewish people who could afford to escape were beginning to seek refuge in England. Two women came, one after the other, to stay at Dibleys. The Donnisons' encounter with them was a prickly one. Edith, Vernon and Ruth all spoke some German — Vernon fluently. The house had bedrooms to spare, and Ruth was Jewish. So they should have been well-equipped as hosts. But these were urban, fashionable women who were accustomed to being waited on by servants, whom they treated with disdain. They were not allowed to take money out of Germany, so they had converted what they could into expensive clothes and fur coats, stuffed into big suitcases which they dragged into the house with them. The Donnisons lived a fairly simple, rural life, and Vernon's mother, though persuaded by her son and daughter-in-law to do her duty, did not like Jews. The ladies eventually departed, as much to their relief as their hosts' I'm sure. But I can still recall the aura of fear and anger they carried with them.

Although only ten years old, David had some idea what they were frightened of. At Oldfeld, his school, teachers read to the younger children in their dormitories before turning the lights off

at night. Arthur Hickson, the Headmaster, read to David's dormitory and he chose Nora Waln's book, *Reaching For the Stars*,[1] a
shrewd, Quakerly account of the fear spreading through
Germany after the Nazis murdered many of their political oppo-
nents in the "night of long knives". Later he read for himself Jan
Valtin's book, *Out of the Night*,[2] a terrifying account of the experience of working class socialists and trade unionists, divided,
imprisoned, tortured and destroyed by the Nazis.

Joseph Roth later explained some of the things that the hosts
of such refugees needed to understand. "Émigré German Jews
are like a new tribe. Having forgotten how to be Jews, they are
learning it all over again. [But] they are unable to forget that they
are German... [so] they are like snails with two shells on their
backs." [Meanwhile the world] "never asks the wanderer where
he's going, only ever where he's come from. And what matters to
the wanderer is his destination, not his point of departure."[3]
Vernon and Ruth too were in a few years time to learn what it is
like to be refugees.

As the time came for him to return to Burma, Vernon wrote to
his friend Donald Petch to find if any jobs were going in the
Secretariat – the headquarters of government in Rangoon. All his
postings, thus far, had been to up-country places – the kind he
liked best, but outside the mainstream of Burma's political life.
Sooner or later, to gain promotion, he would have to work at the
centre of power. Donald said that if he could get back by the end
of February there should be one or two jobs to be filled. But
Vernon's sister, Yseult, her husband Ken and their three boys
would be visiting from Australia during that month. It was fifteen
years since he had seen her, twelve since he had seen Ken (now a
law professor at Melbourne university) and they had never met
the boys – aged about six, eight and ten. So he arranged to fly back
to Burma, which was expensive but took five days instead of the
four-week journey by boat. It was the first time any of the family
had been in an aeroplane. David's memories of the Baileys' visit
were happy, but when Vernon left at the end of February 1937

Ruth found it increasingly difficult to share a home with her mother-in-law and sister-in-law. She moved with the children to "Wayside", a rented cottage on the far side of the village: another half-timbered, low-ceilinged house, smaller than Dibleys, and with a long, narrow garden running down to a clear-flowing stream: "Wind in the Willows" country, marvellous for an eleven-year-old.

Ruth had intended to leave Annis at David's boarding school and with the Snows during the holidays. But the broken elbow must have changed her mind for she was soon seeking another governess to help care for her back in Burma. A German and an Austrian woman were her first choices. Both stayed at "Wayside" for a while, but each seemed to have secret and rather disturbing lives. Ruth and Vernon wondered if one of them was actually a spy. The other presented simpler problems: she drank the best sherry when left alone in the house and – worst of all – topped up the bottle with water. Eventually Ruth found Frances Turnbull, an attractive young New Zealander, who came in response to an advertisement. They set off with Annis to rejoin Vernon in October 1937, and David returned from school to the Snows for the Christmas holidays.

RANGOON

In Burma's journey to independence 1937 was a crucial year. The Parliament set up in 1923 had given Burmese Ministers some power over most departments of government, but no financial control. That remained with the Lieutenant Governor, advised by a nominated – not elected – Legislative Council. Local government was introduced for the bigger towns, but remained fairly corrupt and chaotic in most places outside Rangoon. The vote was given to men over the age of eighteen and to women over 21. To qualify, they had to pass a literacy test.[+] More than 70 per cent of men and 20 per cent of women were at this time able to read and write a simple letter in Burmese – three times as many as in

India.[5]

The British had for years been moving towards a separation of Burma from India — a step strongly resisted by nationalists who feared they would be left out of the constitutional advances promised to the Indians. But in 1935 the Government of Burma Act overrode these objections, creating a full Governor, accountable directly to Whitehall, and setting up, in 1937, a House of Representatives: 132 of them. There was also a Senate; half of them elected by the lower house and half appointed by the Governor. He retained discretionary powers over monetary policy, foreign policy, defence and — most important — the hill peoples and their territories around the edges of Burma. The constitution was designed to compel politicians to seek alliances between the different ethnic and religious groups in Burma and to prevent any one of these groups from achieving political dominance.

Many parties contested the elections, but the arguments between them dealt, not with the policy conflicts expected by their British mentors, but with personal loyalties to rival factions, each competing to be the most forceful agitators for independence. Boycotts of foreign goods and strikes — particularly in the oilfields and the schools —became their favourite political weapons, not parliamentary debate. Meanwhile the main Parties were recruiting private armies with Fascist tendencies. The soothsayers had forecast that 1938 would be a propitious year for revolt. (In the event, bloody pogroms against Muslims were the main result.) The first prime minister was Dr. Ba Maw. Like several of his colleagues, he was a lawyer who had taken a leading role in defending those charged after the Saya San rebellion of 1930.

A lot of anxious thought had gone into the construction of this constitution, but one Burmese historian has argued that it was not the first step towards independence but the last throw of a Victorian liberal tradition which so discredited Western forms of democracy that it destroyed hopes of parliamentary government in an independent Burma.[6]

The younger generation of activists, with Aung San prominent among them, found their main arena in Rangoon University. Launched in 1920 with good academic standards but no popular roots, the University had become increasingly politicised. Only Medicine fully maintained its standards – protected by the need to retain the approval of the British Medical Association. This was the turbulent world that Vernon was entering as he stepped off the aeroplane and joined the half million people – mainly Indians – who lived in Rangoon.

The job he was given was that of Secretary to one of two Financial Commissioners who stood between the spending departments and the departments raising revenue for them. "My first chief" he recalled, "was Charles Cooper: slim, elegant, a leading Rangoon socialite and a polished tenor singer. His handwriting was slenderly cursive – the smallest I have ever seen. But he was soon succeeded by Ernest Pattle: short, burly, untidy and lacking all social graces. His handwriting was large and round – executed, one felt, straight from the elbow. His method of drafting was to put down one idea at a time in vast, circular script and in no particular order, each on a separate sheet of foolscap. He would walk into my room in shirt sleeves, thumbs tucked into his braces, and think aloud as he paced around, scattering disconnected sheets of paper on the floor, leaving me to pick them up, arrange them in whatever order seemed best, add linking passages and develop them into a final draft for his approval. Our work dealt with difficult cases referred by officers on the ground, or arising from appeals against their decisions. It was a new and lively task, calling for the formulation of principles, policies and general rules. I gained considerable affection for Ernest Pattle. He had a good brain, but above all it was his integrity and honest humility that drew one to him. He had a gentle, kindly but ineffectual wife, Beattie, whose cloud of pale gold hair led to a certain pudding, crowned with spun caramel and much beloved of Indian cooks, being known throughout Burma as Beattie's Hair. Ruth discovered later that she spent the middle of each day locked indoors because when Ernest set off for the office their servants shut up the house and went off duty till tea time."

With Ruth still in England, Vernon lived first in the Pegu Club and then in a rented house. He played golf and squash on Saturday afternoons and very early on Sunday mornings; played his flute and a gramophone; and discovered the pleasures of choosing intelligent friends who shared his interests, rather than learning to make friends with pretty unlikely people because they were the only Europeans around. As a Deputy Commissioner he had been responsible 24 hours a day for coping with any emergency that cropped up, alert to pick up word of any local development, and compelled to choose his friends with the care required of a public personage. Now, as an office worker in a big city, he could have a private life. But if he wanted to make friends with Burmese people he would have to seek them out, for they were not admitted to the Pegu Club, the golf course or the squash courts; nor were they invited to most of the parties given by Europeans.

It was precisely in Rangoon, where radical young Burmans were stoking the furnace of their resentments and conspiring to shape a different future for their nation, that the British most needed to mingle and make friends among the people of the country – and were least likely to do so.

When Ruth, Frances Turnbull and Annis joined Vernon towards the end of 1937 they rented a succession of houses in the Rangoon suburbs. Unlike those provided by the government for its staff, these had tennis courts in their gardens and usually stood on the shores of a lake. Annis was given a canoe as soon as she could swim a hundred yards. Their suburban houses enabled Vernon and Ruth to invite Burmese people home who might have been too shy to venture into the government quarter. Later, as these friendships grew stronger, they moved in among the civil servants, and people of all ethnic groups came to see them there. As in previous years, they held great parties with hilarious games. Vernon recalled a treasure hunt leading, indoors and outdoors, from clue to clue. The last but one required competitors to get into one of a number of boats they had assembled with the help of

Vernon and Annis at Lawk Sok

neighbours and row on a bearing to pick up a final clue from a bottle anchored out in the lake.

One evening each week, Vernon would take Annis for a walk in some part of Rangoon little known to Europeans. They found an illicit still on one of these expeditions. When holidays came, they drove not to the resorts most frequented by officials but into the mountains.

"One evening in July 1938", Vernon recalled, " I was driving home from the office past the Rangoon General Hospital. As I drew near a cross-road, I realised that something was amiss. The road was unusually empty except for an untidy group of monks and young men. They had sticks in their hands and there were stones and bricks on the road. I spotted one of the men throwing a brick at my car and was able to swing right, away from the crowd and out of trouble. When I got home we learnt that widespread attacks by Burmans upon Muslims were going on. There had been no violence against Europeans – yet. The riots spread over much of the country and it was some three weeks before order was restored. Two or three weeks later there was a further, briefer outbreak of rioting confined to Rangoon. To ascertain the facts and relax political tension an inquiry was set up under a High Court Judge, Mr. Justice Braund, working with two Burmans and two Muslims. I was to be their Secretary."

Vernon had to organise the work of this committee. After hearing evidence in Rangoon they spent six weeks touring the most affected districts – mainly in the Irrawaddy delta and further up the river– using the Governor's river steamer. This enabled them to work as they travelled, to shed the pressures of their social milieux, and to get to know and trust each other. That, coupled with the skill and charm of an able chairman, enabled them to produce a unanimous report. Vernon made continuing friendships with two members of the committee – one of them a Burmese barrister, the other later becoming Pakistan's ambassador in Brussels.

The committee reported that 192 Indians had been killed in

the riots and 878 injured; 171 people – mostly Burmans – were injured by the police in restoring order; and there was massive looting and destruction of shops and houses. "The riots", Vernon concluded in his own book, quoting from the Committee of Inquiry, "were deliberately caused by 'a piece of unscrupulous political opportunism' which played upon and inflamed religious and nationalist sentiment and racial jealousy and dislike, in order to embarrass the ministry in power."[7] Burmese political parties were not operating in the way the British had hoped for.

After this, Vernon was made official head of the Judicial Department, responsible to a Burmese Minister but with direct access to the Governor on matters for which he retained powers. "This Department – probably the least significant of all of them – conducted the Government's relations with the High Court (which were sometimes uneasy) and administered all the lower courts, besides other generally unimportant matters." This must have been a trickier job than Vernon suggests. Crime and unrest were increasing; and of some 200 judges and magistrates only 13 were British. In the lower reaches of this service there was a lot of corruption and confusion.[8]

"My most troubling task", Vernon recalled, "was to advise the Minister and Governor how to exercise their prerogative to commute sentences of death passed by the High Court. As soon as a death sentence was passed the records of the case would be sent to my office, coming at once before me, distinguished by a red label, without any recommendation from my officials. All other papers were examined in the office first and submitted to me with recommendations. When a red label appeared I would take the case record home and put everything else aside in order to soak myself in the facts and background of the murder. In the past, commutation of sentences had been rare" – and nearly thirty more years were to pass before the British abolished the death sentence in their own country. "But, taking into account the fact that I was advising a Burmese Minister to whom, as a Buddhist, all taking of life was wrong, and drawing on my own convictions about the

death penalty, I sought to distinguish between premeditated murders, and murders committed in the heat of passion,
recommending that the death penalty be enforced for the former
only, and commuted for the latter. These recommendations were
accepted in virtually every case, although I think that on a few
occasions leniency was exercised despite my recommendations to
the contrary. The Judges of the High Court were strongly critical
of this policy, feeling that they knew more about the cases than we
did. In their position I might have held the same view but, looking
ahead to the rapid approach of self-government for a Buddhist
Burma, I think the line I took was right."

When Vernon had been a Deputy Commissioner up-country,
Ruth had been expected to take on all sorts of voluntary work just
because she was the D.C's wife. "But in Rangoon, where she had
no ex-officio jobs, we knew that senior ladies would press her to
work for the Blind School or the Deaf School or take part in
sewing parties for this or that, or sell flags in aid of some cause
that was of little interest to her and of none to the Burmese. She
wanted to do something more connected with reality and Burma"
and, Vernon added, "she was never very good at being bossed
around by rather stupid women." With a little help from him, in
his role as the Judicial Secretary, she became a lay magistrate in
the Rangoon Juvenile Courts, which gave her an insight into the
lives of children on the streets of Rangoon. "It also introduced her
to Tee Tee Luce, another lay magistrate, the remarkable Burmese
wife of Gordon Luce, a Rangoon University don. Gordon was a
shy, gentle and immensely learned scholar. When he married Tee
Tee, who had been one of his students, he found himself
ostracised by all but a few of the Rangoon Europeans; so both of
them naturally became wary of unknown white people." Ruth
immediately recognised Tee Tee's quality, learnt about the work
of the courts from her, and went to visit the home for abandoned
children that she and Gordon had set up — a home they had started by bringing waifs and strays into their own house. A strong
bond of friendship grew up between them. Feeling the courts

needed much more information about those appearing before them to help them make better decisions, Ruth learnt about the work of the probation service in Britain and, with a bit more help from the Judicial Secretary, secured authority to select, appoint and pay a man and two women to help the courts in this way.

Meeting the headmistress of the Diocesan School for Girls at a party one evening, Ruth learned that she was short of a science teacher. Next day she offered to fill the gap and became a part-time teacher. She consulted Professor Meggitt at the University who was very helpful, providing advice, specimens for dissection, and lots of encouragement. She was a good teacher. Meggitt later examined her students and was very complimentary about their work. Ruth and Vernon were still in touch with a few of them thirty and forty years later.

A VISIT FROM DAVID

It was at this time that David took a term off between schools and came out to Burma for six months, flying with one of Vernon's colleagues — T.L.Hughes, who had been Secretary to the other Financial Commissioner, and was later to be the Governor's political secretary. This was an unforgettable experience for a thirteen-year-old. They took off in a K.L.M. aeroplane from Croydon in the evening and flew through one of the most breathtaking sunsets David ever saw, surrounded on all sides by great swathes of colour — reds, oranges, blues — which gradually darkened into dusk as they came in to land at Amsterdam. There they were taken to a hotel for the night. Next morning they flew to Athens, landing in the early evening which gave them time to visit the Acropolis. You could walk freely around this marvellous ruin in those days and David stood out on the front terrace, watching the twinkling lights come up across the city as the sun went down and listening to the taxis — their under-inflated tyres screaming as they rounded the corners. Next day they flew to Basra and another hotel — blinding heat was his main memory of

David aged 13

Annis aged 9

this stop – then to Karachi for a night, and finally, on a fifth day, to Rangoon. Mingaladon Airport was close to the golf course some ten miles north of the city. David stepped out into a green and steamy evening – and there were his family.

They were still living in one of the lakeside houses and David did a lot of canoeing and some sailing in a dinghy; lots of drawing and painting; a little rather ineffectual Latin, taught by a friend of the family; some Burmese – a few words of which I still recall – and visited marvellous places. He went to Yenangyaung, where he had been born, and where he walked in blinding heat among the wooden oil derricks and saw native oil wells; and to Taunggyi where he climbed to the top of the crag behind the town and watched a Sikh signalman tapping out messages on a heliograph to a winking pinpoint of light on a mountain ridge sixty miles away. Family picnics took him to mysterious rivers that flowed underground through limestone mountains – into, and out of, great caves in the rock.

While he was with them, the family moved into town to a house in the government quarter – a tree-lined street, nostalgical-ly named Windermere Park. That made it easier to visit the Shwe Dagon – the great, graceful, gilded pagoda crowning a hill, sur-rounded by clusters of smaller pagodas, shining with different colours at different times of the day: the most breath-taking holy place in the world. He would go with his mother to the Scott Market, seething with people buying and selling marvellous things. These six months were an education, not just a long holi-day. He discovered too that he had a lively and intelligent nine-year-old sister who was a great swimmer and diver.

Vernon seemed to work as hard as ever, shut away early and late in the room called his office, and seeing little of David who was taken out to explore the country by Ruth, her friends and the family's servants. Dinghy sailing on the lake – a marvellous new experience – was made possible by their neighbour, Denis Phelips – a larger-than-life character who swore freely as they battled with the wind. David did not know till sixty years later that

Vernon must have been wrestling with decisions about men's lives on some of those evenings. He did not talk about his work. But it was clear that he and Ruth felt increasingly overshadowed by impending war. "I'm afraid we've got to fight the Nazis", he said. A month later the war began. They did not have a radio, but Denis Phelips next door did, and David used to lean against the fence listening to the news.

Everyone expected Britain to be bombed, and wives and children began filtering back to Burma to seek a safer place. Others already there set off for Australia and New Zealand. Vernon and Ruth had a difficult decision to make about their own children. They resolved to keep Annis with them and to send David home to take the place he had secured at Marlborough College – there being no boys' school in Rangoon that sent students on to British universities. Annis – nearly five years younger – was sent to the Diocesan School for Girls where her mother became for a while a part-time teacher. Apart from a few "country-born" white children, all the other girls there were Burmese, Indian or Anglo-Indian. Her parents' conviction that David should go home was reinforced when he got dysentery, late in his stay. It was, fortunately, the bacterial type which is fiercer but easier to get rid of. With no anti-biotics available at that time, he lay in bed for days in the Rangoon General Hospital where he was fed nothing but liquid chalk and glasses of whey – the disgusting fluid left when they have taken all the good things out of milk. He was so ravenous he leafed through magazines to find advertisements that pictured food and gazed hungrily at anything that looked eatable. But the treatment worked, and he set off to fly home in January 1940, a few days after his fourteenth birthday. A few months later, France fell and there would have been no safe way home.

David was on his own this time, there being no-one his parents knew among the passengers. They took the usual route, stopping at hotels each night. For a marvellous half hour he was invited to sit alongside the Dutch pilot in the cockpit, looking out at blue skies, passing clouds and hazy glimpses of the earth below. But the war meant that they could fly no further than Rome. There, passengers heading for Britain collected their suitcases and were taken to a hotel. Big posters of Mussolini looked down from peeling, yellow walls. Early next morning their small party went to the station and caught a train heading northwards through one of the great tunnels under the Alps: then onwards increasingly slowly across France. As night fell, David curled up to sleep in a top bunk that was pulled down over the bench seat below where an elderly Englishman turned in. It was the coldest winter for many years, and next morning he awoke to look out at thick snow that lay upon the land and was breaking big branches off trees and bringing down telegraph poles. The man in the bunk below was whimpering with apologetic embarrassment. He must have been overwhelmed by incontinence during the night for the floor of their compartment was awash with urine that flowed back and forth as the train rocked its way onward. David gathered up his things, climbed down and tip-toed out through the lake to find a seat elsewhere.

Passengers bound for Britain had planned to get a flight from Paris to London, but when they got there they were told that all the aeroplanes were grounded. They must get to the station early next morning and catch a train for Dieppe where there would be a boat going to England. That meant staying in another hotel where David managed to change some money, and early next morning he found his way through the streets to the right station, got his ticket and boarded an unheated train that drew slowly out.

As they left Paris there was nothing to be seen outside but snow. He became so cold that his teeth were chattering although he had put on all the clothing he could wear. So he dragged his case along the corridors till he discovered one heated compartment at the tail of the train and gratefully sat down there. Men came in and told him he must go away because these seats were reserved for the train crew. In desperation, he summoned all his ignorance of French, acting dumb and helpless. They let him stay. But the few words exchanged told him that he would have to change at Rouen and catch a train to Le Havre. The boats could not get in to Dieppe that day. He had long ago lost all the other people travelling with him, but got off at Rouen and made it to Le Havre and the boat, which took him to Southampton. Crossing the channel, he slept all the way. There he got another train for London, wondering what to do if no-one met him at Waterloo Station. Mrs. Snow had come to London to collect him and was going from station to station meeting every train coming from the channel ports. He caught sight of her with relief and handed her a five-pound note; all the money he had left. (I still sometimes have to remind myself, when I start slipping into travel neurosis on a simple journey from Glasgow to London, that I'm no longer a fourteen-year-old finding his way across wartime Europe.)

A few days later David was starting as a schoolboy at Marlborough which is a cold place even in mild winters. Each night water froze in the bathroom tumblers and ice encrusted the inside of the dormitory windows. He learnt to wear clothes and a dressing gown in bed, fold back the cold sheets and sleep between the blankets − prickly but warmer. Straight from the tropics and days of starvation in hospital, his fingers swelled with chilblains, blood seeping out from cracks in their skin. Then he got 'flu and was taken into the sanatorium, grateful to be warm at last. By the time he had recovered, the snow had gone and the sun was coming back.

David had been put into the Upper Fourth − a modest starting point. His progressive primary school did not reckon to prepare youngsters for the classic public schools. But his capacity for work and for making friends enabled him to find his way into this new tribal society, which I will say more about in a later chapter.

THE STORM GATHERS

The Japanese were becoming interested in Burma. Colonel Suzuki, already renowned as a warrior, gained approval from his high command for an undercover operation in the country on the grounds that supplies sent along the Burma Road since it was opened in 1938 were prolonging the war with China. He also argued that nationalist movements in Burma were looking for foreign support and should not be allowed to fall into the hands of the Chinese, the Germans or the Italians. Since the Japanese knew very little about Burma he asked permission to set up a secret mission there to make contact with the most promising people.[9] There were already lots of Japanese spies in Burma, as Vernon and his colleagues were well aware, but Suzuki was a more formidable operator than most. His story resembles that of many men who have worked with rebels and resistance movements in foreign countries. Starting out as a straightforward, patriotic soldier, he fell in love with the rebels he worked with and was eventually brought to heel by his own high command. The Lawrence of Arabia of Japan. Like others in this business, he found that if you are looking for men prepared to risk their lives as rebels, established politicians and civic leaders who have a good deal to lose are no use to you. The best resistance fighters are usually found among trade unionists, communists, students, criminals and others with little to lose – men who are accustomed to clandestine collective action, and familiar with violence.[10]

Aung San, who in 1936 had led the University strike which brought down the Principal, helped to set up the All-Burma Students' Union and became its President in 1938. He worked with various, feuding nationalist groups who sought to make the country ungovernable. None of them gained much support in any elections held at this time. Those on the more violent wing of the movement saw that they would need arms, and in 1940 Aung San, at the age of 25, was sent out with one comrade to seek help from the Chinese Communists. They were brushed off by Chinese leaders, wandered around for a few months, and were eventually picked up by Japanese agents of Colonel Suzuki who had sent his people photographs of the two young men. Aung San and his comrade were persuaded to fly to Tokyo and meet the Colonel himself.[11] They did not know that he failed at first to convince his superiors that they were of any significance and put them up at his own expense. But he was eventually allowed to set up a team to work in Burma with them and other nationalists.[12] Aung San returned to Burma in 1941 with promises of arms and money. Soon after, a group of thirty comrades were smuggled out in several ships to Hainan Island where the Japanese gave them rigorous military training to turn them into hardened soldiers. The Burma Independence Army was formed with Suzuki as Commanding Officer and Aung San as Chief of Staff. Their training must have been an odd affair. It was conducted in bad English, the only language the Burmans and their instructors shared, with unfamiliar weapons captured in China, to ensure their Japanese links would not be discovered.

Meanwhile the Burmese Government had asked for Dominion status in 1940 and twice more in 1941, appealing to the Atlantic Charter which in that year promised "the right of all peoples to choose the form of government under which they will live". Churchill refused them. U Saw, the Prime Minister, then turned for help to the Japanese and was arrested and detained till the end of the war. No-one in Burma seemed to notice. Political parties and their leaders still had very shallow roots in the society.[13]

To understand what the British authorities in Burma were doing at this time we have to remember that 1940 and 1941 were years of direst danger at home. While Britain's cities were being bombed and invasion was expected any day, it is not surprising that they had few resources to spare for a distant colony. They believed their ships commanded the Indian Ocean, and major forces would not be able to get through the mountainous jungles along Burma's eastern border. A British military historian records that "In August 1940 the Chiefs of Staff reviewed the situation in the Far East and concluded that... the invasion of Burmese territory would ... be a... remote threat. ...the defence of Malaya had to have precedence..." [14] Even after the Americans broke Japanese codes in June 1941 and warned the British that the Japanese intended to invade South East Asia, nothing was done.[15]

The British had been committed to handing power over to the Burmese ever since 1922, and they had made impressive progress towards "Burmanising" their services. The Indian Civil Service – the "officer class" of officials – had been almost entirely British when Vernon first came to Burma in 1922. By 1942, when the Japanese invasion got moving, only 15 per cent of them were white men who had actually been "bred in Britain". The same pattern was to be found in the police and the magistracy. Although there were many Indians among the non-British members of these services, the bulk of them were Burmese.[16]

The Armed forces were a bit different. For a start, there were very few of them. Figures for 1938 showed that, within a total of about six thousand men, more than half the officers were British, but among the other ranks half were from Burma – mainly Karens and other minorities – and a quarter were Indians. Scarcely any were Burmans – the majority community of the country. The Burman, the British still believed, "would never make a soldier". Indeed, in 1927 a conference of Indian Army Officers, not one of whom had served with a Burmese unit, resolved to exclude Burmans from the regular Army – and did so for ten years. By the eve of the Japanese invasion these numbers had all dwindled as men had been sent to other theatres of war, and – critically – there was only one squadron of rather unwarlike aircraft to support them.[17]

The East Indies fleet still looked formidable, led by its impressive battlecruisers, but the British seemed not to have noticed that their own Fleet Air Arm, flying rather primitive aeroplanes, had sunk a large part of the Italian navy in the Mediterranean. They presumably thought the "Eyeties" were easy meat.

LEARNING TO BE A FOSTER CHILD

Meanwhile David was finding his feet in a boarding school and a foster home. Most of my story about his life there comes from journals he wrote between the ages of 14 and 21: sixteen little note books which have been gathering dust for the past sixty years. When first left in England at the age of six and then again at eight, he had found it easier to forget his parents – guiltily hiding a growing pile of their unopened letters – rather than suffer the daily pain of living without them. To be told that his father would come home every three years, his mother every eighteen months, was like talking to an adult about the time when the sun will cool down – interesting perhaps, but not affecting *him*. By the age of fourteen, time horizons expand. It was a comfort to hold his parents in mind and read their letters. That comfort held up, even when France fell a few months later and no-one could be sure that he would see them again.

Marlborough, where he went to school, is an attractive market town lying midway on the old Roman road from London to Bath. In 1940, with London to the east, Southampton and Portsmouth to the south, Swindon and Coventry to the north, and Bristol and Cardiff to the west, this was a safe place, surrounded by southern Britain's main targets for German bombers. Wrangway, a small cluster of farms and cottages on the Blackdown Hills, where David spent his holidays with the Snows, lies high on the edge of a moor that divides Devon from Somerset. It was another safe place, within sight of the flicker of bombs and gunfire when night raids were made on Cardiff or Swansea.

When Britain's Forces were driven out of France they placed some of their main bases and training camps around Marlborough. The open downland was ideal for tanks, airfields and artillery; the woods for concealing ammunition dumps; and all were close to the ports from which the invasion of Europe would eventually be launched. Other bases were scattered westwards into Somerset. Thus the military, their men and hardware, were a constant presence through David's boyhood.

His journal begins on the last Thursday of the autumn term in 1940 with the words: "Air raid, 9.30 am – 1.30 pm. Weight [his own] 8 stone, 8 1/2 pounds." Next day comes: "Lecture on [T.S.Eliot's] 'Murder in the Cathedral'", and a note of post cards

They are very angular and fairly heavily armoured.

Slits to see thru'

4 feet approx.

Head lights. Bullet proof Tires (more or less)

It has a sort of turret which is open as a rule with men inside.

Monday

History. Chapter 9.

Today it is very dreary. Much rain fell during the morning and there is little sun anywhere.

Last night we were told that the Bismark, 40 miles from her home. was still being pursued by cruisers and planes. At least one hit has been scored

Sidney Tuik, was killed by blast from a land mine. I am writing to her today.

Also to Mrs. Snow, concerning her visit here, and when and where it will be spent.

We are still holding Tobruk, and at Sollum we have pushed the Germans back slightly. Some days ago it was announced that General Wavell now has 500,000 men under his command.

Yesterday I saw two Westland "Whirlwinds" the first I've ever seen.

The main characteristics are the very tall rudder with elevator mounted high

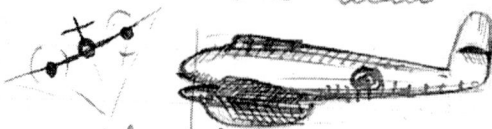

he sent to family friends and his grandmother, followed on Sunday by "Carol service in Chapel" where 'Murder in the Cathedral' was acted, and "air raid 7.15 – 11 pm".

On Tuesday David records his train times and travel costs for the journey back to Wrangway and the Snows. "Bus to the station 6d. Marlborough to Taunton 19s 8d. Taunton to Wellington 1s 2d. Breakfast at Swindon 5d. Lost my sponge and sponge bag. Left my gas mask behind." Then, on the next line: "19 ships sunk. 87,000 tons in last week. (Well below average)" he adds in a reassuring bracket. Then comes a note about American fighter aircraft being sent to Britain, followed by a shopping list for a trip to Taunton – to post a small present to his girl friend, and buy an "egg timer and ping pong balls (if possible)" – probably Christmas presents for the Snows.

The story continues with descriptions of heavy snow falls and curious ice formations, carefully illustrated with a pencil drawing. As the water level in reedy moorland pools fell each day, it formed a thin new layer of ice each night, building successive glassy floors downwards which were penetrated by reeds that thrust upwards through holes they created in each deck as they shimmered in the wind above. He was fascinated by the beauty of this delicate, natural architecture. (Indeed, I've never seen anything like it since.)

During the coming days David describes a small drama created for the family Christmas party by him and the three McCracken children whose parents were also in Burma. He also tells how he and "Nicho" Snow explored an army firing range on the moor, where there were notices saying "Danger. Keep Out". They brought back shiny spent bullets and a small unexploded bomb (*probably* only a smoke bomb) which they left on top of the water butt by the front door. And, as always, there was the war news: lots of Italians captured in Abyssinia, air raids on London, submarine warfare... He returns to school next term, taking a long, bitterly cold train journey and seeing anti-aircraft fire in the sky on the way. "Have left behind eye prescription and savings stamp book." He often had painfully sore eyes and headaches at this time.

46

Mr. Evans.

The light is coming from a
Tilley lamp to the left on a
level with the top of the paper,
and a fire to the right on

47

is level with the seat of
the chair.

Mrs. Evans
(knitting
while she
was drawn)

I should explain who the Snows and the McCrackens were —
all, in various ways, part of the British Empire. The Snows had
four children: Elizabeth, Audrey and Nicholas — all older than
David — and Ursula, the youngest. Dick Snow, their father, was in
his sixties. He had grown up in a family of West Country craftsmen who had little luck: both his father and then his stepfather
died when he was young. But he won himself an education
through scholarships that took him to Oxford and a first-class
degree in "Greats" — classics, ancient history and philosophy. He
could have become a university don had he not felt obliged to earn
money to support his mother and pay for his younger sister's
schooling. That took him to Burma as a school inspector, and in
time — after war service with the Army in Mesopotamia — he
became head of Burma's Education Service, with a reputation for
scholarly intelligence and wit. On the way, he married and had
four children. "Why" he would ask, in a characteristic joke, "is it
always so cool in Windermere Park?" — a road of Government
houses in Rangoon where the Snows, and later the Donnisons,
lived. "Because there is a little Snow there every year". Dick hated
Burma and his job, and when his service was brought under
Burmese Ministers who expected him to ensure their sons all got
pass marks in their exams he retired early.

Una, his wife, was eleven years younger. Coming from a
devout Anglican family, she got a good degree in History at
Oxford and worked during the First World War in Intelligence —
although she never said anything about this to anyone. After the
war she went to Burma to join a missionary society, but soon
moved into teaching and became head of a teachers' training college. Marrying Dick, she had to give up work and never did a
full-time job again. When he retired, they settled, first, in the
lovely house in Halberton, a Devon village, where David first
went to stay with them and Annis broke her elbow falling off the
see-saw. Later, they moved to the cottage at Wrangway which
belonged to Dick's sister — whom he was still supporting.

The M5 motorway roars close by now, but in those days this

was a pretty remote spot. The people of Wrangway had no electricity, main water supply or cars, and many had no water-born sanitation. These conditions would today be regarded as hardship, but that's because we have come to depend on refrigerators, central heating and the like. Water came down to the Snow's cottage through a pipe from a spring on the edge of the moor above. In dry summers they eked it out with help from the rainwater butt. There was no shop in this hamlet so the family went spinning three miles down the hill on their ancient bicycles to Wellington where they bought the food they could not grow for themselves. Peddling home, they stored perishables in a meat safe under the eaves on the north side of the house. Even the doctor came, when called, on her bicycle. Meals were cooked on a coal stove, and the family warmed themselves around the hearth of a wood fire – the boys cutting logs for it from branches dragged down from the moor above. They listened to the B.B.C's Home Service on a radio powered by a heavy battery, and read books by oil lamps downstairs and candles upstairs. Outside there were long views and great country. It was a marvellous place to grow up in. The children had all that they needed: poverty only arises when economic and social change creates new necessities that some people are deprived of – as, in unequal societies, it repeatedly does.

Most of Dick Snow's pension must have been devoted to sending his children to middle-rank public (ie, private) boarding schools. Una accepted from her foster children's parents only enough money to cover the costs of caring for them. Dick was a sceptical, ironical, depressed man who seemed to David to spend most of his time reading "The Times" or the classics – often in their original Latin or Greek – and listening to the news on the radio. We were listening to the struggle for survival of the empire to which the Snows, the Donnisons and the McCrackens had devoted much of their lives – the empire that provided the pay cheques and pensions on which they all lived. I now believe Dick was anaemic – or perhaps he had what we would call M.E. He loved his own children dearly, but I doubt he was ever asked

whether he wanted four more added to them. For them he had little energy to spare; and his comments could be devastating. When
David, at the age of nine, came proudly home with a school report
that described his "conduct" as "very excellent" Dick exploded,
and never allowed the boy to forget his contempt for a school that
would so misuse the English language.

Una was quite different. A devout, driven woman, I remember
her coming down at six in the morning to say her prayers on her
knees before the stove; digging the garden to raise vegetables for
us; cooking and mending, and going to local meetings of church
and state. When the evacuees arrived from the cities it was she
who organised billets for them on neighbouring farms. All eight
of the children she was responsible for were visited once a year at
their boarding schools where she would consult teachers about
their progress. She peddled up and down the hills on a heavy, old-
fashioned, sit-up-and-beg bicycle; and stayed up late at night to
write letters sending news of her foster children to their parents –
the nib of her pen sometimes trailing across the page when she
fell asleep, exhausted. Her hands were patterned with a network
of blackened cracks acquired from fierce bouts of gardening,
interrupted for cooking and washing. I guess we were, in a way,
her war work – but she gave us more than that suggests. I know
why tears came to my eyes when, many years later, I read Day
Lewis' poem "My Mother's Sister" in which he celebrates

...a distressed

Gentle woman housekeeping for strangers;
Later, companion to a droll recluse
Clergyman brother....
She lived for all she was worth – to be of use.

She bottled plums, she visited parishioners.
A plain habit of innocence, a faith
Mildly forbearing, made her one of those
Who, we were promised, shall inherit the earth.

The McCrackens must have suffered much the same loss of parents that David experienced, but they dealt with it differently. He treated Una like a school teacher; trying to be a good boy and firmly calling her "Mrs. Snow". The McCrackens' rather buttoned-up Scottish parents may have given them less to lose in the first place. Graeme, a year older than David, was at Shrewsbury School where he had acquired an outwardly confident carapace of manliness. John and Alison, a good deal younger, dropped more sweetly into "Aunt Una" and "Uncle Dick" mode.

In those days married women of the middle class were not allowed to work. They believed, with some reason, that the state schools might not get their children into universities – and the Snows had nothing but education to offer their children to carry them through life. Today, a woman as well qualified as Una Snow would take her family to a city, get a good job and send her children to local schools where they would do well. Some things do get better. But in that case David would not have been with them. If he had to be left in England eight thousand miles from home, he was lucky to live with this family: much better than with his grandmothers with whom he had, at best, an uneasily cautious relationship.

When I grew up and had children of my own I came to love and admire Una Snow. But I suspect her own children were short-changed. Sent off to boarding schools, they returned for holidays to find their mother had so many demands on her energies that she economised by type-casting them. Elizabeth was expected to be the flamboyant, passionate, musical one; Audrey the patient, level-headed one who cleared up other people's messes; Nicho the lovable, chaotic one – an athlete who would one day become a talented scientist – and Ursula was ...the youngest; and for a long time *kept* young lest childhood be no longer found in the house. They were entitled to be taken for what they were, there and then. In the long run, few of these expectations worked out. Fortunately for David and the McCrackens, they responded not by resenting those who had invaded their home but by welcoming them into the holiday-time gang that together they formed.

David's journals recall summer picnics on the moor, and the whole family cycling to the river Culm where they swam in a pool by a small weir before falling upon the sandwiches; carol singing at Christmas time when the children walked from farm to farm through the frosty darkness, carrying the musical instruments that most of them played; the lamp-lit ritual of Christmas dinner, solemnly listening to the King's speech on the radio, and the opening of presents by one child at a time – the youngest always starting first and the oldest coming last. I recall the division of tasks – sexist, we would now say – girls helping with the cooking and mending, boys cutting wood for the fire, cleaning and polishing shoes, digging in the garden and repairing bicycles... There were tensions and quarrels too, but David stood back from these, telling his journal "*our* family was never like this!" (An illusion of course.)

I will tell the term-time story of his life in a later chapter.

IN CONCLUSION

What were Vernon and Ruth doing as Burma moved towards the abyss? Their memoir records the kinds of things they had always done. He mentions a marvellously varied gallery of friends of various backgrounds and professions. They included Geoffrey Wood, an engineer, who married Annis's governess, Frances; Captain Seagrim of the Burma Rifles, later to die in a Japanese jail, who came to concerts Vernon helped to organise; Rene Vachet-Beeston, their excellent French dentist, musical and sophisticated – of whom I say more later – Rex Sharpe, an English High Court Judge who came to their house to apologise for the behaviour of the Chief Justice who retired to a dug-out and refused to come out for fear of bombs; and Mi Mi Khaing, an able and charming Burmese lady, then a student in the Teachers' Training College.

When it became clear that there would be no holidays in Europe for them, Vernon and Ruth bought a tiny cottage in their beloved Taunggyi and set about extending it a bit. The house gave them opportunities for getting out of the heat for a few days, finding peace, and forming new friendships among Shan people.

Along with other officials, Vernon was sent on a fortnight's course to toughen them up for war. He recalled being made to dig trenches in the full noonday sun while wearing gas masks – "an exasperating and particularly pointless exercise". The General in charge came down the line inspecting the officials and asked Vernon whether he had any previous military experience. "Yes, Sir" he was able to say. "Two years with the Grenadiers in France". As part of another exercise to familiarise civilians with the military culture, he was sent, with an old friend from the Burmah Oil Company, to sit at the Army Headquarters for a fortnight simply to learn all they could. This may have been useful later when he had to work closely with the Army and eventually join it, but it did not increase his respect for the military.

It was music that inspired Vernon's most vivid recollections of these years. There was no orchestra in Rangoon and good music was hard to find. He had become secretary of the Rangoon Gramophone Society, which was open to anyone with a good gramophone, a room capable of taking their twenty members, and a willingness to give a record concert followed by drinks. After several years of these happy evenings, he was invited to play his flute in a small orchestra assembled for some charitable occasion. Mr. Galimberti, a good professional cellist in the group, remarked as they left that "We ought to have a proper orchestra in Rangoon". Vernon took him up on this and together they searched for musicians. Galimberti knew the professionals and Vernon looked for amateurs, stopping people in the street who were carrying likely-looking instrument cases, and knocking on doors in the evenings when he heard sounds of a western instrument being played with some skill.

They both knew that the only man in Rangoon capable of conducting an orchestra was Mr. Dumble, a trained musician who had got a job in the Army during the First World War, ending up in Burma and taking an office job there, spending his evenings with a cheroot and a tumbler of whisky, playing chamber music to himself. He was eventually persuaded, and under his direction they assembled about 40 musicians with various ethnic backgrounds. They ranged from jazz and dance band players to military and police bandsmen and students – Kelly Isaacs, aged eighteen, was one of these, later to become a distinguished London performer[18]. They borrowed music from various places – some of it from the Calcutta Orchestral Society – and practised together once a week. After a year's work they performed, in November 1940, in the Rangoon City Hall: a Mozart overture, Beethoven's Symphony No. 1, songs by Gounod and Quilter, Bizet's Arlesienne Suite, some violin solos arranged by Kreisler, and two Spanish dances by Moszkowski. I think Vernon recalled every player and every note.

The Governor himself agreed to come to their concert and they gave his party the best seats, ten rows back from the stage. Then Government House said it would violate protocol if anyone sat in front of the Governor, so they had to remove all the seats between him and the orchestra.

"What an excitement it all was! And really it didn't go badly. No-one had thought it could be done in Rangoon." There was such enthusiasm in the town that they set about preparing for a second concert, to be held in December 1941. Rehearsals began and continued through the year till, on 8 December, the Japanese invaded.

Fiddling while Rome was on the point of burning, some might be tempted to say of this project. Others felt that, in the face of barbarism, they had upheld a civilised tradition and the cross-cultural relationships which make it possible.

My foreboding account of these years owes a lot to hindsight.

Across most of the country things went on much as before — sometimes well, sometimes badly. In the last year before war came to Burma, Ruth played a part in a small incident which reflects both aspects of a world approaching its end. She was on her own for a few days at Taunggyi, sitting in the sun in their cottage garden knitting, with a kitten on her knee. Suddenly there were shouts in the road outside and an Indian leapt over the style, running for his life across the lawn to escape a group of Burmese soldiers who were tearing up the road after him, armed with dahs — big, sharp knives. Ruth went straight to the style and confronted their leaders, still holding the kitten and her knitting on her arm. "There's no way through" she said firmly in Burmese. Slowly they backed off and melted away as their quarry disappeared into safety. Going back to her chair, she was suddenly aware that she was shaking all over. Being at her best in a crisis was a capacity she was going to need again before long.

NOTES

1   Nora Waln, *Reaching For the Stars* (Reprint Services Corp., 1991)

2   Jan Valtin, *Out of the Night*, New York, Garden City Publishing Co., 1942.

3   Joseph Roth, *The Wandering Jews*, (Trans. Michael Hofmann), London, Granta Books, 2001; page 124.

4   F.S.V.Donnison, *Burma*, London, Ernest Benn, 1970; page 115.

5   G.E.Harvey, *British Rule in Burma 1824-1942*, London, Faber and Faber, 1946; pages 45, 79-80.

6   U Maung Maung, *From Sangha to Laity. Nationalist Movements of Burma, 1920-1940*, Delhi, Manohar Publications, A.N.U. Monographs on South Asia, No.4, 1980.

7   Donnison, 1970; page 121.

8   Harvey, 1946; page 58. These figures are for 1942.

9   Izumiya Tatsuro, *The Minami Organ*, Tokyo, Tokuma Shoten, 1967.
    Translated into English by U Tun Aung Chain of Rangoon
    University.

10 For a British study of resistance movements and their foreign
    backers, see William Mackenzie, *The Secret History of SOE, the
    Special Operations Executive, 1940-1945*, London,
    St. Ermin's Press, 2000.

11 Aung San Suu Kyi, *Freedom From Fear and Other Writings*,
    Harmondsworth, Penguin Books, 1992).

12 Izumiya Tatsuro, 1967; pages 21-25.

13 Harvey, 1946; pages 87-95.

14 S. Woodburn Kirby, *The War Against Japan*, pages 11-12; quoted in
    Frank N. Trager (ed.) *Burma: Japanese Military Administration,
    Selected Documents, 1941-1945*, Philadelphia, University of
    Pennsylvania Press, 1971; page 9.

15 Trager, 1971; page 9.

16 Harvey, 1946; pages 42 and 31.

17 Trager, 1971; page10.

18 Kelly, who later called himself Maurice, Isaacs became a life-long
    friend and later played at Ruth's and Vernon's funerals. He died on
    4 May, 2003. His obituary appeared in the Independent on 22May

VII

DISASTER

On the eve of the Japanese attack, the British were well on the way to handing Burma back to its own peoples. If you had assembled British officials from every Department of Government, British officers from the Police and the Army, and the British managers of firms operating in Burma, the whole lot could have been fitted into one railway train.

Wondering, in Chapter III, how such handfuls of men managed to run the largest empire the world has ever known, I described their authority as a sort of confidence trick that worked so long as the Royal Navy commanded the oceans of the world, so long as the British could still recruit loyal officials and soldiers from the people of conquered lands and raise sufficient taxes from them to pay for the whole enterprise, and so long as the Empire's forward momentum was maintained and every setback avenged. Establishing British rule was often a bloody business; but, once established, it was generally less violent and arbitrary than the regimes it displaced. To keep their magic working, however, the imperialists still had to be prepared to kill people when necessary.

Once the British were committed to giving their country back – some day – to the Burmese, imperial power began to unravel. It was destroyed altogether by Japanese infantrymen in six months – not only in Burma, Malaya and Singapore, but also in the Dutch East Indies and ultimately in French Indo-China too. In this chapter I shall tell how an empire disintegrated. The backdrop to the drama is drawn from the history books; the action played out on the stage comes from one family's memoirs, letters and journals.

JAPAN INVADES

The Japanese invaded China in 1931, and ten years later they were still trying to subdue that vast country. Always short of fossil fuels, they were planning to take over the oilfields of the Dutch East Indies, and calculated that would require the capture of Malaya, Singapore and Southern Burma to protect their supply lines. Meanwhile the Chinese fought on with the help of munitions sent in by rail from French Indo-China and later in trucks that came up the Burma Road that was completed in 1938. The French were compelled to close their rail route when they were defeated in 1940, and the British, with their backs to the wall, followed suit for a year. But when the rains stopped in 1941 they reopened their road. That was when Army and Navy chiefs in Tokyo authorised Colonel Suzuki to set up an organisation within Burma that would contact Burmese rebels. He had already been promising them arms and support without saying anything about this to his superiors.[2] Later, the 30 comrades trained by the Japanese as freedom fighters were sent to Siam to recruit supporters and prepare for the invasion of their country.

The Japanese attacked Pearl Harbour on 8 December 1941, and took over Hong Kong and Siam and invaded Malaya and the Philippines during the following days. On 28 December, in Bangkok, Aung San's group formed the Burma Independence Army in an oath-taking ritual that involved sharing and tasting each others' blood, making Suzuki their Commander and 25-year-old Aung San Chief of Staff. They had already recruited some 3,500 Burmese who had come across the border into Siam.[3]

Next month small groups of lightly armed Japanese soldiers clambered through the jungle-covered mountains to enter Burma at several points, heading for Moulmein as their main target. This town, with a population of well over 50,000, was quickly taken. Burma's long southern coastline, intersected by rivers and with few roads, was impossible to defend with the few troops stationed there – mainly units of the Burma Rifles who tended to desert under fire.[+]

Vernon recalled these first days vividly, and – unless attributed to someone else – it is from his memoir that the passages in quotes have been taken. "It was almost a relief", he wrote, "to shed our feelings of guilt for taking no share in the war." For two weeks all was quiet in Rangoon. Then, on 23 December, came the first air raid. "It caused heavy casualties because people who had never experienced bombing stood out in the streets to see the fun." Next morning Vernon drove Annis to the Diocesan School as usual. There was a notice pinned to the gate saying that the school was closed until further notice. The Japanese had complete command of the air and many more raids followed. At first the family took refuge in a slit trench in the garden during daylight; under the stairs after dark. But as it became clear that the docks, the railway station and the city centre were the bombers' targets, they gave up these precautions. Ruth went to work each day in the cipher office at Government House.

Annis, aged eleven, wrote an account of the first raids for the magazine of the school in India to which she was soon to be sent. When "the ground had stopped shaking and I did not feel so scared...Father shouted 'Look! There is a parachute', and, looking out of the window we saw... a parachute was floating down...We could see the cords attached to a dangling black dot – the airman! Then... we saw another parachute as well as a falling plane [which]... turned over and over in the air looking like a falling leaf... whole except for a missing wing..." In the second raid "a Jap plane dropped a stick of bombs in a straight line... and about twenty crashes followed each other appallingly quickly."

The Japanese soon cut off Mergui, in the far south of the country, which had been Vernon's first District. He later recalled what happened to some of the people he had known there. The rather ineffectual tin miner and his irascible wife whom I described in Chapter IV got away on the last boat to leave for Rangoon. They arrived, gloating that Jubb, their devious but unsinkable rival, had been left behind and would at last get his come-uppance, along with his Burmese wife and children. But Benjamin Bateson Jubb filled his motor launch with tin ore, got his family aboard, and steamed 400 miles to Rangoon with nothing but a school atlas to navigate by. There he sold his tin for a profit and made his escape to India.

Government officials were at this stage instructed to stay put, await the Japanese, and do their best to protect their people during the occupation — a pointless gesture, for Europeans were all immediately imprisoned. That policy was soon abandoned. Captains of the ships that plied along the coasts between Singapore and Rangoon — the men who had helped Vernon to make up a football team when they called at Mergui on a Saturday — were ordered to keep going, even when Japanese command of the air and the sinking of the *Repulse* and the *Prince of Wales* made it clear that they could be offered no protection. More than thirty of these civilian ships were lost, along with most of their crews.

Europeans in Burma depended heavily on their servants to keep their households going. Kitchens, bathrooms, laundry and many domestic tasks were organised in ways that called for native skills and lots of manual labour. When bombs began to fall, many families awoke in the morning to find their servants gone. Public services in Rangoon — a predominantly Indian city — tottered as their staff began to escape. More than half a million Indian refugees eventually got back to their country, mainly from Rangoon and the surrounding area. Thousands more perished on the way.

Vernon and Ruth gathered their servants together when the raids began and suggested that they might want to send their wives and children to a safer place up country. Their cook, Nikunja, said he had relatives at Bassein and they agreed their families would go there for a while. Nikunja set off with them and Vernon said to Ruth that evening "That's that: you won't see him again." But Ruth was confident he would return, and indeed he did. Two or three weeks later Vernon suggested to the men – cook,

butler, and two personal peons – that they should take it in turns
to go to Bassein to make sure all was well, but they refused to go
until Annis had been sent to safety.

Fleur Lecky Thompson, an old friend of the Donnisons –
white but "country born" – came to ask Ruth's advice. "She had a
sister in Calcutta who kept urging her to come over with her two
children. 'Should she go?' she asked. 'If you've got anywhere to go
– go' said Ruth, adding 'I only wish that I could get Annis away'.
'I'll take her' said Fleur without hesitation. In that case, we said,
Lecky (her husband) must come and stay with us."

But how were they to get away? "There were Japanese submarines in the Bay of Bengal and few ships sailing. Air passages
were all booked. But we were told that unscheduled aircraft were
still landing at Mingaladon and taking off as quickly as possible,
sometimes with a few empty seats. If we could get our party to the
airport as soon as we were telephoned, we might be able to get
them away. So we packed suitcases and kept a car loaded for departure in the porch. We raced to Mingaladon four times in the next
ten days and thought once that we were going to be lucky: then
Wavell arrived with his staff officers to fill the aeroplane – returning to India after one of his pep talks. On the evening of 30
December, with Ruth feeling increasingly desperate and me trying to reassure her that our luck must turn eventually, the
telephone rang. A flying boat had come down on Rangoon River
and would leave at dawn for Calcutta. It had brought officers on a
mission to Army headquarters, and if they had not completed
their work by next morning there might be seats for our party.

"We drove down to the seaplane terminal before dawn, casting
lethal looks at every officer entering the hall – and got the seats.
Fleur and the three children went off in the launch to the great
flying boat floating out on the river. Ruth had told Annis, 'David
had his great adventure when he flew home alone in 1940. This
will be your great adventure'." Vernon, Ruth and Lecky drove
down to Monkey Point where the estuary opens out to the sea.
"The sun rose, and the flying boat took off, throwing out a bow

wave and a great plume of spray as it gathered speed and climbed into the sky." I do not think it crossed their minds that Ruth might have gone too; partly because they wanted to stay together; partly because they disapproved of the people who sent their wives out at this stage. It conveyed a defeatist message.

Fleur and the children reached Calcutta safely and stayed for a few days with her sister in what Vernon described as a typical Anglo-Indian household. Annis was puzzled. She had never before been in a house where there were no books. Then they travelled to Darjeeling up in the hills where she and Fleur's daughter Joan entered St. Michael's, another Diocesan Girls' School, run by Protestant nuns mainly for Anglo-Indian children. It was "somewhat inhibitive and mortificatory", Vernon later recalled. But they were grateful to have found a relatively safe place for Annis, with Fleur nearby to keep an eye on her.

DAVID AT MARLBOROUGH

Meanwhile David, a schoolboy at Marlborough, had only the vaguest notions of what might be happening to his family. He coped with his anxieties by staying fiercely active, and by talking to himself in the little note books in which he wrote his journal.

The school, he reported early in 1942, had survived another bitter winter, coping not only with snow and ice, but also with measles, whooping cough and chicken pox. Patients overflowed from the sanatorium and boys who remained well had to be shifted from house to house to make room for the sick. "All our books [for school work] were burnt in London last holidays [in the blitz], along with the orders for them, so things are rather slowed up."

Keeping the school going must have been a demanding task – complicated by rationing, the loss of many of the best teachers and domestic staff to the forces, and the evacuation of the City of London School to Marlborough. This could have been an opportunity for two good but very different schools to pool resources and learn from each other. The C.L.S. was a big-city day school with a high proportion of Jewish boys and businessmen fathers – good academically, but with little time for games, other than boxing. Marlborough was a classic public boarding school, surrounded by playing fields with marvellous country beyond, teaching the sons of civil servants, doctors, gentlemen farmers, Church of England clergy and the like. Snobbery and tribalism kept the schools apart. They each used classrooms, labs, playing fields and dining hall at different times of day. David knew that the C.L.S., viewed by Marlburians with a hostility often tinged with anti-semitism, was the school where his Singer grandfather and great uncles had been educated. He was disturbed by the snobberies around him, but his journal focussed on more practical matters. "The butter in hall has been distinctly cheesy in taste and smell."

Letters continued to get through from Burma, but took six to eight weeks on the way, sometimes arriving in the wrong order. A cable came from Rangoon for David's sixteenth birthday in January 1942, saying simply: "Birthday love from Father Mother Annis Donnison." News bulletins about air raids in the West, which he recorded in his journal, made no mention of those wreaking havoc in Rangoon. "I wish", he said, "that one could get decent news more quickly from Burma. I wish the time would go more quickly. But then I wish such a lot of things..."

Boys knew the names and makes of tanks and aircraft on both sides as well as they knew the names of the cars on the road. When David saw a new one he would draw it in his journal. Then, one day, "The air raid warning went as we came out of hall [from lunch]. On the way to house shelters heard an aero engine. It did not sound powerful, and I thought it was an Anson, but I looked round, and coming over very slowly and very low was an He 111k. At first I got quite a shock and thought it would machine gun us (one could plainly see a machine gun sticking out from underneath) but nothing happened. When he had gone over everyone burst out laughing and went on to the shelter. The all-clear went at 1.30 and now (1.50) the warning is sounding again." Later he reports "We are now wearing gas masks every week for a quarter of an hour after lunch on Wednesdays."

Despite losing the best of its younger teachers to the forces, Marlborough did a great job of deploying the rest to fit the evolving stages of a boy's development. David began in the Upper Fourth with Mr. Pepin: a tough disciplinarian, who never forgot he was teaching boys, not subjects. His thirteen- and fourteen-year-olds learned that they had come, not just to a school but to a place – a place with a long history. They read about the ancient Britons, walked their green roads, explored their earth works on the downs, and wrote imaginative stories about the people who built them. They learnt about the Roman road that ran past the school gates and the development of farming, and saw how the water meadows worked. They sharpened up their arithmetic by using ordnance survey maps – finding hill tops by their map references and working out whether you could see one from another, despite the ridge lying between them. With a sudden flash of private warmth at the end of the year, Pepin told David "Your father would be proud of you!" It had never occurred to the boy that Pepin had taught his father too.

Next year – promoted two forms higher – David was working under Mr. Dee, who drove boys through the School Certificate examinations which he treated like a military assault course. Arid, but effective. After that grind of rote learning, he found himself in the sunlit uplands of a form led by Mr. Jennings, who was also his housemaster. Jennings would surprise his boys with some new challenge each week. "He has given us each a mythical £100 to invest and reinvest as we choose" – which obliged them to learn about stock exchanges, study share prices in the Times each day and keep an exact record of their imaginary transactions. "He is offering two shillings and sixpence to whoever makes the most money by the end of the month." The moral drawn by most of them from this game was not to gamble on the stock exchange. A week or two later Jennings brought in an old copy of the Times and read from the small ads which used to appear on the front page of that newspaper. "Take notes, and work out the date of this paper". This involved discovering when public authorities changed their addresses, and when new London post codes and telephone numbers were introduced. The paper was, I think, from 1912.

After two more terms David was moved up again, to the History Sixth which was led by a tall, frail man with a high voice – acquired when he barely survived a gas attack in the previous war. Mr. Wylie was a real scholar who taught his young men to use the library, enticing them to move on from wars and heroes to constitutional history – the study of power and its workings. He dismissed the Higher School Certificate (what we would now call A-Levels) with contempt: all but a few of his less able pupils worked for scholarships – at Oxford and Cambridge of course. And how they worked! Till two in the morning and later.

But, to return to the start of his time in the school, it is clear that in the first years David had lots of mates but no close friends. Burma was still the centre of his world, and even among his teachers few people knew exactly where it was. "The other side of India" he would explain. He was proud of being half Jewish: his mother had given him that, explaining that Jewish mothers were the best in the world – how else could the Jews have survived centuries of persecution? (A sense of humour was not her strongest suit.) The school allowed scant time or space for its younger boys to make real friends. They were kept constantly active from seven in the morning till 10.30 at night, with work, games, cadet corps and chapel, interspersed with domestic chores taken over from a dwindling staff. All had to be out of doors every afternoon. If not listed for organised games, they would work in nearby forests for sixpence an hour, or go for long runs. "Sweats" they were called. Although he enjoyed academic work, he treated it as a competitive game – determined to climb the form orders. He abandoned the school's Christianity for a passionate pantheism of the wilderness – enraptured by the breath-taking green of beech trees in spring, sunbursts breaking through the rain, the rolling ridges of the downs that were like some vast sea in motion. His creed, he said, was "to do as much as possible as well as possible". But on a later page he writes "How I long to sleep!"

The boys had to devote a good deal of their time to military training in the Officers' Training Corps — since renamed the Cadet Corps — which meant rifle drill, square bashing, and learning all sorts of military lore. He records with irony a field day, with small boys wearing hot, prickly uniforms and carrying rifles much too big for them under a blazing sun, ending with "the band playing, flags flying and a lot of military spirit". They were reviewed by a Brigadier who insisted "on saying a few words" to them — "using an exact copy of Churchill's style. 'Marlborough is a school with fine traditions. You fellahs will be the leadahs of the nation when we have won this war.' Then a lot of waffle about the old school tie. He finished up by saying that he had asked the Master [the Head] for an extra half-day holiday. Everyone suddenly woke up and cheered."

David was not forgotten by his family. Besides the letters from Burma came occasional messages from Una Snow. "Grandy Dibleys" — his father's mother — sent presents when she could. "Two small cakes and lots and lots of chocolates! Where she got them from I can't think. I haven't seen anything of the sort for more than a year." But his diaries and letters show a boy with less and less understanding of his parents' increasingly stressful lives — partly because they spared their families back in England the more frightening things in their story.

During the summer holidays of 1941 David went with other boys from various schools to his first farming camp. Coming next morning to the farm he had been assigned to, he was led by the farmer down a lane and through a gate opening on to a field of potatoes. Their green leaves stretched unbroken to the skyline. The farmer — a man of few words — gave him a fork, pointed to a pile of sacks, and said "Dig 'em up, and put 'em in t'bags." There was no-one else in sight. So he began, and in time found he was learning the hypnotic pleasure of rhythmic manual work.

Someone in the school must have been aware that Britain was

changing because, next term, there was a big debate on the motion "This house would welcome a Socialist England after the war". It was resoundingly lost. "I voted for the motion" David recorded. Hopeless though the struggle might be, he knew which side he was on. He was becoming convinced that in power struggles the 'good guys' always lost: the Chinese devastated by the Japanese, Spanish Republicans by the Fascists, the Abyssinians by the Italians, the French by the Germans, and, worst of all, the fate of the Jews. Meanwhile, at home, the Labour Party, which spoke for the underdogs, lost elections. But it still seemed natural to him that Indians and the colonial peoples of the empire should be ruled by Britain – a view reinforced by the feeling that it was now Britain's job to defend them against Fascist invaders.

COLLAPSE IN BURMA

As communications in Burma disintegrated and the courts ceased to function, Vernon's work as Judicial Secretary dried up. He was sent to Thaton, where he had previously been Deputy Commissioner, to help Ian Wallace, the new D.C., stiffen morale and organise evacuation from a District that lay in the path of the Japanese advance. Locally recruited staff – policemen, clerks, village headmen...stayed put, but those whose homes were elsewhere were to be got out.

"Our task", he wrote, "was to keep the administration going as long as it could be of service to the Army. For some, the war was still an amateur affair. I recall members of the Rangoon Auxilliary Force (part-time, volunteer soldiers) coming through in an elderly armoured Rolls Royce and heading on towards the enemy. A few hours later they returned with one of the party dead and the others looking very shaken. There was a tremendous amount of bombing, mostly with incendiaries that started fires all round the town. A later raid set the town centre on fire and we realised there were prisoners in the police cells there. We managed to get through and let them out. There was a wounded

Burman nearby and we carried him away from the flames on a piece of wooden fencing, but he died of his wounds."

Eventually, as the area they controlled shrank, Ian and Vernon agreed that Vernon should return to Rangoon: there was not enough work left for both of them. The railway was still working, after a fashion, and he managed to get his car on to a train of empty flat wagons that had brought army trucks to the town, and returned to Rangoon across the bridge over the Sittang River. Sitting up in his car, he was the only passenger on the train.

The Japanese were heading for that bridge – and getting more intelligence and support on the way from Burmese people than the British could get. The army of Indian, Burmese, British and Ghurka troops opposing them was not well led. General Wavell, their supreme commander, was based in Java. Always under-estimating the Japanese, he flew to Rangoon from time to time and berated his officers for not showing enough fight. General Hutton, who was responsible for Burma's defence, knew little about the country; and Major General Smyth, the local field commander facing the Japanese, had only recently arrived in Burma for the first time, and was soon a very sick man. More fundamentally, the Army had been given no clear war aims – only a general expectation that they would hold on to territory – and no convincing reasons for laying down their lives to defend one empire from another. The Japanese were well prepared, battle hardened, constantly aggressive, and knew exactly what they had to do – kill and drive out the British. Slim reflects revealingly on the differences between these armies.[5]

The Sittang River, one-and-a-half miles wide in its lower reaches, was the most defensible natural barrier on the road and rail routes to Rangoon. The Japanese were preparing to launch their assault on the bridge when, at dawn on 25 February, the British blew it – not completely effectively as it turned out – leaving most of their troops and weapons on the far shore. It was the first great disaster of the campaign.

Meanwhile, an Australian division, promised for the defence

of Burma, was ordered home by Curtin, their Prime Minister, to defend Australia itself. Another, on its way to Burma, was diverted to Singapore where it arrived two days before the surrender of that great imperial fortress and went straight into the Japanese prison camps.

Vernon rejoined Ruth in Rangoon. She had transferred to the cipher office at Army Headquarters in Rangoon University. What she experienced there must have seemed like a microcosm of the whole rather unmilitary force. "Procedures were slapdash, compared to Government House. Although unauthorised persons were kept out of the University grounds, vendors of tea, cheroots, betel-nut and sweets clustered along the railings. When there were air raids office workers took cover, but no-one bothered to put away the secret papers on which they had been working and these would be scattered by the breeze to blow about the compound. It must have been the simplest thing to pass them through the railings."

ENTER THE CHINESE

After reporting back, Vernon was given another job. Chiang Kai-shek had offered Wavell the help of Kuo Min Tang troops from Yunnan. Wavell had at first refused, fearing the political difficulties they might create within Burma. But the War Cabinet in London feared the international difficulties that might be created by a refusal. "So Army Headquarters began forming a Chinese Liaison Section to work with the expected Chinese forces. The military side of this, headed by Brigadier J.C.Martin who was in overall command, was to deal with operations. The civil side, headed by me, was to provide local knowledge, to smooth relations with Burmese people, and, above all, to supply rice to the incoming Chinese. I recruited a team of sixteen officers wherever I could find them – mostly among forestry workers. I attached them to Chinese formations and spent most of my time going the rounds to instruct, answer questions, and redeploy my men from time to time."

The Chinese entered Burma from the North East and came southwards to defend the road and rail routes coming up the Sittang Valley to Mandalay. The British-Indian forces they relieved could then concentrate on defending the Irrawaddy valley, running parallel to the Sittang on the west. "I was told" wrote Vernon, "that Taunggyi would be the best base for my headquarters, which suited me well. It was on the route that the Chinese would take, and we had a cottage there. But I did not want to leave Ruth in Rangoon which was being bombed and might soon be cut off and captured. I quickly found she would be welcome to do the same kind of cipher work in Taunggyi, so we prepared to move together.

"Official pronouncements at this time asserted that Upper Burma would be held even if Rangoon and Lower Burma were lost. So we loaded about two-fifths of our possessions into a railway waggon – some trains were still running – and, with Lecky and another friend, set off in three cars. Some of our servants came with us; others went by train."

They threaded their way northwards by back routes to avoid road blocks set up by the Army to prevent refugees clogging their communications. Even on these roads they were stopped several times and "it took a good deal of argument and brandishing of my orders to proceed to Taunggyi to get our small convoy through. North of Pegu we pulled off the road in the dark for a rest. Some of the party slept but I could not. Huge, six-wheeled American trucks with Chinese drivers thundered by all night, making a last, desperate effort before Rangoon was lost to get munitions up the Burma Road to Chungking. Soon after dawn we approached Pyinmana where we were looking forward to a good breakfast of bacon and eggs in the railway station's refreshment room. As we approached, a vast column of black smoke was rising from the centre of the town with fires burning everywhere. There was no railway station any more. We brewed some tea by the road side, had something to eat, and pressed on to Meiktila and Thazi where we turned into the hills and got away from the trucks. It was about here that Tha Det, one of our servants who had come with me to Thaton, called out 'Look, our cat is dead!'. They had refused to leave the cat behind because it was Annis's. Now it appeared to be a corpse. But Ruth gently opened its mouth, put water on its tongue and it revived."

Two weeks after the Sittang Bridge disaster the Japanese were at the gates of Rangoon, expecting a great battle at last. But the British had already pulled out. General Alexander, sent by Churchill to replace Hutton, ordered the withdrawal, and was nearly captured, along with his staff, as they fled northwards from the city. With the East Indies fleet driven off the seas, and with coastal airfields and the port of Rangoon in their hands, the Japanese began to bring a much larger army into the country — some 300,000 men eventually.

Vernon and Ruth moved into their cottage in Taunggyi and she started work in the local military headquarters. He spent nearly all his time touring the areas where there were Chinese forces, recruiting and instructing liaison officers and placing them in Chinese units. Their job was "to secure rice, billets and transport for them, to protect the Burmese so far as possible, and do their best to prevent friction." One of his first trips was to Toungoo to which the Burma Division was withdrawing, in hopes of handing over to the Chinese Army and moving across to join the Seventeenth Indian Division who were holding the Irrawaddy valley. On the road he met Major-General Bruce-Scott, commander of Burma Division, looking tense and tired, with a wounded staff officer in one of his party's cars. Vernon managed to find two Sino-Burmese Forest Officers to prepare the way for the approaching Chinese. They came down the railway and took over the defence of Toungoo where they fought a gallant and bloody battle for several days. But they were eventually overwhelmed and withdrew, "very bitter about the lack of air support from the British, which they said had been promised them. When it soon became clear that the Seventeenth Indian Division were not going to be able to hold the Japanese on their side of Burma, the heart very understandably went out of them. They fought on, but never with the same determination as at Toungoo." Slim described the loss of Toungoo as the second great disaster, after that of the Sittang Bridge. It sealed the fate of Burma.

"Communication with the Chinese was difficult. Few of us spoke their language and none of them spoke ours. All armies loot – except possibly the Germans. But for the Chinese the officially recognised method of supply was to live on the country. My organisation (if such an impressive word can rightly describe our improvisations) did its best to provide rice and some vegetables, but inevitably there was widespread looting. Villagers were terrified and villages deserted. The American General Stilwell was supposed to be in command of the Chinese forces in Burma but wielded only occasional influence on them. I met him and his staff of American advisers at Pyawbwe, and soon realised why he was called 'Vinegar Joe'. An acid and unlikeable man." (General Slim gave a kinder account of Stillwell, but admits that to understand the true quality of the man you had to talk to him privately.[6]) "It was here too" said Vernon, "that I found that the local Chinese Commander and I had a language in common: German.

"But it didn't matter whether one could converse or not: no reasoning or argument made the slightest impact on them. They moved or stayed according to inscrutable decisions of their own. A train bringing a badly needed Chinese unit down from Mandalay stopped at Kyaukse and nothing any of us said could get it moving again. Eventually we were told that they could go no further without express orders from Chiang Kai-shek in person. We requested Army Headquarters to try to prevail upon the Generalissimo. Then suddenly, without warning or explanation, the train resumed its journey south. But the general movement was northward."

Rangoon had fallen, resistance was crumbling and it was becoming clear that the British were going to lose the country.

"We would have to get Ruth out to India — if that were possible. She was reluctant to go, but we agreed that I might not be able to make it and one of us must get back to the children. We expected she would probably have to walk; but in mid-March word came to Taunggyi that arrangements were being made to get Army and civilian families out. Frances Turnbull — now Frances Wood — who had come out with us four years before to look after Annis, was staying with us in Taunggyi with her first baby, born only ten days earlier. Her husband Geoffrey, an engineer who had built a lot of the Rangoon docks, had last been heard of blowing up all his handiwork there. No-one knew if he had got out, and he did not know he was a father."

At this point in the story I draw on another memoir, written by Phyllis Latimer, English mother's help to Mrs. Ford and her family of five children. Their father, Frank, was an Army officer stationed in Taunggyi. As the Japanese advanced, more people sought refuge in this small town, bringing wild rumours with them. One — a Lieutenant who had until recently been a Rangoon University professor — came to tea with Ruth, Frances Wood and the Fords, and "told us a story of how all the convicts had been let out of the Rangoon jail, and had armed themselves with tommy guns stolen from an army dump, and were laying in wait for every European they could see... Imagine telling such tales to a woman who had no news at all of her husband and who was recovering from childbirth ten days... earlier!" Ruth interrupted him, saying" 'You happen to be talking to... three very level-headed, sensible women and we have a shrewd idea of what is going on... but I advise you not to go round talking to other people in such a way." They reported him next day to Frank Ford for spreading alarmist rumours.

RUTH ESCAPES

Vernon contrived to be in Taunggyi when a party of two or three hundred women, children and invalids were gathered together and sent off to the railhead at Shwenyaung – Ruth, Phyllis and Frances among them. The train they were put on moved slowly through the night to Thazi which was in flames and full of looting mobs. There the driver deserted. After a long wait an army sapper was found to work the engine. Indian Army troops came aboard to guard the passengers, and to patrol the platform, keeping off Indian families, crammed in cattle trucks nearby that were going nowhere. After many anxious delays – the children crying with thirst in their hot and waterless train – they reached Shwebo, there to be placed in a barracks where most of them had to sleep on the floor. "My chief impression', Phyllis Latimer recalled, "will remain with me always. It was the crying of the children. The whole barracks echoed with it. Poor little things, so many of them were far too young to understand what it was all about. ... How they missed their [native] nannies, poor mites, and were not consoled by any mere mothers."

Ruth had made it her job to take care of Frances and her baby – who had lifted their spirits by giving them his first smile during the worst part of the train journey. At Shwebo she got them into one of the Bombay Burmah Company's houses. An elderly Dakota had somehow been secured to make three or four trips a day between Shwebo and Chittagong which lay over the mountains on the eastern fringe of India. Ruth, Frances, Phyllis and the Fords got on to a flight on the second day. Before boarding, they had to stand, holding children and all their baggage in blazing sun. Phyllis recalled that "if the heat outside had been terrific, in the plane it was infernal... It was a Douglas troop carrier. We sat in bucket aluminium seats. There were no seats for the children..." When the plane took off it became mercifully cooler and the pilot, an American, "took all the children into the cockpit, and many of them were allowed to sit on his knee... Many Anglo-Indians, probably through sheer nerves at the thought that they were flying, began to be sick. The only utensil was a communal kerosene tin. ... Ruth Donnison...went round, giving them glucose, handing them the tin and comforting them. One old woman she made lie down on the floor while she ministered to her...."

They were placed in a refugee camp when they arrived in Chittagong. There they were found by T.L. Hughes, who had brought David out to Burma in 1939, and had been the other Financial Secretary working alongside Vernon in the Secretariat. He brought them news that Geoffrey Wood was in Calcutta. They had both escaped from Rangoon by sea in the final evacuation, and Hughes was now heading back to Burma to report for duty. Ruth gave him a letter for Vernon to say they had arrived safely and he got it to him within a few hours. She and Frances travelled onwards for two days – by train, then boat, then train again – to Calcutta where they were placed in the Loretto Convent and given some food, and mattresses on the floor. They could wash too, if they did not mind doing it in public.

Many families had to stay for weeks in barracks and convents, caring for children and babies in nappies, using fly-infested, communal washrooms, often with no waterborne sanitation, and encountering for the first time the mixed feelings the British have for refugees – even those of their own kind. Phyllis recalled W.V.S. ladies who were "most unsympathetic. On a Sunday morning they brought their husbands round to visit us. It was like the Lady Bountiful visiting tenants. It never seemed to occur to them to offer to look after the children for a morning or to invite us into their homes." Gradually, as news filtered through that husbands were walking out, and then beginning to arrive in India, the morale of these families began to recover.

Geoffrey came to collect Frances, and after a night or two in the convent Ruth went to stay with an English couple. She was soon on her way to Darjeeling to see Annis, but, said Vernon, "she could not bear to sit there doing nothing. So she came back to Calcutta and found work in a Government of Burma office set up to identify government servants who were coming out of the country – mainly Anglo-Burmans, many of whom she knew. She would provide papers for them, make sure they got some pay and put them in touch with others they knew. She also visited the

Loretto and other convents each day to meet incoming refugees, pick up news and offer what help she could. She was happy to do this – despite Calcutta's exhausting heat – because she felt she was doing something for Burma and its people." She was also in the best place to pick up news of Vernon and their friends. In a letter to her mother she said it was a marvellous relief to have no possessions, and no responsibilities except the work to be done each day – "like being a student again".

The stories she picked up must have been frightening. She made friends with a doctor in the Indian Medical Service who returned occasionally from the frontier areas where he was responsible for meeting and helping the starving Indians who were walking out. He had to learn fast and make dire calculations. When he started to lose more of the coolies carrying food along tracks leading into the jungle than the lives he was saving by feeding the incoming refugees he had to shorten their journeys by pulling back his improvised reception centres. He found that starving people standing in a crowd of strangers would die rather than eat food that did not accord with the rules of their religion. So he would make soup with whatever ingredients he had, place it in two big cauldrons – one labelled "Hindus" and the other "Muslims" – and everyone ate without asking questions. His centres were so short of food that staff had to learn to spot those who were going to die anyway and refuse to feed them. He found that people long deprived of food cannot digest it. They throw up and may die. But powerful emotion starts their digestive juices working; so the latest arrivals at his reception centres were made to stand and wait while those who had arrived before them were fed. When the newcomers were shouting with rage they could be fed with much better chances of survival.

FREEDOM FIGHTERS AND TERRORISTS

When Colonel Suzuki first picked Aung San and his comrades as the most promising group of rebels to back, he knew exactly what he was doing. In December 1941, as the invasion began, he wrote a paper stating his aims, the first of which was "to stir up disturbances throughout Burma in order to hamper the enemy's operations and to induce the Burmese to co-operate whole-heartedly with Japan." Eventually, when the country had been conquered, "the new regime shall have on the surface the appearance of independence, but in reality it shall be induced to carry out Japanese policies." In another paper, written three months later, officials of the Army's Military Administration Department were told that "The Burmese… have turned into inactive peoples with almost no vigorous aspirations. This is mainly due to the fact that they have suffered long years of tyranny and exploitation…" "It is much desired therefore that we show them a sincere parental affection in guiding and educating them."[7] Imperial policies and their supporting myths seem to be much the same everywhere. I guess there are similar papers about the Iraquis in the Pentagon today.

The Burma Independence Army (the B.I.A.) formed in Siam, recruited Burmese young men already in that country. Others came across the border to join them, and to carry arms and supplies through the jungle to their comrades who were crossing into Burma. "Dobama! Dobama!" was their constant cry – "We Burmans! We Burmans!"[8] Following the Japanese troops into Burma, they were at first treated with hostility by people in the hill country, most of whom were Christian Karens. But once into the Burman lowlands they gained recruits – and still more when Burmese units fighting for the British began to desert and surrender. They set up a Burmese administration in Tavoy to replace the British. The regular Japanese forces were suspicious of them, and there was a nasty incident at Moulmein, so the B.I.A. outflanked the regulars and got into Rangoon ahead of them. Colonel Suzuki and his Burmese officers demanded that they be given Government House as their headquarters – a potent symbol of power for the Burmese. But the Japanese Army refused. Suzuki was coming passionately to believe in his young men and in

Burmese independence which, he said, should be "recognised", not "given".[9]

But there were quarrels among the B.I.A's leaders, and in Karen areas they went on the rampage, killing and looting indiscriminately. The village Headmen left behind by the British were often given a rough time, and one of them was crucified and publicly executed by Aung San himself. His widow, whom we shall hear from again, survived. Nevertheless, this amateur army fought one serious engagement, in company with Japanese troops, at Shwedaung, where they lost half their men – killed, wounded or deserted. That gave them a sense of achievement, although their part in the battle was never mentioned in Japanese official histories.[10]

Disturbed by the threat it posed – both to them and to public order – the Japanese disbanded the B.I.A., which, at its peak, numbered about 23,000 men, and formed a smaller "Burma Defence Army" of 3,000, still under the command of Aung San but tightly controlled by Japanese "advisors". Suzuki's organisation was disbanded and the Colonel sent home in July 1942 to Tokyo where he was given a ceremonial job of no significance – but he did gain audience with Prime Minister Tojo and tried, unsuccessfully, to get him to recognise the independence of Burma and the Phillipines. Before leaving Burma, he held a meeting with Aung San and his staff, told them they would have to fight his countrymen for their freedom and suggested they should start by killing him.[11] Aung San refused. Although he knew he would eventually have to fight the Japanese, it was much too early to strike. He waited another three years. After Suzuki's departure, he seems to have had a breakdown in health and went to hospital for a while. He met a nurse there who became his wife – and mother of Aung San Suu Kyi.[12]

By the end of May 1942, British Indian forces had been driven out of Burma. The Japanese found Dr. Ba Maw, Burma's first prime minister who had come to office after the 1936 election – the only one ever held. He had been imprisoned for sedition by the British in the Mogok jail. In August they made him premier of a puppet government − choosing him partly because they could rely on him to control Aung San and his soldiers.

Resistance to the Japanese began − and was always strongest − in the hills. In Karen, Chin, and Kachin areas men were left with a rifle, fifty rounds, three months pay and a promise that the British would return. By the end of the war these guerillas had killed some 12,500 Japanese soldiers.[15]

THE END OF EMPIRE

As Vernon returned to his liaison work, after seeing Ruth off, it became clear that the situation was crumbling fast, both in the Irrawaddy and in the Sittang valleys. Once the Japanese had captured Toungoo there was an easy and virtually undefended road leading 100 miles northwards, straight to Taunggyi. It was at about this time that General Slim, fighting his way out, recorded in his diary that "if somebody brings me a bit of good news, I shall burst into tears", adding drily in the book he later wrote: "I was never put to the test".[14]

Vernon planned to head for Mandalay and Maymyo further north, along with officials of the civil administration who were moving out. As he was about to set off, their head man asked him to go back down the road to Kalaw and persuade the principal British official there to report to the Commissioner in Maymyo. "He was drinking very heavily and quite unable to cope with his work. I asked what authority I had in this matter and we agreed that all I could do was to try to persuade him. It was like coaxing an animal into a cage. Several times I got him as far as my car, but each time he shied away and went back into his house for another drink. At last, by bringing the one unfinished bottle of gin with me, I got him into the car and we set off down the long hill towards the plains. On the way the empty bottle was tossed out into the jungle. He was an Irishman, and fastidious with words even when drunk. He would try to say something; reflect for a moment, and then say 'No, that wasn't the right word', feel about and find a better one. Approaching Kyaukse we passed through irrigated fields with clear water in grassy ditches. He stopped me so that he could get out and pour water over his head and sober up a bit. Finally I got him to Maymyo. When I next saw him, months later, he was reunited with his wife in Delhi. She was a splendid Irishwoman of great character – an ex-nurse who kept him more or less sober. He seemed to bear me no ill-will."

Vernon abandoned the remainder of his family's possessions in Taunggyi and gave what money he could spare to the few servants remaining with him. Years later, he and Ruth learnt what happened to Nikunja, their cook, and his wife. She tells the tale: "Without work and harassed by the Japanese, they decided to return to her home in Mergui at the southern tip of Burma. They set out to walk there, with four young children and such possessions as they could carry. It must have been about eight hundred miles through a devastated land. Only Ma Hkin Su, his wife, and the two boys survived. Nikunja, who had always been lame, died on the way with the little girls." In 1960 Vernon and Ruth were able to visit Mergui. "Ma Hkin Su came out to meet us. In eighteen years she had changed very little; still the sweet, gentle smile, the dainty figure, the smooth skin untouched, it seemed, by time or suffering. Her two boys were doing well and she lived in a fine house with a cheerful elder sister, making cotton jackets to sell in the bazaar. She had always been a wonderful needlewoman and sales were evidently booming."

Vernon continues his own story. Later, in India, he was to write a report covering every day of this experience, and the following pages are derived from that document.

The Japanese were held for a few days at Kyaukse by Seventh Armoured Brigade who still had some tanks; but not for long. Mandalay, the old Burmese capital some twenty miles to the north, was already in flames, and those who wanted to get away knew they would have to cross the Ava Bridge over the Irrawaddy before it was destroyed.

"On 26 April, I went into Mandalay to meet some of my liaison officers. They reported that the Chinese were now completely out of hand and there was little we could do for them. The Japanese bombed the town again and there were terrible casualties among refugees waiting on the river foreshore. The launches that could take them across were damaged or destroyed and the men who could work them were killed or wounded. I went back to Kyaukse and got the same story about the Chinese from other members of my team. There was talk of re-establishing a line north of the Irrawaddy, but my appreciation of the situation was that this could not be done – the retreat had become a rout. In that case, there was nothing more we could do, and the sooner we got out the better, both for ourselves and for others who would be trying to escape along the same routes later." He felt he should report to Brigadier Martin, who was responsible for liaison with the Chinese, before closing the civil branch of it down, but Martin was up in Lashio and might never get back to them. "I was afraid and made up my mind that we should all head for India, so I took my team across the Ava Bridge and we slept at Sagaing. Or the others slept. I lay awake the whole night, full of doubts and shame at having been frightened into my decision."

Next day they went to Monywa where they put their names down to get on a launch going up river. They were told they might get off in two days time. Vernon consulted such colleagues as he could find. All of them told him he should go. Completely exhausted, he broke into tears with one of them who urged him, yet again, to leave and consoled him by offering him a cigarette. (Vernon never smoked.) "Finally, I went to see Ian Wallace, and although he too urged me to go, it was then I found the strength to do what I knew I ought to do. He had had a worse time than me, he had a dearly loved wife in India, and reasons as good as mine for leaving. But he had stayed. How could I face him in future if I left now? I went back to my Liaison Officers, told them they must go, but that I was going to stay – feeling rather foolish for changing my mind. A few moments later, word came that there was a

launch due to leave that would take them. I dined that evening
with two of the men I had consulted. They got rather drunk, but I
felt at peace at last.

"Early next morning, 29 April, I left for Shwebo further north,
looking for Army Headquarters there, and failing to find anyone
to come with me. Travelling alone was becoming risky. An Army
chaplain had been attacked by dacoits and left for dead (but survived). The town was on fire as I approached but I found Brigadier
Martin. 'That's the end of Civil Liaison' were his first words. I told
him I had already sent my team away and added, by way of con-
fession, that I had nearly gone with them. Martin explained that
the decision had been taken to get the British-Indian Army out,
via Tamu on the Indian frontier. The Chinese were breaking up.
Some were heading up the railway line northwards to Myitkyina,
about 300 miles away. Some were trying to get back to China
across the Shan hills to the east. We had no idea what would happen to three more divisions left in the plains. We calculated that
20,000 Chinese would try to get out along the railway line. And
there was no food for them. They would simply starve in the
forests, we feared. Martin asked me to go to Myitkyina as his representative, find three or four tough characters who knew the
country well and who could help to guide the Chinese out, and do
what I could to organise supplies of rice along the route. Here, at
least, was a job to do; so I went to the station to find if there was a
train going north. There might be one during the night, I was
told." Vernon slept uneasily, listening for the train, but it did not
leave till the following afternoon. For the next four days he took a
nightmare journey as the last remnants of imperial authority
unravelled around him. All over northern Burma others were
having similar experiences.

Officials, soldiers, clerks and a servant or two competed with
crowds of refugee families for a foothold on the train, travelling in
trucks – some carrying dismantled machinery, now of no use to
anyone. "One had to practice the most despicable stealth to get on
before there was a rush." Later, railway officials found seats for

Vernon and some of his colleagues in a coach, turfing out refugee families to make room for them – "a very unpleasant business". Their train started and stopped repeatedly. Early in the small hours of next morning he found the engine driver who said he was running out of water. If he uncoupled from the train he could just get his engine to the next station to pick some up. So Vernon went on the footplate with him to make sure he came back. All through the next day they proceeded a few miles at a time. There was desperate congestion on the line as more and more rolling stock was pushed northwards. Trucks and coaches were being run into sidings, and right off the line down embankments and into the river. Offered space on a troop train ahead of them, Vernon and a few colleagues were transferring their gear onto it when it suddenly started, leaving them behind. That gave them an opportunity for walking half a mile across fields to a stream where they had their first wash for three days. Sauntering back towards the station, they saw their train pulling out and had to run hard to catch it. Some Chinese troops had persuaded the driver to move at gun point. They went through a village that was on fire, and there were shots in the night that passed close to them, fired by dacoits – bandits.

On 3 May they reached Indaw, nearly half way from Shwebo to Myitkyina where the line comes to an end. There they got stuck for a day and a night, with little hope of getting further. No-one had any reliable information – only wild rumours . Vernon had to recognise there was no chance of doing what he had been sent to do. The talk was increasingly about the best routes out; and when the rains would break, making travel impossible. Vernon did his best to help people who were trying to organise refugee camps at Indaw. Wives and children of his colleagues were coming through, along with the other refugees.

When railway staff began planning to walk out the Chinese put them all under close arrest – convinced they were deliberately refusing to keep the railway working. At a conference in the middle of the night British officers, military and civil, decided they could not leave their railway colleagues in the hands of the Chinese, nor could they rescue them. The Chinese had more men and more guns. So, as a way of convincing them that the railway was done for, they sent a delegation offering to do whatever the Chinese wanted. "The first requests made by the Chinese were easily met, but soon they were in difficulties, and even they had to recognise that the railway *could* not work. Next morning railway staff were released and allowed to set out for India." That was 5 May.

WALKING OUT

"Indaw would soon be a target for the bombers and we were anxious to get away. At 7 am. I set out in a fine new American car that had been abandoned. With me were two colleagues, Sammy, the Madrassi servant of one of them, an army driver and his mate (both English) and a dog. We cut down kit and provisions to a weight that we could carry ourselves – as we expected to have to do before long."

They were heading westwards towards Tamu on the Indian border, more than 100 miles away as the crow flies; and then 50 miles north-west to Imphal and the railhead. But the tracks they would follow would wind, rise and fall – climbing to six thousand feet – and there might be a day or two on a boat going up the Chindwin River. Vernon took with him a rain-proof army cape, a light, knitted blanket, his revolver and his flute, a bag of rice and some Glucose – together with a bag containing the family silver. If they had to make for China this would be useful currency.

It took them nine days to reach Imphal – days of blinding heat and growing exhaustion, coming close to delirium. The party Vernon was with fluctuated as some went ahead and others fell behind, but he and his friend Donald Petch stuck together and helped each other through the worst stretches. Many other men and women were on the same route. Indian families, unsupported by coolies, were dying one by one as they struggled on, their bodies left to pollute the air and the streams. It has been estimated that between ten and fifty thousand of them died on the various routes out.

Setting out from Indaw, they followed a rough, slow road till it petered out, talking on the way about the best route to take when they started walking. As a small party of pretty fit men they chose the shorter but more mountainous of those on their map. It was less used than most, which might save them from the cholera, malaria and blackwater fever that broke out on more crowded routes. Finding shelter in a rather dirty rest house at the end of the road, they sent the car back for Donald Petch who had been completing work at Indaw. It returned with him later that night. Early next morning they abandoned it and started walking, with some coolies they had managed to collect to help them carry their stuff.

"Oh, the relief of throwing away all cares except the single one of getting oneself alive to India! That was not going to be simple, but doubts and conflicting duties could at last be cast aside." Their only enemies would be the rains and the Japanese – both approaching fast.

That evening they made camp on a sandy river shore, and talked again about their plans. Some of the party felt that the coolies had held them back and wanted to press on without them. They decided they would do better to lighten their loads by throwing out gear that they could do without – which just meant that the coolies collected what they discarded and carried it for themselves instead.

Starting in the dark next morning at about 4.30 am., to get as far as possible before the heat became too oppressive, they climbed 1,000 feet before daylight and walked 25 miles, finding shelter in a charming village where there was a Forest Rest House. It was the hottest time of the year and "everyone felt the heat dreadfully. Donald and I were getting pretty footsore." Vernon was only wearing light, canvas shoes. Now it was clear that they were heading for India, and would need to cut their loads to a minimum if they were to get there, Vernon took his bag of family silver and stuffed it into a hole in a tree.

Their journey next day, 8 May, was much the same, but they had a refreshing bathe in a stream on the way, and another where they made camp. The following day, in a party of about a dozen people, including three who were walking wounded, they managed to get a boat whose crew paddled them down a stream towards the River Chindwin. It was a big, dug-out canoe, giving them the choice of lying crowded in its filthy bottom under a matting roof, or out in the sun. "I lay down inside and remember little about the journey except that we were much frightened by two aeroplanes that kept on sweeping up and down the river a few hundred feet above us. It was so long since we had seen friendly aircraft, we feared they must be Japanese. We learnt later that they were American Volunteer Group 'planes looking for Stillwell's men."

They camped on the bank that night, then set off up the Chindwin river at 4.30 am next morning in their dugout. Creeping along the bank, their three boatmen could scarcely keep the boat moving, so Vernon helped with a punt pole and others took it in turns to relieve the men at the oars. They overtook other boats, going even more slowly, and met a steam launch coming down river with men aboard who told them "they had no information about the Japs, but thought our route would be all right for a few more days. They had a wireless transmitter on board and took all our names to send word to Calcutta that we were well on the way." Ruth got the message an hour or two later.

Next day they had to leave the boat and start walking again, westwards. "We had to climb some 1,500 feet through thin forest, stopping exhausted every few hundred yards to rest for ten or fifteen minutes in whatever shade we could find." Finally reaching a small village, they were told that coolies had returned from Tamu on the Indian frontier and reported seeing the Japanese flag flying there. Since that was at least two or three days walk, the Japs might be anywhere by now. Spurred on by this news, they walked five miles further — fortifying themselves with horlicks and glucose on the way — to sleep on the pebbly shore of a stream, along with between a hundred and two hundred other people heading in the same direction.

"In the small hours it rained on us. I was too cold to sleep and got up at about 4 am. I climbed into soaking clothes and shivered. We made very heavy weather of lighting a fire, but eventually got ourselves a little hot tea and some biscuits. We stumbled off along a slippery path in the rain and darkness, with one or two hurricane lamps between us: a foretaste of what would happen to us if the rains broke, as they might do at any time.

Before dawn they had crossed from Burma into India, although there was nothing to show for it. Soon they began climbing along jungle footpaths into the big hills ahead of them, eventually reaching a mule track that ran along a ridge at 3,000 feet. A triumphant moment: "tired though we were, there would be no more sweating through the steamy plains. We were on top of the world with magnificent views on either hand." They reached a village of the Naga head hunting people where their Burmese coolies refused to go further. So they recruited Nagas instead, who were a terrible nuisance in many ways — disappearing suddenly when they scented villages where there might be alcohol or drugs — but moving faster than the Burmese and capable of carrying at least twice the loads. In the afternoon they came down from the ridge and camped by a stream in the valley, along with many other people.

Next day, 13 May, they climbed 4,000 feet up and walked along exactly the kind of track the Japanese would have used to outflank the defenders of Imphal. They were relieved to find no sign of them.

The day after, starting an hour before dawn, they went up to 6,000 feet where there was a wonderful sunrise but it was too cold to stop for long to look at it. "Donald and I had very sore feet. He did not know if he could keep going, and I began to feel so sleepy I could not walk straight." Vernon fell asleep on the ground every time they paused. As they came off the ridge later in the morning, each had to go at his own pace and the party got split up. Fearing they had lost Donald, Vernon turned wearily back up the hill and found him — "hobbling. He told me he was finished and burst into tears. I seized him by the shoulder and said we would find a way of getting him along, but it was hard to restrain my own tears. I told him how I had broken down in the same way at Monywa, only a few days earlier." They reached a party of Indians who were very kind and helpful. One of them was a doctor who dressed Donald's feet. They started making a chair to carry him in, but Donald eventually got on his feet again. Eight miles further on, down narrow and increasingly hot valleys, they caught up with the rest of their party. At last there was a rough road before them, and their comrades had secured three bullock carts — at an exorbitant price. After a little food, they climbed into the carts and set off for Imphal, dropping into an exhausted sleep despite the rough and rolling movement.

Waking at about 2am, they found they had halted in a village square. "On the far side of it was a man dancing and staggering about, waving a hurricane lamp and rolling stones and bricks across the ground at us. Behind him were some crazy-looking houses dimly visible in the flickering light of his lamp. He was clearly mad. Pulling myself together sufficiently to get out and ask why we had stopped, I found we were about a mile from Imphal and our drivers had halted because they feared they would be shot by sentries if we tried to enter the town by night."

The party eventually got into the town, which had been bombed recently, and had to assert themselves aggressively against others — anxious soldiers, competing refugees, a drunken man... — till they found the local Political Officer (the Government Representative) who kindly fed them tea, Ryvita and fruit, prepared with his own hands. His servants had fled. With a crowd of other refugees they managed to get into a truck which drove them eighteen miles to the railhead at Manipur Road. After some tea in a refugee canteen, they were put on a train — women and children in closed wagons, the men in open ones – where they had to sleep overnight because they did not start till next day. The makeshift train then proceeded with many starts and stops, the sun beating down into the open trucks. Indians gave them some food when they stopped and Indian troops on a passing train threw them cigarettes. Vernon managed to send Ruth a telegram from one of the stations. By the end of the day they reached a ferry crossing at Gauhati where the wounded – of whom there were many on the train – were taken across a river. They were promised that the ferry would return for them, but it did not. So they had to spend another night in the open. There was a lot of anger about. The aggressive determination the refugees had learnt to mobilise to get them through the jungles and over the mountains was on occasions like this turned on anyone who seemed obstructive or incompetent.

On the ferry next morning, to make amends, the crew provided a splendid breakfast of bread and butter, bacon and eggs. Vernon's party ate theirs and then ate the same breakfast over again. They were ravenous. The station master on the far shore attached two coaches to his train – one for the Europeans and their servants, the other for "respectable" Indians and Anglo-Indians. The "coolie class Indians" went in wagons and trucks if they were lucky, but many of them had to wait a day for the next train. The precarious comradeship of the jungle trails did not long survive in India.

This local train reached Parbatipur at 3am. on 18 May. Here Vernon's party had to get a mainline train to Calcutta. He sent another telegram, giving their numbers and location, and there were more altercations before they managed to get aboard the Assam Mail, later in the morning. It had a restaurant car, where again they fell upon the food, and after a long day it brought them into Calcutta at 4.30 pm. And there was Ruth.

IN CONCLUSION

"Where was my kit? Ruth asked. I explained that the small bundle I was carrying, wrapped in an army gas-proof cape, was all I had in the world. She took me in a taxi to a friend's flat and there was afternoon tea with a succulent, chocolate iced cake. I fell on this with a craving — we had been so short of sugar — and was violently sick a little later. My feet were dreadfully sore, and that night I was delirious. But I began to pick up strength in the coming days. Ruth felt she could not leave her colleagues in the office without warning, so we remained in Calcutta for a fortnight of exhausting heat while I rested and bought some clothes.

On 31 May, 1942, David, aged sixteen, received a letter from his father, posted from Taunggyi many weeks before, and another from his mother in Calcutta. But a few days earlier Una Snow — always the family's lynch pin for communications — had sent word that she had received a cable to say that Vernon had arrived safely in India. David wrote that "It was the best bit of news I had had for ages." Reginald Jennings, his housemaster, was more graphic. Having called David to his study to give him Una's news, he wrote to his mother, telling her "the whole boy wagged". Later, Vernon sent him a long letter describing his walk out of Burma.

Meanwhile, in India, Ruth and Vernon "took a train to Darjeeling where we rented rooms in a private house close to Annis's school. It was a joy to see her. But Oh, the black stockings, the long, dark blue skirt, and all the rules...!"

The high country and the cool air began Vernon's recovery. His strength came back and in a few weeks time he was able to walk twenty miles in a day through those wonderful mountains. Ruth too needed an opportunity to recover. She had plunged straight into work at the height of the hot weather when she reached India and was suffering the exhausting effects of jaundice, still continuing when she got to England two years later.

The remnants of the Army continued to struggle out of Burma. Slim was proud of his men. "On the last day of that nine-hundred-mile retreat I stood on a bank beside the road and watched the rearguard march into India. All of them, British, Indian and Gurkha, were gaunt and ragged as scarecrows. Yet, as they trudged behind their surviving officers in groups pitifully small, they still carried their arms and kept their ranks, they were still recognisable as fighting units. They might look like scarecrows, but they looked like soldiers too."[15] It was among the non-combatant units that discipline too often broke down and bad things happened.

Slim was brutally honest in asserting that it was the men's leaders who had been responsible for the disaster. They had been given, and they conveyed to their troops, no clear aim or purpose; and they failed to formulate any effective response to the enemy's tactics of repeated, aggressive, penetration and encirclement.[16]

The survivors of this war often remember the Japanese as callous and cruel − which they certainly were. What is often forgotten is that the demands they made on all conquered people were equally brutal − far more Asian labourers than British prisoners died in the course of building the Burma-Siam railway. The demands they made on their own men were extreme too, and accepted without question. Japanese soldiers were given no instructions about what to do if captured, and not a single regular army officer was captured in the four years of the Burma war. Of the few men who surrendered, most were too sick or too severely wounded to resist.

Sakurai's Division, who drove the British back over the Chindwin with much slaughter and booty, had "marched for 127 days, taken part in 34 battles, and covered over 1,500 miles, some of it − on foot − at the rate of thirty miles a day."[17] Meanwhile, a Japanese Colonel Uno had been writing a Haiku:[18]

> Our food is exhausted,
> Already for seven days
> We have been gnawing at
> The banana tree's core;
> Into battle.

These men had in six months destroyed the claim of western empires to fulfil the basic responsibility of every ruler – to protect the people from enemies. "Vinegar Joe" Stilwell summed up his feelings at the end: "We got a hell of a beating. It was as humiliating as hell. We ought to find out why it happened and go back."

Vernon was already aware that, whatever happened in the coming years, things could never be the same in Burma again. The spell had been broken. Who would eventually take over the Guardians' responsibilities? And with what chances of success?

A British Colonel, Graham Cherry, was writing a poem of a different kind.

DEFEAT

Oh the flower, the flower
Of the land is dust

In a bankrupt hour
Of a spendthrift season
Purpose, dying, cries:
I am a broken thing
If this was privilege
If this was power
I have done with both

Call off the battle
Haul down the banners

Music is fallen
The skies run blood
Exploit crumbles
Honour's a mock
Silence the drummers
Silence the trumpeters
Send them away away

. . . .

The laurels are burning
Round the sepulchres
The birds cannot fly

Where are the heralds
Where are the champions
Gone with the goblins
Drunk in the temples

Call up the torturers
O strip Beauty bare
Tear the flesh from Truth

...Leave me alone, alone
. . . .

For the flower, the flower
Of the land is dust.[19]

NOTES

1   G.E.Harvey, *British Rule in Burma 1924-1942*, London, Faber and Faber, 1946; pages 31 and 42.

2   Frank N. Trager, (ed.) *Burma: Japanese Military Administration, Selected Documents, 1941-1945*, Philadelphia, University of Pennsylvania Press, 1971; Chapter 1 and Izumiya Tatsuro, *The Minami Organ*, Tokyo, Tokuma Shoten, 1967. (English translation by U Tun Aung Chain, Rangoon University.) Page 21.

3   Martin Smith, *Burma: Insurgency and the Politics of Ethnicity*, Dhaka, The University Press, and Zed Books of London, 2nd. Ed.,1999; page 59.

4   Much of my account of the war comes from William Slim, *Defeat into Victory*, London, Cassell, 1956, and Louis Allen, *Burma. The Longest War 1941-45*, London, J.M.Dent, 1984.

5   Slim, 1956; page 118.

6   Slim, 1956; page 51.

7   Trager (ed.), 1971. Document 1, December 1941, and Document 9, 23 March. 1942.

8   Tatsuro, 1967.

9   Tatsuro, 1967; pages 171-74.

10   Louis Allen, 1984; page 62.

11   Tatsuro, 1967.

12   Aung San Suu Kyi, 1992.

13 Trager, 1971; page 14.

14 Slim, 1956; page 97

15 Slim, 1956; pages 109-10.

16 Slim, 1956; pages 118 et seq.

17 Allen, 1984; page 79.

18 Allen, 1984; page 111.

19 Graham Cherry, (Lieutenant Colonel, 60th Rifles) in *Poems From India by Members of the Forces*, Oxford University Press. Published in India, 1945; in England, 1946. Page 128.

VIII

A FAMILY SCATTERED

Like millions of other families at this time, the Donnisons were scattered by the war: David in a boarding school in England, Annis in schools in India, and their parents Ruth and Vernon in Delhi – until he set off to return to Burma with the Army. Unlike many others, they all survived and were eventually reunited. This Chapter focuses on the period between mid-1942, when the British were driven out of Burma, and early 1944 when the campaign to recapture the country was launched.

INDIA IN PERIL

When the battered remnants of British, Indian and Chinese forces crossed the Ava Bridge over the Irrawaddy on 30 April 1942, blowing it up behind them, it was clear that Burma was lost. Thereafter it was a matter of getting as many men out as possible – Chinese northwards, British and Indians westwards – before the Japanese and the monsoon finished them off. Soon the monsoon became the more formidable foe. Slim, looking back on this disaster, concluded that "the only test of generalship is success, and I had succeeded in nothing I had attempted... In preparation, in execution, in strategy, and in tactics we had been worsted, and we had paid the penalty..."[1] Meanwhile, behind them, the Japanese were already sinking British ships in the Bay of Bengal, and the Indian National Congress was mounting a "Quit India" campaign which compelled the British to arrest and intern their leaders and deploy growing numbers of troops around the country to control the situation.

Beautiful though it was, Arakan, to which the British had withdrawn, was appalling campaigning country — impassable during the monsoon except by boats patrolling its many swollen rivers. When the 1943 dry season came the British launched an offensive to recapture Akyab where there was the only airfield capable of taking aeroplanes that could reach into central Burma. They had regained command of the air and had a five-to-three superiority in men, but were humiliatingly repulsed, suffering much heavier losses than the Japanese. Disease claimed even more of their men.

One of Slim's officers reported to him that:

"... our troops were either exhausted, browned off or both, and ... did not have their hearts in the campaign. [They were]... scared of the Jap and generally demoralised..." "They fear the jungle, hate the country and see no object in fighting for it, and also have the strong feeling that they are taking part in a forgotten campaign in which no-one in authority is taking any real interest...". "To sum up, ... the seasoned and highly trained Jap troops are confronted by a force which, though impressive on paper, is little better, in a large number of cases, than a rather unwilling band of levies."[2]

If this army was defeated again it might break up altogether. The High Command already believed that Burma could not be recaptured through the jungle and they would have to make seaborne landings in the south. Some of them were turning to the idea of an invasion of Sumatra, by-passing Burma altogether.

Then new men came on the scene who changed all this. First came a distant portent: in August and September 1942, the Australians had defeated the Japanese at Milne Bay, New Guinea, in jungle country much like Burma's — the first allied soldiers to break the spell of Japanese invincibility.[3]

Mountbatten, the new Supreme Commander for South-East Asia, arrived in August 1943. "Youthful, buoyant, picturesque, with a reputation for gallantry known everywhere", he could talk equally convincingly to men of all backgrounds.[4]

In October of that year Slim was given command of the Fourteenth Army, responsible, with Stillwell — still commanding the Chinese on the North-Eastern fringe of Burma — for the whole Burma front. He laid stress above all on morale, which had to be rooted in his soldiers' conviction that their cause was just, necessary and feasible. He trained them in patrolling that was to make every unit — even the clerical and medical staff — familiar with the jungle, confident in hand-to-hand fighting and responsible for their own safety. Commanders who failed to care for the health of their men were sacked, and the numbers reporting sick came down to negligible levels. Weapons and supplies of every kind were organised in detail — right down to the number of meat meals a week a soldier needs to fight on, and the different kinds of meat Slim's multicultural army would require.

The greatest public impact — reverberating around the world — was made by Orde Wingate who led his first, airborne sweep through the jungles behind the Japanese lines from February to May, 1943. In cool, statistical terms it was a disaster. He lost one-third of his men, and only blew up a bridge and some railway lines that were replaced within days. But he had shown that, with proper training, even very ordinary troops (as his were) could fight their way through difficult country, supplied by air drops. The British could "beat the Japs at their own game". His men also learnt that they could not trust the Burmese: *someone* in a Burmese village always betrayed them to the Japs. It was hill tribesmen like the Kachins who gave them food, loaned them boats to cross rivers, and came with them through the jungle as guides.[5]

Churchill insisted that Wingate be promoted. A religious crank, a skilled self-publicist, admired as warmly as he was hated, he made merciless demands on his men and was killed in an air crash in the early stages of his next and larger operation. He had helped to turn the tide of war.[6]

Meanwhile the Japanese High Command were arguing about

the next steps they should take. They had not planned to attack India, but American victories at Okinawa and Guadalcanal meant that a success was badly needed. General Mutaguchi, who believed he had played a key part in launching the original "China incident", was determined to transform the defence of Burma into the conquest of India. Wingate's invasion of territory that the Japanese had regarded as safely theirs strengthened his hand in these arguments.[7]

The British had learnt that fighting the Japanese called not for conquest of territory but for the killing of Japs. Killing their enemies had always been the aim of the Japanese. Both sides resolved that the plain around Imphal — the small frontier town through which Vernon and thousands of others had struggled to safety — should be the killing ground. Beginning in March 1944, the battles for the Admin Box, Imphal and Kohima were the bloody but decisive settlement of that argument.

Had the British lost again — as they nearly did — the Japanese would have gone streaming into India, taking with them the Indian National Army they had forcibly recruited from captured Indian soldiers to raise rebellion all across the sub-continent. But British, Indian and Gurkha forces, supplied by an air force that generally retained command of the air, had learnt to stand their ground and fight back when surrounded. Their patrols had for some time been coming off best in jungle encounters with the enemy. By June there were the first few desertions by Japanese soldiers, and Indian troops of the Indian National Army were coming in to surrender in large numbers. Major General Tanaka was still calling upon his crack 33rd Division to counter-attack with an Order of the Day that said "Our death-defying infantry group expects certain victory….it must be expected that the division will be almost annihilated….[but] a man guilty of any misconduct should be punished at once… a commander may have to use his sword as a weapon of punishment, exceedingly shameful though it is to have to shed the blood of one's own soldiers on the battlefield…"[8] They were repulsed, and defeat turned into rout as British forces struggled forward into Burma along tracks knee-deep in the monsoon mud.

As they lost the initiative, serious failings began to show up among Japanese commanders: quarrels between senior officers, incapacity to change tactics when their enemy learnt how to respond to them, and death-or-glory commitment to unattainable objectives. Their appalling treatment of prisoners and the wounded continued, now arousing fierce resistance from an increasingly confident enemy. A Major in the Cameronians, who had written a verse about defeat, was now writing:

> "The fallen die in victory at last;
> The camp fires of the living glow more bright
> For all the sorry darkness that is past.
>
> This is our battle and our hour, nor evermore
> Shall we pass through the mountains in retreat."[9]

THE DONNISONS IN INDIA

Vernon, Ruth and Annis, marooned in India, had been lucky to survive the disaster in which many of their friends had perished. But it was not a good time for them. Defeat divides a society, stirring up conflicts between soldiers and civilians, the people and their government, in ways that may eventually lead to revolution. The immediate difficulties the Donnisons faced were those experienced by refugees everywhere. They were utterly exhausted by months of stress and hardship, and all of them became ill with mysterious infections — with 'flu (twice), threatened heart problems and german measles for Annis, malaria and then a threat of diptheria for Vernon, german measles and a more lasting anaemia for Ruth. They found that many Europeans in India resented the refugees from Burma who competed for servants, and for housing which became very scarce. Vernon recalled that "It was even held against us that we all had new clothes. If we hadn't, we would have had only the filthy, tattered rags we walked out in. Above all, we were a standing reminder that there was a war on. Europeans in India had suffered nothing from the war, and for the most part wanted to ignore it."

The refugees at first spent a good deal of time seeking news of old friends, and offering each other help where they could. Meanwhile, the rebellion called for by the Indian Congress Party was leading to attacks on railways and police stations, and for some days the situation in Bengal and Bihar was dangerous. Europeans became very anxious for a while, provoking mild contempt from the refugees who had been through much worse than this. But the Army, the Police and railway managers got things under control before long.

The Donnisons made for Darjeeling in the hills as soon as they could to recuperate and be with Annis, aged eleven. She was at a boarding school there run by Anglican nuns for pupils of many different ethnic origins: Vernon recalled it as "...repressive and rather narrowly religious. Annis had to wear a long, dark blue skirt and black stockings."

As he regained sufficient strength to walk in the mountains, Vernon started looking for a job. He and Donald Petch, with whom he had escaped from Burma, had talked about their plans on the way – expecting, if they got out, that there would be no work or pay for either of them. They resolved to apply to the British Council. This they now did, and both got offers, but Vernon was forbidden to accept by the Burma Government-in-exile which had been set up in Simla. He protested with great anger at this enforced idleness, but his friend Ian Wallace assured him that plans were being made for him. He was soon invited to Simla to receive his instructions. "I was to go to Delhi as representative of the Government of Burma, attached to the Government of India and Army Headquarters... to advise and inform on Burma matters, and, as far as possible, to safeguard the interests of Burma and the Government of Burma."

The family was offered rooms in a hotel in Delhi, and knew

they were lucky. Others were living in tents. Vernon recruited a P.A. – an excellent Indian who had also walked out of Burma – and some clerical staff. He found a second-hand typewriter, some office furniture, and bicycles for all the family – for no cars were available. Ruth and Annis joined him and they got an Indian servant "with a presence so overpowering we began to wilt under it. We felt that nothing less than Government House would measure up to his dignity and importance, and found ourselves longing for a Burmese servant who would be prepared to turn his hand to anything and who would laugh with us…" They found a Shan from Myitkyina in the far north of Burma who had been making his way across country through Japanese-held territory to visit some of his family when he had the misfortune to learn too much about British Army dispositions, so he was picked up and flown out to be held in a detention camp in Northern India. Hsi Nan, a bright and cheerful man, spoke enough Burmese to communicate with the Donnisons and, although he had little education, picked up new skills very quickly. Since he had to spend a good deal of time hanging about doing nothing Ruth taught him to knit, and within a day he was making socks for himself. He seemed to like the Donnisons and must have realised that Vernon might eventually get him back to his family.

To take account of the Indian climate – which in most places is cool for a quarter of the year and very hot for three quarters – boarding schools in the hills had one nine month term and one three month holiday each year. Annis came to join Ruth and Vernon in Delhi for the cool weather and was then sent for nine months to a school in Simla – another Diocesan school but more liberal than the previous one. "We felt much happier with Annis there" Vernon recalled. He did not recall that Annis became ill as soon as she arrived and the school, fearing she had a heart weakness, shut her away in the sanatorium for days. She recovered, but memories of the hospitals in England where she had been confined with a badly broken elbow flooded back. With no familiar voice or face anywhere, she thought she had been lost and forgotten for ever. It was a bad time.

Perhaps the most useful thing Vernon was able to do during these months was to organise a programme of lectures — many of which he gave himself — to troops who would be fighting their way back into Burma. Burmese people had collaborated with the Japanese, revealing British positions to them, and sometimes killing their soldiers and the officials who remained loyal to them. "The Burmese, not unnaturally, had come to be looked upon as 'traitors', and there were many reports of the troops having sworn to wreak vengeance upon them when they returned." Vernon recruited two other men who were likely to carry conviction with soldiers and the three of them went to speak at barracks through-out India, telling their audiences that "the Burmese were not really so bad, and that it would in any case pay to be friendly to them." "When the Army went back into Burma there were no atrocities and no revenge. While it cannot be proved that this was due to our lectures, I think we helped...."

After that, Vernon and Ruth managed to get some leave to go to the "blissful fairyland of Kashmir" where they had a marvel-lously healing time, exploring the lake in a houseboat, seeing a few old friends, and walking for days among spring flowers and through high, snow-covered mountains.

In the train on their way back to the heat of the plains they "were burnt a dark brown and somewhat disreputably clad. When we got into the first class compartment in which we had reserved seats, there were two Englishwomen, very much the memsahibs, who clearly decided we were Anglo-Indians and a distasteful intrusion. They would not turn their dogs off our seats until I insisted they do so. It became clear from their conversation that they were 'in oil'. How we lost India..."

In Burma, relations between soldiers and civil servants had often been difficult, as Slim makes clear[10] and these tensions per-sisted in India. Vernon wrote "I remember drinking with Brigadier Jehu, the Army's Public Relations man, and Jehu saying to me that he had been told to use Dorman-Smith [Governor of

Burma] as a scapegoat and to pin all blame for the collapse in Burma in 1942 on to him, so as to divert attention from the Army's failures. He did his work well – at the cost of great injustice to Dorman Smith who, little as I liked him, was in no way responsible for what had been a straightforward military failure."

The civil and military top brass were planning to create a Civil Affairs Service that would work with the Army and the native population as the invasion of Burma got under way. Beyond that, they had to have some plans for the future of the country. Dorman Smith was widely regarded as a rather unsuccessful Conservative Minister of Agriculture who had been sent to govern Burma as a way of getting him out of Westminster. Like most of his officials, he was determined that Civil Affairs staff should be civil servants, saying that they were likely to be more acceptable than soldiers to the Burmese. "But the essential reason" Vernon later confessed "was that our experiences in 1941 and 1942 had left us with a deep distrust of the Army's competence and judgement" – a distrust reinforced by the ignominious failure of the attempt to recapture Akyab at this time. The Army were equally determined that the service should come under their control. Vernon accompanied the Governor to several meetings with Field Marshall Wavell where these matters were discussed. "Dorman Smith kept on saying things that I knew would anger Wavell. Each time he said them I could see a deep purple flush rise above the collar of Wavell's bush-shirt and spread up the back of his neck into his hair. It would subside again as the conversation moved on to less dangerous ground."

Just when it seemed that the Army's view would prevail, the whole policy was reversed by diktat from London. Churchill, Vernon later discovered, had encountered Sir Roger Lumley – once Governor of Bombay, and not a man he liked – wearing a Major-General's uniform acquired in the course of his job in AMGOT (Allied Military Government of Occupied Territories) the civil affairs service formed to work in Italy. This provoked "a furious Churchillian minute, asking what this was all about, and ending with 'We can't have hordes of sham Major-Generals, preening themselves all over the place' and a complete veto on the commissioning of any more civil affairs officers." This left Vernon, who was due to join the service, as a civilian in a military world, unable to attend any of the key meetings and having to rely on colleagues, recruited earlier to military rank, who brought back news of the matters discussed. Eventually, "after a decent lapse of time to allow memory to fade, commissioning was resumed" and he became a Colonel.

But before joining the C.A.S., Vernon did a four-month spell in Simla as Secretary to the Governor. The best part of this was the opportunities it gave him and Ruth for seeing Annis. The Government-in-exile was planning the "Reconstruction" of Burma. "Never was there more of a South Sea Bubble since the days of the Bubble itself" commented Vernon. "All departments were invited to make proposals... and to plan for the best, regardless of cost... Predictably, all began with a statement that the importance of their Department had never been appreciated, and went on to propose a vast expansion... It did not for one moment occur to these Utopians that the Burmese themselves might like things otherwise. This is not written merely with the benefit of hindsight. Indeed, it was part of the reason for the frustration I felt while working in Simla." When he was posted to the Civil Affairs Service in Delhi, he "went, with relief, to a harder, more realistic atmosphere".

But first he was given a few weeks holiday in Britain. Before they became enmeshed in another campaign, the Government was anxious to get its people away on leave. Vernon, like most of his colleagues, had not been home for seven years. Ruth had already gone ahead of him with Annis, taking her to start at another boarding school and to place her with new foster parents. Ruth had also been asked to play a small part in the Burma Government's reconstruction plans by visiting juvenile courts, remand homes, approved schools and borstals, and writing a report proposing how such services could be developed in postwar Burma – which she did, earning an M.B.E. for her labours. Their journeys home took roundabout routes on overcrowded troop ships which sailed round the Cape and far out into the Atlantic before swinging back to join convoys escorting ships into the Clyde. Leave in wartime Britain, with no opportunities to travel abroad or even to drive a car, passed unmemorably. David, by now in the Navy, was able to join Annis and his parents for a few days before his father was called suddenly to an airfield and sent back to India in a bomber.

DAVID AT MARLBOROUGH

Until he left to join the Navy, David's life centred on his school. Like all youngsters of his age, he was trying to work out what kind of person he wanted to be. Others look to their parents and neighbours for answers to that question, but his parents were too far away to offer much help, and his school friends were the nearest thing he had to neighbours. When I compare his life with the way his grandchildren live today, his seems an odd mixture of sophistication and innocence – reflected in the careful record he made of his expenditure. Books, followed by stamps and stationery (mainly for letters to Burma and then to India) were the main things he spent his money on. "A.E.Housman, *Collected Poems*, Bernard Shaw, *Adventures of the Black Girl in her Search for God*, Michelangelo's, Donatello's and Rodin's *Sculptures* (the big books published by Phaidon) and Liddel Hart, *The British Way in Warfare*, were a few of those he was buying and reading in 1942. "The style of Ruskin", he wrote in his journal, 'is magnificent after the babble of the many little streams of modern literature... like an irresistible river sweeping all before it... Even the most trivial points are set forth in towering argument that frightens the reader into submission."

Political concerns are never far below the surface of his thought. He writes enthusiastically about Tom Paine, quoting his response to Benjamin Franklin's 'Where is liberty, there is my country' – to which Paine replied 'Where is not liberty, there is mine'. He wrestles repeatedly with ancient dilemmas: What is truth? Is it whatever we believe the evidence shows us to be true? If so, it must be different for each person… then, in the next line, he records "This afternoon I have seen 117 tanks go past; nearly all 'Valentines' but some 'Crusaders'. More are still coming", and draws little pictures of them. If a policeman had picked up this journal, with its carefully illustrated notes about the movements of military hardware he would have assumed it was the work of a rather amateurish spy; although he might have found the next lines puzzling: "Snobs frighten me. They make me fear for the future of England. Yet some of them really are the nicest people imaginable." (There were quite a lot of those at Marlborough.) He was sceptical about the Church and was one of the few boys in the school who did not get confirmed. But he had a strong spiritual sense, although his pantheism was losing its raw edge: "If you see God in beauty you may make beauty your God. … See the work of God in a spring morning; do not make the spring itself a God."

The dogs that don't bark in these pages reveal gaps in this boy's life that would surprise his grandchildren. He rarely goes to a shop, other than those selling books or stationery; and would be shy about entering a café to ask for a cup of tea. Pubs he never enters. As for girls – he maintains an occasional correspondence with a stunningly beautiful lass he fell in love with at his primary school, and once cycles 70 miles each way to see her, but has no idea what to say or do when he gets there. Next year, when he is just seventeen, Elizabeth Snow – the flamboyant, passionate, musical one – takes her foster brothers, one at a time, into her bed, and the first touch of her leggy nakedness, wrapped only in her long silky hair, sends an explosion of such power through David's body, it almost blows his head off. But he never links these two experiences of passion or sees either as posing questions about the other.

Many people expect life in a classic public school to be laced with sodomy, and I have read an account of Marlborough during these years which claims the place was full of it. But although he met a good deal of ribald humour about homosexuality David never saw any evidence of it in practice. Yet, shortly after he left, a housemaster at the school killed himself when his abuse of small boys was discovered. I guess we all see what we are looking for – and what we ask for. A tirelessly active boy with a rather puritanical, homophobic outlook was unlikely to be propositioned.

Deep friendships which may have had sexual undertones became increasingly important to him during his last terms in the school when he had the privacy afforded by a small study and the right to stay up working or talking as late as he chose. He developed a powerful David–and-Jonathan comradeship with several other young men. They worked together, read poetry together, played games together and stayed up through the night talking and drinking cocoa in each other's studies: loving bonds for sure, but without overt sexuality.

The war offered many opportunities that our children will never have. Today it would not be so easy to get jobs on farms and in factories, and cycling on main roads has become a dangerous way to travel. Petrol rationing had driven most of the cars off the roads, and David soon learnt to ride his bicycle more than a hundred miles a day along routes carrying little but trucks and military traffic: source of another love affair with the slopes, the highways and changing weather of his country. He rode 90 miles to school at the start of each term, and back to Wrangway again for the holidays, sending only heavy luggage by rail.

To summer-time farm camps, where boys helped to bring in the harvest, Marlborough added forestry camps at Pitlochry and spells in a factory in Manchester – "William E. Carey, Spring and Axle Manufacturers", whose works stood on a street described by Engels in his great book on *The Condition of the Working Class in England in 1844.* It hadn't changed much. Carey's was a roaring, blazing, smoke-filled cavern where newcomers took two days to learn to hear and understand people shouting to them from a few inches away. Amidst its soot and sweat David discovered a new kind of hypnotic working rhythm.

Here and on the land he found great kindness among working people – particularly, he said, in the North of England. He describes with warmth "the land girl who is such a straightforward, hard-working person. She used to work in Woolworth's ... now very thick with the tractor driver. They'll probably get married after the war and should do very well." He describes lorry drivers who gave lifts to him. And "Joe Clark – a happy-go-lucky, knock-about fellow, aged 76...never depressed or defeated. He slept in his clothes up in the hay loft; worked eight hours a day and kept very fit. Then, after a few months, he would collect the money due to him and go off to drink – useless for anything – but returning to work after a fortnight. Down in the village lived his children and grandchildren, but he would not stay with them, although he liked to talk to the grandchildren ... He bade me a fond farewell: 'I'll meet ye at Hell's gate, lad.'"

David came to recognise and respect the codes of those who had to survive as best they could in a hard world. Fathers of families that never had a bank account – their money all spent by Thursday. Boys, unlike their counterparts at Marlborough, who did *not* want to be called up by the Army. The man at a lathe who cast counterfeit half crowns when there was no work coming down the line – adding a teaspoon of cod liver oil to give them the yellow tinge required to mimic the well-worn coin he was using as a mould, and selling them for two shillings each to his work mates.

David turned a cooler gaze on middle class people. One man, he said, "you often see driving in a big open car round these lanes. When he has gone by, the smell of his cigar hangs still in the air. A doctor – he has had two sons killed, and a third remains at home with him, a poor creature – young, yet ageing... arrested in his development. He is a wild and lonely man – his glance fierce and brief. His wife is a chatty, sociable woman; a musician... 'We cannot help each other' was all she said when their second boy was killed."

Soon David was in the Home Guard and going on night manoeuvres. His journals contain drawings of small arms, and instruction on street fighting: "Nine-inch brickwork is not proof against small arms. Cut loopholes low to expose less of your body, and strengthen the walls with sandbags. Put another layer on the floor in case they get underneath you. Booby trap the house next door to give you warning of their approach... Tanks will come in close support of infantry, but they cannot see you above the first floor." He then lists the kinds of bombs to drop on them, and continues: "Place automatic weapons low – well back, behind netting hanging from the ceiling – and single-shot weapons high where they cannot be rushed... No matter how small your force, always keep a counter-attack reserve..."

He admired pacifists and some boys joined the Friends' Ambulance Unit, but he described them as being "a thousand years before their time". He wanted to join the Indian Army and wrote to his parents to say so. A painfully baffling correspondence followed. Vernon and Ruth believed that their family should strive to join the high achievers and tackle the more demanding tasks in any field they entered. As a former Guardsman Vernon knew what that meant in the Army; and as a man who had just spent six painful months watching British-led Indian forces being humiliated by the Japanese, he knew this was not where the high achievers were at that time to be found. But he could not say so, because he had to work with the Indian Army and letters from India were censored – by Indian Army officers. So David's journal records his growing frustration at the unexplained hostility to his plans that his parents' letters conveyed. There was nothing military about his motives for joining the Indian Army; he just thought it would give him the best chance of seeing his parents again. It was for the same reason that he chose the Navy when finally persuaded to abandon his army plan.

But first he had to win a scholarship to Oxford, not because he could get there in no other way, but because coming top had become an addiction. Winning the approval of teachers was perhaps a substitute for parental love. (If he had been better at games he might, like his father, have become an athlete instead – but captaining the school's second fifteen was the furthest he got in that department.) When news came that all four of Hubert Wylie's candidates had won major scholarships the old man's feet momentarily left the ground altogether.

Leaving school was a poignant experience, full of farewells between young men who had lived hard together and would now be setting off to join different branches of the armed forces. For David – still seventeen – this latest gang in his life had provided an anchorage through the years leading from boyhood towards manhood.

TED AND DAINTIE

Vernon and Ruth had lost touch with his cousin Ted when they had paid for his passage to London about six years earlier. And they never knew Ted's sister Daintie, a nurse who had come to work in Burma when her brother was serving a life sentence there. (I think it was she who traced her brother's I.C.S. cousins and sent them photographs and an unsigned letter telling them they had a cousin in the jail.) In a once-imperial country, most of us have cousins of various characters and colours in many parts of the world – descendants of freebooters and black-sheep uncles. They, too, are part of our story.

Ted was a skilled mechanic – largely self-taught in the jail, I think. With help from one of Ruth's friends, he got a job in a London garage and soon married a young woman who quickly had a baby – too quickly, he later concluded, for it to be his. Once on her feet, she made off to Canada and he never saw her again. But for eighteen years he loyally sent her a payment for the child every month.

Ted's sister Daintie was eight years younger than him. A spirited little woman, only four foot six inches tall, she eventually left her hospital in Burma and went to London for a year to take a

278

course in midwifery. Returning to India, she arranged a marriage by post with a Boer farmer in Rhodesia (now Zimbabwe). He was an older man who had fought the British in the Boer War, and been captured and sent to a prison camp in Ceylon. But when the First World War began he had fought with the British against the Germans in Africa, and been rewarded with the Rhodesian farm.

Daintie, setting forth as a "mail order bride", boarded a boat for Beira, and first met her farmer when she got off the train in Salisbury (now Harare). They were married at once and she had a baby ten months later. "That" she later told her daughter, "was part of the contract". But the partnership seems to have become a happy one, for she described her next as a "love child".

When the Second World War began, Ted joined the Army again and was soon running a repair shop in Nigeria, keeping army trucks on the road. After a couple of years he got two weeks leave in London. There, through a marriage bureau, he found and married Margaret before going back to Africa. She already had a daughter (all sorts of things happened to you if you worked night after night through the blitz on the switchboards of the London Fire Service) and Ted was happy to accept the child as his own.

Margaret followed Ted to Nigeria as soon as she could, bringing her daughter with her from the children's home in which she had been placed. The child was soon sent to foster parents and a boarding school in South Africa (David and Annis would have recognised the pattern). I will tell more of their story at the end of this book.

BURMA UNDER NEW RULERS

Although their towns were burnt up by both sides in the course of the war, most Burmese people lived in villages where life under Japanese occupation went on much as before. Supplies of manufactured goods — things like knives, cooking pots and (most important) textiles — disappeared, but food and shelter were sufficient. In the hill tracts, where people depended on subsistence farming, little changed unless armed forces came their way. But in the towns life was harder. There, Japanese brutality soon alienated the Burmese. Aung San's daughter has written that "The soldiers of Nippon, whom many had welcomed as liberators, turned out to be worse oppressors than the unpopular British"[11]. Colonel Suzuki, described in the last Chapter as becoming devoted to the young nationalists whom he recruited to the Burma Independence Army, was sent home to Japan and his organisation was disbanded. Business men and administrators, who had learnt how to deal with conquered peoples in China and Korea, arrived to take over the country, and "…disappearances, torture, forced labour" became "part of everyday experience".[12] Far more Burmese labourers than allied prisoners died building the railway to Siam.

The Burma Independence Army was cut down drastically in size, brought under tighter control and renamed the Burma National Army — with Aung San still in command under the Japanese. He soon recognised that the Burmese would have to fight the new occupiers if they were to win their independence, but he had to hold diverse and quarrelsome groups together and to avoid frightening his Japanese masters. Those manoeuvring to take over power after the war ranged from old politicians to young nationalists, from Communists to neo-Fascists, and from Burmans to the minority groups in the hills. Aung San did not lead his men out of Rangoon to fight the Japanese until the end of March 1945, when Mandalay, Burma's old capital, had already fallen to the British. Two years earlier, he had sent two of his men out to India to make contact with the British. They had been members of the Thakin Party; young, educated and left-wing — a violent group which had been very unsuccessful in elections. The Burma Government in Exile, whose two remaining Ministers were relics of those who had won the elections, were hostile to them, as were their civil servants. But the young men found their way to Colin Mackenzie, the one-legged head of Force 136 — cover name for the Indian branch of the Special Operations Executive (known as

S.O.E.) which worked with resistance movements in occupied territories. The S.O.E. came under the Minister of Economic Warfare, which gave them direct access to Churchill, and were not subject to military or India Office control. Without informing the soldiers or the civil servants, Mackenzie set up two units — one to work with the Karens and another to work with Burman groups. (They had been killing each other, so they had to be dealt with separately.) Before long, he was sending arms, money and radios to both.

When they got to know what was happening, civil servants like Vernon, now being recruited to the Civil Affairs Service, protested that Mackenzie's people were "dangerously ignorant of the realities of political life in Burma" and "playing with fire", leading to "the danger that the Thakins would be enabled after the war to demand an altogether unjustifiable share in political power". Men like Aung San, who had murdered Burmese officials loyal to the British, would very likely be prosecuted when Burma was reconquered. On later reflection, Vernon wrote "I still think that S.O.E. were playing with fire. On the other hand, I doubt whether their efforts appreciably affected the course of events. The fire had been lit by others and would have burnt up the past any way." [15]

I guess Mackenzie, like Suzuki, knew that if you need tough resistance fighters you do not go to successful, respectable, middle-aged citizens of the sort that senior officials and politicians are accustomed to deal with. They have too much to lose — and are not fit for guerrilla warfare. Mountbatten, who had worked with resistance movements in Europe, backed Mackenzie.

Ultimately, the British would have had to leave Burma even if Force 136 had never existed. But Makenzie's choice of the people to whom he sent arms played a part in determining who would succeed them.

NOTES

1   William Slim, *Defeat into Victory*, London, Pan Books, 1956;
    pages 120-21.

2   Louis Allen, *Burma. The Longest War 1941-45*, London, J.M.Dent,
    1984; page 115.

3   Slim, 1956; pages 187-88.

4   Slim, 1956; page 192.

5   Bernard Fergusson, *Beyond the Chindwin*, London, Collins, 1945.

6   Louis Allen tells the Japanese side of the story well in
    Burma. The Longest War 1941-45.

7   Allen, 1984; pages 152-54.

8   Slim, 1956; page 337.

9   P.R.Boyle, in *Poems from India by Members of the Forces*, Oxford,
    Oxford University Press, 1945; page 130.

10 Slim, 1956; page 31 et seq.

11 Aung San Suu Kyi, 1992; page 16.

12 Aung San Suu Kyi, 1992; page 16.

13 Memoir by F.S.V.Donnison in Hugh Tinker, (Ed.),
    Burma. The Struggle for Independence, 1944-1948,
    London, H.M.S.O., 1983; Vol. I, pages 1,000-01.

IX

PYRRHIC VICTORY

In 1944 Sir Reginald Dorman Smith, Governor of Burma, was sitting in Simla with a few officials and two Burmese Ministers who had escaped with them from the Japanese. This Government-in-exile was confident that Burma would be reconquered and they would have at least seven years to get the country back on its feet before handing it over to the Burmese who would wish, they assumed, to remain within what was now called the British Commonwealth. They were preparing voluminous plans for post war reconstruction; plans eventually sent to the Westminster Government which must have been far too busy fighting the war to read them. They were accepted, but with a warning that this entailed no financial commitments – and thus no promise to do anything.

Vernon Donnison was brought in for a while to work with this team, but he had seen imperial authority unravel through six humiliating months as the British failed to protect the people from the horrors of conquest. After two years under brutal Japanese rule, it was not surprising that the Burmese wanted their latest conquerors to leave. But they had got out of the habit of being ruled by the British. It was that habit which had been the foundation for the imperial confidence trick which had enabled young men in their twenties to lead public services staffed almost entirely by local people, to appoint and dismiss chieftains and village Headmen, to walk unarmed through huge tracts of the country they ruled, and to sleep soundly at night, needing protection only from the mosquitoes. Whatever the future held for the

Burmese, Vernon knew that his countrymen had lost the right to plan it for them. Imperial authority could not be rebuilt. So he was relieved when he was posted to join in the more urgent and practical work of the Civil Affairs Service that was to play its part in the reconquest of Burma.

Could the British reconquer the country? There were powerful military voices saying at this time that Burma would have to be written off until the war was won on other fronts. And if the British did return, what would happen when they found that they could never again resume the role of "thakins" – masters?

The Burma war has been well described elsewhere and I shall only sketch in enough of its main events to explain what the characters in my story were doing. That calls for an account of the Civil Affairs Service in which Vernon Donnison was engaged. This may sound like a side show, but the disastrous experience of the greatest military power on earth, unfolding as I write in Afghanistan and Iraq, should remind us that "civil affairs", which means the military government of occupied territories, may decide the outcome of major conflicts.

MOUNTING THE ASSAULT

As the Japanese attempt to break into India was beaten off in the summer of 1944, Admiral Mountbatten, the supreme allied commander in South-East Asia, had to decide what to do next. He was holding a precarious alliance together. The Americans were working with the Chinese through General Stillwell who was commanding a ragged but battle-hardened Chinese army on Burma's North-Eastern frontier. They wanted to build a road across Northern Burma and pour in supplies that would enable China to stay in the war, and eventually provide air bases from which the Americans could support their own forces in the Pacific and attack Tokyo itself. But they wanted nothing to do with the rebuilding of the British Empire and were not much interested in central Burma unless that proved to be the only way to their

China road. British officers working with "Vinegar Joe" Stillwell commented that he seemed determined to fight the War of American Independence all over again.

Chiang Kai-Shek, leader of the Chinese Nationalists, was fighting the Japanese and his own country's Communists who were supported by another British ally — the Soviet Union. He must not be alienated; nor the Americans either, for they had brought a growing number of supply planes and smaller support aircraft to this theatre of war and these would be needed to back a British advance. They had already been used to rescue the Indian Army when it got into trouble in Arakan on the western fringe of Burma.

After painful negotiations, it was agreed that General Slim, leading the Fourteenth Army on the Indian border, and General Stillwell, leading the Chinese, would be jointly responsible for the assault on Burma. Slim was one of the few senior officers who could work with Stillwell. But he had other problems.

To keep his Army supplied through some of the most impenetrable country in the world would be a formidable task. There had never been a road from India to Burma until the Army built one. The fighting would have to be done mainly by the multi-cultural Indian Army — one of the Empire's great creations, whose men spoke different languages, believed in different Gods and ate different foods — without consulting their countrymen back at home who were demanding increasingly vociferously that the British quit India. Lack of intelligence was another problem. The Japanese had good intelligence through the Burmese and from their agents in India; but it was difficult for the British to get reliable information from tribesmen in settlements sparsely scattered in the mountains through which they would have to advance; and the Japanese, until the last days of the campaign, never surrendered, so there were few prisoners to interrogate. Slim knew very little about that most vital factor — the personalities of the generals he would be up against. His troops even had difficulties in identifying their enemies: as they moved through the jungle,

Burmese, Chinese and Japanese all looked pretty much the same to them.

But the British also had some advantages. The Japanese were operating at the outer limits of the vast empire — roughly the size of the whole of Europe — which they had captured from the British, the Dutch and the French. Behind them, the Americans were winning victories in the Pacific which were beginning to threaten the homeland itself. It was not only for the British that this was the forgotten war. Japanese assault troops had sometimes to be withdrawn to scavenge the jungles for food to feed themselves and their starving comrades.

Both sides were shaking out their top brass as they drew breath for the next stage of this war. The Japanese had staked everything on the battles for Kohima and Imphal and when that gamble failed most of the generals involved were sent back to Tokyo in varying degrees of disgrace. The fanatical Mutaguchi, who had been a leading spokesman of those determined to conquer India, was one of those sent home.

The British were seeking leaders with the aggressive flair that would be needed for the assault.[1] Japanese fighting tradition meant this would not be a war for territory or position; the enemy had to be killed — in large numbers. Slim was prepared to speak sharply about civil servants[2] but his reluctance to criticize in his writings soldiers of any rank in any army was one of his endearing characteristics. He described Scoones, who commanded Fourth Corps, which was to bear the brunt of the fighting, as "steady" and "far-sighted"; but to this Louis Allen added "and slow off the mark"[3]. He was promoted back to India and the Corps gained an altogether different commander. Even Stillwell was removed at last. Slim was sorry to see him go because he knew that, if Stillwell said his Chinese would fight, they probably would; but Chiang could stand his disloyalty no longer.[4]

The first plan of action agreed by Mountbatten and his generals called for a southward drive by the Chinese down the east side of the country to Maymyo where they would link up with the

Fourteenth Army driving in from the north-west across the Chindwin and Irrawaddy Rivers to Mandalay. Between them would lie the Shwebo "plain", north of Mandalay, which was to be the killing ground on which the Japanese Army would be destroyed. (It was not really a plain — just a bit flatter than the surrounding hills.) Meanwhile, a combined seaborne and airborne assault would be launched on Rangoon. Few people were confident at this stage that the allied Armies could fight their way right across the country to the capital.

CIVIL AFFAIRS

Before Mountbatten came on the scene in August 1943, Field Marshall Wavell had been preparing for the government of the territories to be liberated. For this purpose, and to secure his lines of communication, a Civil Affairs Service was to be created which would operate until power could be handed over to civilian authorities. Although a properly organized service of this sort had not been set up before, the job it had to do was not a new one for the British. It was by treating conquered peoples with respect and paying for any supplies secured from them that Wellington gained the support of Spanish guerillas who helped him win the Peninsula War. Meanwhile the French who expected to live off the land, leaving the peasants to starve, soon found that every despatch had to be accompanied by a squadron of cavalry if it was to arrive. The soldiers who appear in Goya's drawings and paintings which so vividly record the cruel brutality of that war are French, never British.

I have already explained that the organisation of the Civil Affairs Service was held up by Churchill's warning that there must not be "hordes of sham Major-Generals preening themselves in all directions", but the arguments that seethed around its birth dealt with bigger questions than the uniforms of its members. The Service originated in the mountainous fringes of Burma where British officials left behind in the retreat tried to maintain some kind of order and mobilize resistance against the Japanese.[5] They received occasional supplies brought in by air or along jungle tracks. Their only roads led down into Japanese-held Burma. Sometimes these officials got involved in the fighting, and some were killed. One, an Anglo-Burman, managed to evade the Japanese and make his way to the British lines where the officer in command said he had never heard of a civil affairs service and intended to shoot him as a spy – and nearly did.

How could such confusion be avoided? Who could order men to undergo such risks? Would their dependants be entitled to compensation if they became casualties? If they had to take drastic steps to maintain order, by what authority would they be acting, and to whom would they be accountable? Such questions concentrated the minds of all concerned.

Meanwhile, in North Arakan, still in British hands, similar questions were being posed. This is a coastal strip, 150 miles long and about 40 miles wide, laced by rivers and arms of the sea, which has always been linked more closely to India than to Burma. Slightly more than a million people lived there in 1941: about 600,000 Arakanese, who were Buddhists of mixed Indian and Burmese descent speaking their own Burmese dialect; about 200,000 Chittagonian Indians, who were Muslims speaking the language of Chittagong; and another 200,000 consisting of hill peoples and smaller groups living along the coast. As the Japanese approached and nothing more could be done to help the Army, "British" administrators – mainly Indians, Anglo-Indians and Anglo-Burmese – left for India. But most of the people who constituted the administrative "machine" of clerks, policemen, messengers and the like remained on the ground – leaderless. Were the British needed at all in such places?

At first the answer to that question seemed to be "no". The people set up "Peace Committees", headed by local notables, to keep things going as best they could – a task complicated by the fact that the frontier between British-Indian and Japanese forces swung violently and unpredictably back and forth. Soon conflicts, never far below the surface, broke out between Buddhist Arakanese and Muslim Chittagonians. There were pogroms. Farmers were driven off their land; pagodas and mosques were destroyed, and the use of minority languages was banned. Smallpox and other diseases spread. A Deputy Commissioner, gallantly trying to maintain order, was murdered. A unit of the Burma Independence Army came through, looted 23 million rupees from the Treasury and distributed them to the poor — who naturally became their supporters. Peace Committees financed themselves by confiscating cattle and other goods from terrorised minorities. One of them conducted public floggings, amassed quite a lot of arms, and — as a readily understandable insurance policy — began negotiating with the Japanese. All coherent authority collapsed.[6]

Meanwhile the Army, desperately short of men, was trying to recruit an irregular force of local Muslims who would form a screen along the frontier to gather information and absorb the first pressure of any Japanese attack. But they found that those who had been so zealous in murdering Arakanese Buddhists were now fighting among themselves and could not be entrusted with arms. The Army could do nothing until some sort of order was established, so they asked the Burma Government in Simla for help. Dorman Smith sent them an experienced civil servant — Denis Phelips, an old friend of Vernon, previously glimpsed in this story when he took thirteen-year-old David sailing on one of the Rangoon lakes. The Army made him a Lieutenant-Colonel, and — to make it quite clear that he was their man — forbade him to communicate in any way with the Burma Government. Then they sent him into Arakan, with no staff, no administrative authority, and no declaration of martial law to legitimize his actions.

Since the Japanese now commanded the sea which was the usual route to this outer fringe of Burma, Phelips walked about 50 miles down rough tracks along the coast from Chittagong into Arakan, arriving in August 1942. There he was joined by a few other officers sent in by the Army who set about recruiting and training what became a very effective irregular force while Phelips gradually persuaded the Peace Committees — mainly with offers of money — to accept his authority. He rebuilt a police force, organized courts and created his own "law" for them to administer. It became known as the "code Phelipe". Punishments included executions. Villages had to be moved to make way for airstrips and military operations, and their people resettled or compensated. Movements of people trading goods between Japanese and British territory had to be restricted to prevent them carrying intelligence to the enemy. Vaccinations were carried out to stop the spread of small-pox; a veterinary department was set up to help farmers; and refugees were sheltered. Phelips did battle with the authorities who were trying to reinstate Burmese money in the area, arguing that his people depended on traders bringing goods down the coastal tracks from India, and they had to be paid in Indian money. He also resisted pressure to start raising land tax from them, arguing that this was the least they could do for people who had been so badly let down by the imperial power — and anyway he had none of the staff or records required for this purpose.

This wild-west frontier would eventually have to be brought under control, but that had to wait on the outcome of a top-level battle between the "civilians" — Dorman Smith backed by officials in the Burma Office — and the "soldiers" — Wavell, the Commander-in-Chief, backed by the War Office — in which Ministers on both sides became involved. Eventually, at a meeting in Delhi in November 1942, the Governor and the Commander-in-Chief were told that a military administration would be established with a duty to hand authority over to civil powers as soon as the Force Commander felt this could be safely done.

Vernon commented later that the Army had always feared that civilians would be too protective towards unruly groups in the native population, while the civilians feared the Army would alienate the natives by their brutality. Ironically, right across South East Asia, it proved to be the generals who were prepared to work with rebels and the civilians who sought to repress them.

Dennis Phelips and other pioneers were at last brought within the framework of a recognized, properly empowered, reasonably supplied regime. They had shown what "civil affairs" meant, and what kind of men it would require. Vernon said later that "Even if disguised as soldiers it was well known that they were not 'real' soldiers. Whether endowed with military rank or not, their influence depended upon character and personality. Fortunately, Civil Affairs Officers in Burma usually had an abundance of both."

Slim's account of Phelips describes a man the soldiers could work with. He "was invaluable, not only in the work for which he was appointed, but in the effect that his courage, energy, resource and devotion to duty had on all of us. ... His laugh was like a battle-cry to us, and, I am sure, to the Japanese too, for they must often have heard it. Phelips was the embodiment of the highest tradition of the Indian Civil Service; ... an example to us soldiers."[7] But he and his pioneering colleagues were not altogether grateful for being brought within the system.

Vernon recalled the transition. Knowing that they were nobody's responsibility had "exhilarated rather than daunted them. It meant freedom from the tyranny of paper and precedent, from the need to refer to remote and often uncomprehending authority before taking decisions, from the criticism of press and politicians". That brought an "emancipation of the spirit, a release from trivialities, born of the sickness and weariness that were their frequent companions and of the collapse of the society they had known. ...With freedom went pride, pride in their knowledge of the people and the country ... pride in their tested toughness and resource, pride above all in doing without assistance from others a supremely difficult task...". Their comradeship "was seasoned with 'laughter's gusty squalls', laughter without which the difficulties and frustrations could hardly have been borne, laughter which showed perhaps how near the breaking point had sometimes come." Now "the dead hand of official control, particularly of financial control, was to fall on

Ruth about 1944

their shoulders. Military administration might [bring] official
recognition, equipment, even transport; it would never give them
again the satisfaction and pride of these early days."[8] In these last,
chaotic years of an empire they had briefly recreated the spirit
and tradition of its eighteenth and nineteenth century pioneers.

This was the service that Vernon was to enter. Ruth went
home with Annis and he was made a Colonel – "red tabs and all"
– setting off by train from Delhi to Calcutta and then by air to
Imphal. There he joined the headquarters of Fourth Corps, commanded by General Scoones who was preparing to move forward
into Burma.

"I do not think Scoones liked Civil Affairs Officers" Vernon
recalled. This led to absurd irritations. Scoones had decreed that
all his officers must wear topees – the old imperial pith helmet.
Looking out one afternoon from the mud hut that served as his
office, he "saw three captains walking towards the main
gate...One was wearing a hat ... that made him look like a scoutmaster.... Another had almost snow-white hair... and no hat of
any kind. The third officer wore a battered forage cap. The
General summoned them to his office. When he had them standing, more or less at attention, in front of his table" he asked each
of them in turn "Why aren't you wearing a topee?" to which the
"scoutmaster" replied "I have only been commissioned three
days, Sir", the white haired man, "I haven't worn one for years,
Sir" and the owner of the forage cap "Please, Sir, I lost mine in
Malaya". Civil Affairs had met the military.

Fortunately, Frank Messervy soon took over command of the
Corps. Vernon described him as "an old Etonian, tall, a little...
unkempt in appearance, a tough fighting soldier, who had commanded a Division in the Western Desert. At the fall of Tobruk
his Division had been overrun by the Germans, but Messervy told
them he was the sanitary man and while they went in search of
more important prisoners he escaped and walked back to safety
along the coast. More recently, he had commanded 7 Division in
Arakan, making history by allowing himself to be surrounded by

the Japanese, and then, with the help of air supply, fighting and winning the Battle of the Admin. Box.." (The Japanese were so sure that the British would once again run away when surrounded that they had brought extra gun crews without any guns, confident that they would be able to take over abandoned British weapons and forge on into India in ten days.) Messervy, Vernon continued, was "no intellectual", but he had "a terrifying capacity to single out with great speed the crucial factor in any situation." He knew he was going to need civil affairs officers and invited Vernon to join A Mess where he himself fed and talked with his brigadiers and colonels. "A small matter, but it made a great deal of difference to one's standing in headquarters".

Vernon was a Formation C.A.O. attached to Corps headquarters and moving with it. But most of his colleagues were Territorial C.A.Os, organized in small teams to be dropped off as the Army advanced – taking charge of captured territory a few hours after the Japanese had been cleared from it. Although given military titles, each team consisted of "the equivalents of a Deputy Commissioner, a District Superintendent of Police, a Medical Officer, an Engineer of the Public Works Department, and such assistants as could be provided, together with transport, rations and office equipment."

Vernon's job was "to provide such information about Burma as the Corps Commander might require, to act as his mouthpiece in relations with local inhabitants, to make contact with village Headmen and other administrative officers uncovered by our advance, to ensure that the appropriate teams were called forward, briefed and dropped off to set up administration in their areas, and thereafter to advise and instruct them and try to resolve any problems they might have".

To help him he had two staff officers and one or two clerks. One of his staff officers dealt with relief supplies, for the whole of Burma had been starved of necessities of every kind. The other – Pat Rathbone – helped with everything else. Originally a young I.C.S. official, he had spent two years in the Army, leading irregulars in the Chin Hills: a hard and dangerous life.⁹ He was "a great charmer who knew far more than I did about the workings of the military machine". A friendship grew between them that lasted for the rest of their lives.

Fourth Corps headquarters moved forward as the advance began, and soon they were into Burma. Vernon lived in a tent with a camp bed across the back and an office table at the doorway with a telephone on it. Eventually he secured a jeep, and a small truck to carry his staff and their equipment. An airstrip would be laid down nearby for landing supplies, and mail from England reached them in the depths of the forest in five days – faster than in prewar Burma. To visit his more remote officers he would get a lift in a light plane that could carry one passenger. "When I needed to see Judson Carrott at Homalin on the Upper Chindwin we flew much of the way along the river below tree top level. We circled over detached units operating in the jungle and the pilot called to me to throw mail bags out to them. I spent a night with Carrott and was fetched back next day. After we had done our business the villagers put on a *pwe* with all the customary Burmese verve and humour. There was a fine take-off of Jud and myself."

MASTER STROKE

On Christmas Day, 1944, they were in Myintha, on the eastern side of the River Chindwin. Slim came from Army Headquarters, spent the whole night in conference with Messervy and his staff and left next morning. "We were then told of the big change of plan that had been decided upon." The Chinese were no longer involved but Slim had been following a modified version of Mountbatten's original plan in which "33 Corps was to advance steadily from the Tamu area to Shwebo; meanwhile Fourth Corps would swing widely out to the left, cross the Irrawaddy below Kathar, and turn upon Mandalay with a powerful left hook. Together they would encircle the main Japanese forces in the

Shwebo Plain. But it had become clear that the Japanese were already withdrawing southwards across the Irrawaddy. Fourth Corps would encounter little resistance, fail to encircle them" — and territory was not what this war was about.

"Accordingly it was decided to swing Fourth Corps to the *right* of 33 Corps, send them south down the Kabaw and Myittha valleys to reach the Irrawaddy near Pakokku, south-west of Mandalay, where they would cross the river and strike for Meiktila — a vital communication centre for the Japanese, well behind their Mandalay front. The Japanese would be encircled in the Kyaukse area instead of the Shwebo plain.

" The leading Division of Fourth Corps — 19 Division — had already been launched across the Chindwin River and could not be recalled, so it would continue its advance and come under command of 33 Corps. The rest of Fourth Corps would move with all possible secrecy down the Myittha Valley. All movement would take place under cover of darkness. All wireless communication would cease so the Japanese would not know the scale of the forces involved, and a great deal of dummy wireless communication would be transmitted on the left flank where Fourth Corps had been expected to go."

"We were all swept into the excitement of this stroke." Japanese generals later described it as the "master stroke" of the war. "The leading Division — 7 Indian Division — set off at once down the Myittha Valley, covered by a light screen which was required not to reveal the weight of the forces behind it."

Vernon recalled driving with the rest of the Corps' headquarters "through the nights, with severely blacked out headlamps, on a rough and not always obvious track", and finding resting places in forests that were beginning to thin out. "Almost before you had finished putting up your tent, the signalers would run a line along from tree to tree and put a telephone on your table." Southwards they went to Kalemyo where he wanted to climb a mountain in the Chin Hills — officially because he had a C.A.O. there, but mainly because he had never climbed in the Chin Hills "and it was my experience that expeditions of this sort were seldom wasted. They enlarged one's knowledge of Burma and often helped one to take a sensible view of the problems arising." It would have been the last of his many journeys into the wilderness, but the pace of the advance left no time for it. They moved on to Kan where he had to deal with claims for compensation by cultivators whose fields had been taken for the usual airstrip, and then to Ondaw near Pauk as the Corps gathered itself to cross the Irrawaddy and drive eastwards to Meiktila.

They were now out of the jungle and into "low hills sprinkled with thorn bushes. It was February and the weather was beginning to stoke up. ... It was here that Lady Mountbatten, who was in charge of Red Cross work in South East Asia, visited Corps headquarters. A messenger came to say that she wanted to see me, making it clear that he would rather not be in my shoes. I found an angry Lady M. who came straight to the point. She had visited a civilian hospital and found it scandalously short of equipment. I told her that the hospital in question was not in my area, but quickly added that if she had visited one of my hospitals she would have found equally scandalous shortages, and the reason for them was the very low priority accorded to civilian needs by the military. She got the point in one. 'I see' she said; 'yet another case in which the Army has insisted on taking responsibility but has made no provision for discharging it.' We became allies, and as soon as she got back to Calcutta a Major-General was hussled off to the black market to get the supplies needed for our civil hospitals.

"The Irrawaddy crossings followed and a bridgehead was established at Nyaungu. Within 48 hours I was over to visit our Civil Affairs people and to talk to a number of Burmese officials who had taken shelter from the battle among the clusters of ancient pagodas at Pagan. Stepping into the jeep that would take me there I found the driver was that cheerful rascal Maung Kyin, who had been the driver of my first car on the oilfields. I guess he had been driving for the Japanese. We greeted each other with much warmth."

Vernon found old friends among the officials sheltering at Pagan. They had gone there "because they were certain the British would not bomb or shell the pagodas. The Civil Affairs Service had indeed provided the Army and the Air Force with lists of pagodas and monuments that were to be safeguarded. But my trust in the Air Force was a good deal less than my friends': it seemed to me that they seldom knew exactly where they were."

"Our meeting was very exciting – emotional indeed – for this was the first time we had uncovered fairly senior, educated people who had held posts of considerable responsibility under us. I stayed the night in a monastery, spending most of it talking with Htin Wa, an old friend. He was still staunchly pro-British and had refused to work for the Japanese – although we would not have held it against him if he had, provided he had done no more than his normal duties. To make a living he had bought a Burmese country boat to trade up and down the river, taking rice to Upper Burma and vegetables and cooking oil back to Lower Burma. He took his young daughter with him to help with the boat, and when British planes came over and began machine-gunning them to stop all traffic on the river the two of them would jump overboard, holding on to a long rope, and swim well away till the danger had passed. He had taken with him copies of Shakespeare and the Bible which he would read with his daughter". (Desert Island Disks for real.) "Now he was worried lest her education would be set back by having missed so much schooling. I laughed. Shakespeare, the Bible, Htin Wa for company and all the life of the great Irrawaddy River … there wasn't much better she could do for an education!"

Vernon got back to his headquarters and took an evening walk by the airstrip on the West bank of the river, "watching the Dakotas flying in and out in a steady stream, disappearing into the sunset over the Arakan Yomas. It was getting much hotter; the season was advancing and we were into the dusty Upper Burma plain." The soldiers were growing increasingly determined to get to Rangoon before the monsoon broke.

Soon Vernon was flying into Meiktila "to visit the Civil Affairs team who had gone with the force that had seized the town and then allowed itself to be surrounded by a strong Japanese counter-attack... At first the besieged force were confined within a shrinking perimeter, but as reinforcements and supplies were flown in the perimeter began to expand. ... It was here that we first came seriously up against the problem of what to do with officials who had done more for the Japanese than we thought justifiable. We decided they should not be employed by Civil Affairs until an inquiry had been held into the nature and extent of their collaboration."

Fourth Corps' headquarters was moved forward to Meiktila — Messervy's men joking that after being encircled at Tobruk and then in Arakan he was hoping to be encircled yet again. But that was not to be, for they were soon making spectacular headway southwards down the road and railway towards Rangoon. Despite being outnumbered and taking what more cautious generals would have regarded as crazy risks by pouring all their forces down one slender line of communication, Slim knew that "we were winning...My soldiers were out for Rangoon, and anyone who...had seen them fight could not doubt that they would get there."[10] Civil Affairs teams were lit up by the fierce enthusiasm of all around them.

Vernon visited one of these teams in Kalaw, very soon after the Japanese had been driven out, and met his friend Ian Wallace there. They found "Myint Thein and his wife Hpwa Hmi. Both were barristers and good friends of Ruth and me. She had been Burma's first woman barrister. We received a tremendously warm welcome. They insisted we should spend the night with them, and Myint Thein went out into the compound, where there were many pine trees, and dug up a bottle of Scotch that he had hidden away for just this occasion. We sat long over our drinks, talking of what had happened to Burma during the three years of Japanese occupation."

These and other Burmese friends whom he was rediscovering were of Vernon's own generation and living in up-country places. But there was a new generation, more heavily concentrated in the country's central plains, whom he learnt more about as his teams spread southwards.

Jan Gillett – a botanist and Communist, son of a banker father who had advised Vernon's mother – was working in clandestine operations behind the Japanese lines with Force 136. Prompted by a message from Ruth who had recently met his parents in England, he turned up when Vernon got to Yamethin. "He had been working with Aung San's Burma National Army." They had just marched out to join forces with the British, four weeks before the fall of Rangoon, and were now turning their Left-wing political alliance – the Anti-Fascist Organisation – into a larger Anti-Fascist People's Freedom League which became known as the AFPFL. "He had much to say about the idealism and integrity of the young Burmans he met in this way."

"Leo Edgerly, who was in charge of the Civil Affairs team for the Yamethin District, had also made good friends with the League and gave me accounts of the patriotism, idealism, and sense of responsibility which these young men displayed. His forces were so thin on the ground that he soon recognized that he could establish control only by working with the AFPFL." Moving further south, Vernon met Hedley Pudden, in charge of the Civil Affairs team at Toungoo. "He too found that he must lean on the AFPFL. It was only through them that he could communicate with many of his Headmen. He saw the dangers of this reliance a bit more clearly than Leo and Jan, but that made it no easier to avoid."

A few days later, Fourth Corps' headquarters moved on to Pegu where, for the first time, Vernon had an office in a house. "The rains were about to break and we were very glad to have something more solid than a tent over us."

RANGOON

The bridges on the way to Rangoon had been blown, so the Corps was held up for a few days while an amphibious force from Arakan were first into the city. "A few days later, I flew in to Mingaladon, the Rangoon airport, over territory not yet ours, to make contact with the Civil Affairs team that would be there and co-ordinate our plans. I also very much wanted to see the places where we had lived and worked for so many years.

"The airfield was peculiarly deserted but two of us eventually found a truck and a driver whom we persuaded to take us the twelve miles into Rangoon. On the way we turned a mile or two off the road to see the golf course – bright green, but hopelessly neglected and covered with vehicles, parked and abandoned by the Japanese. Continuing into the city, I had no idea where to find the Civil Affairs team but we drove firmly up to Government House which proved to be a military headquarters where they told us how to find them. On the way we made a detour to look at our old house in Windermere Park. It was completely empty; the only traces of us being a telephone receiver and the bottom piece of my music stand, lying on the floor of the garage." Vernon had some talk with his colleagues before he had to leave, but soon returned by road – dashing past a burning tank at the roadside on the edge of town lest it blow up.

Rangoon was in filthy, stinking chaos: sewers, refuse collection, water and electricity supplies had all been out of action for months. The Civil Affairs team sent there was a big one, coming straight from the headquarters of the Service in Calcutta. Even with the help they would get from the Army, they had a massive job to do. Vernon, by now a Brigadier, was characteristically unassuming in his approach to them, saying that "we needed to compare notes. Civil Affairs doctrine had been shaped by events. Those of us who had been in the field for the last six months needed to be brought up to date with thinking at headquarters, and the newcomers who had no practical experience of doing the job needed some help from us."

He found time, too, for "a sentimental journey round Rangoon. As I was climbing into my jeep Ian Morrison, the *Times* war correspondent, asked if he might come with me. A gentle and attractive person and a perceptive writer, he later wrote *Grandfather Longlegs* about Seagrim and the Karen underground movement, and was eventually killed with another correspondent in Vietnam when their jeep was blown up. Just as we were about to move off, I was asked if I could take Thakin Than Tun and his gear to one of the beautiful Burmah Oil Company houses where Force 136 had their headquarters." (Than Tun was one of Aung San's close colleagues and was to go with him and Ne Win to meet Mountbatten a month later.) "All that I remember about him was that he was sullenly uncommunicative, and that his eyes had the closed, almost unseeing, look of the fanatic. Clearly we were his real enemies." Vernon took a nostalgic look at the B.O.C. houses where they dropped him off: Ruth and he used to play tennis and listen to the gramophone with good friends there. Then he went on to search for more Burmese friends who had stayed in Rangoon through the occupation. He must have wondered how these friends – civil servants, lawyers, doctors and teachers in the main – would be treated by the new generation of angry and ruthless young men.

A few days later Vernon received a copy of a letter, dated 11 May 1945, from his old friend Jim Lindop. It had been sent to Major-General Rance, the head of the Civil Affairs Service. Lindop, writing in Calcutta, was a Brigadier and a Deputy Chief Civil Affairs Officer, like Vernon. His letter, which claimed to be the authoritative view of the Service, said that there was "extreme political danger in accepting the aid and collaboration of the AFPFL and the BNA" (the Anti-Fascist People's Freedom League, and the Burma National Army.) Both, he said, should be "dissolved immediately by proclamation".

For Vernon, this letter posed a crisis, both political and personal. It "filled me with misgivings", he said, for "events had outstripped the policy advocated by Brigadier Lindop."[11] But he had respect and affection for Jim and was reluctant to challenge him. They had been at Oxford together; they had joined the I.C.S and come out on the same boat as new recruits together, 25 years earlier. That night he had a long talk with Pat Rathbone, and wrote back next morning, 15 May, to Lindop. Although he did not know it, this was the day when Aung San had his first meeting with Slim who described him as "ambitious and [determined] to secure for himself a dominant position in postwar Burma, but I judged him to be a genuine patriot and a well-balanced realist.... The greatest impression he made on me was one of honesty... I had the idea that if he agreed to do something he would keep his word."[12]

Vernon's letter began by recognizing that Aung San's organizations were dangerous and had been involved in some bad incidents. But "there is no doubt that the AFO [the Anti-Fascist Organization, fore-runner of the AFPFL, formed in August 1944] is an organization that is not far from being nation-wide. It now includes many persons of standing and respectability. It has been of assistance... in re-establishing order and everyday life. In some areas it has stamped out... dacoity" (armed robbery).

"The help given by the BNA to our forces is not as great as the BNA asserts, but there is no doubt that it has been of definite... value and this force has been helped and urged on by us.

"Our declared intention has been at all times that we are returning to Burma to liberate the country. If our first action on return is to proscribe the AFO and the BNA, ... we shall, in my opinion, have to face the likelihood of a civil war...

"... after a period of years 'Dominion Status' will be granted to Burma; and ... the persons who will ... probably constitute the party that will then come into power will be the descendants of the organizations now under consideration. It would, in my opinion, be a grave error to throw them now, and irrevocably, into opposition.

"Finally I am convinced that Parliament would not support

such a policy. . . . [It] will not readily accept responsibility for a repetition of events in Greece.

"In any case we must face the plain fact of the matter, which is that we are not. . . able effectively to dissolve and disarm these organizations even if we were to decide that this was the proper course. . . . It would need military forces that I do not think could be made available at the present time. . ." Although the war in Europe had come to an end a few days earlier, the Japanese were still fighting, and were to launch their last big offensive across the Sittang River more than two months later. It collapsed a few days before the first atomic bomb was dropped on Hiroshima on 6 August, but they did not finally surrender to Mountbatten till 12 September.

Vernon went on to suggest things the AFO could be asked to do, like helping to get rice to people in Upper Burma who were desperately short of it.

He concluded by saying "This matter is so important. . . that I would urge with all the weight at my command that the Chief Civil Affairs Officer should establish himself. . . in Rangoon without delay. . . I submit that any decision taken as far away as Calcutta will not be based on the realities of the situation."[13]

Rance, the CCAO, wrote a week later to Air Marshall Sir Phillip Joubert, Mountbatten's Deputy Chief of Staff for Information and Civil Affairs, quoting Vernon's letter and accepting its main arguments. [14] Vernon's clearly reached Mountbatten who dealt with the matter more simply. On 16 June he called a meeting of all CAOs, told them to work constructively with the AFPFL, and said that anyone who failed to do so would be court-martialed. On his way out of the room he turned to Vernon, who was standing near the door, and said "You at least will be pleased with the results of this meeting". "In fact" Vernon wrote later, "I was far from pleased because I had respect, and a great deal of sympathy, for the views of senior and more experienced civil servants which I knew to be honestly held."[15]

Reflecting on this exchange later, Vernon wrote that Lindop's letter and his own dramatized the conflict between two schools of thought. One he described as "... the magisterial section, who liked the Burmese, but liked them in their place, which was, broadly speaking, that of children at school. For this section, it was self-evident, whatever might be the policy of H.M.G., that the Burmese could not govern themselves satisfactorily." They needed a "paternal regime". "There was, understandably, little real friendship between holders of these views and the Burmese.

"The more liberal section recognized the common humanity of the Burmese and was ready to treat them as equals; as mature human beings. Between holders of these views and the Burmese there could, and did, come into being close and valuable friendships.

"I probably fell between the magisterial and the liberal schools. Emotionally, I was unquestionably with the liberals, and am still proud to count Burmese among my most valued friends. But when it came to the practical business of administering the country I was not sure that the magisterialists were not right. Many...were... first class District Officers. On the other hand, politics is the art of the possible and it did not seem possible to me, in the circumstances of 1945, to hope to restore... magisterial relations."[16]

CONCLUSION

If this were a novel, it should come to an end about here. Vernon's letter, which may today seem a statement of the obvious, was written at a point when powerful people had yet to grasp that the world had changed. Churchill, who was still Prime Minister, had no intention of giving the Burmese their freedom, and was later to criticize Attlee from the Opposition front bench for doing so. The Governor of Burma must, I think, have known about Lindop's letter and probably approved it. The French, in Indo-China and Algeria, took many years longer to grasp, after much bloodshed, that the days of empire were over.

Vernon's challenge to the magisterialists owed as much to political realism as to liberal ideals. He was encouraged by the advice of younger men like Pat Rathbone, Jan Gillett and Leo Edgerley who spoke for the new world that was emerging. But his standpoint was rooted in many years experience, going back to his first posting to Kyonpyaw, where he had to fight the floods day and night, and learnt that race and colour have no bearing on the character and quality of a human being. It reflected the determination he had shown to help leading citizens in Yaunghwe rebuild their monarchy and its government without relying on foreign soldiers or policemen; the experience of assembling a multiracial orchestra in Rangoon and playing great music with them; and the warm friendships he and Ruth had forged with people of many races over many years. All that, in turn, goes back further still to the kinds of people the Singers and the Donnisons were.

While a novelist might draw these threads of the story together and tie them into a neat final bow, history and biography do not have neat endings. Vernon was deeply involved in Burma for two more years as the country staggered on towards a tragedy that is still unfolding. Families like the one whose story I have been telling still bear marks of their involvement in the imperial project.

I will try, in two more chapters, to find a fitting way of relinquishing the entwined threads of this story.

NOTES

1   Louis Allen, *The Longest War. 1941-45*, London, J.M.Dent ,1984;
page 386 et seq.

2   William Slim, *Defeat into Victory*, London, Cassell, 1956 and
Pan Books, 1999; eg. page 31.

3   Allen, 1984; page 388.

4   Slim, 1956; page 384.

5   Desmond Kelly writes about the gallant part his father played in
    the Chin Hills in *Kelly's Burma Campaign.*
    Letters from the Chin Hills, London, Tiddim Press, 2003.

6   My account comes from F.S.V.Donnison, *British Military
    Administration in the Far East, 1943-46,* London, H.M.S.O., 1956;
    Chapter 2.

7   Slim, 1956; page 36.

8   Donnison, 1956; page 34.

9   Desmond Kelly tells much of this story in *Kelly's Burma
    Campaign,* London, Tiddim Press, 2003.

10 Slim, 1956; page 485.

11 Hugh Tinker, (ed.) *The Struggle for Independence. 1944-1948,
    Documents from Official and Private Sources,* London, H.M.S.O.,
    1983; Vol .I, page 1002.

12 Slim , 1956; page 515.

13 Tinker, 1983; pages 252-256.

14 Tinker, 1983; pages 278-79.

15 Tinker, 1983; pages 1003-04.

16 Tinker, 1983; page 1003.

X

ENDINGS AND BEGINNINGS

Try though we may to fashion tidy endings for our stories, real life has a more ragged texture. Watersheds in history – points at which the whole world seems to change – occur at different times and have different meanings for different people. What is an ending for some is a beginning for others. How does an empire end? Through what struggles, what betrayals, what redefinitions of right and wrong does power change hands?

NEW WORLD EMERGING

Political leaders may come and go, but regimes – power structures – tend to survive for many years, no matter how incompetent or corrupt they may be. In peace time most people are too busy making a living, building a home and caring for their families to bother much about politics. Meanwhile the small political class are more interested in the power game than in changing the power structure itself. But in the aftermath of war every regime – and particularly those that failed to protect their people from invasion and air attack – is exposed to critical questions. Citizens, who may have had to fend for themselves in desperate times, have lost the habit of obedience.

Atomic bombs were dropped on Hiroshima and Nagasaki on 6 August and 9 August, 1945, and five days later the Japanese Emperor overruled his generals to insist on surrender. Two days after that, Burmese political leaders called a two-day conference on their country's future. Power was up for grabs.

The Japanese had sent more than 300,000 soldiers to Burma, and three-fifths of them — 185,000 men — were dead. The survivors were going home to a country in ruins.[2] All across South East Asia power, for the moment, rested with Mountbatten, the Supreme Commander there, with a million men under his orders. Sir Reginald Dorman-Smith, the Governor of Burma, still in Simla, had recently sent a weighty report on the future of Burma to London. It expressed the views of his officials in calling for massive expenditure to rebuild the country, and in assuming that British rule would continue for at least five more years — perhaps seven — before the Burmese took over. They, it was assumed, would then choose to remain within the Commonwealth. Dorman-Smith had been a farmer; a Conservative member of the Ulster protestant ascendancy, and Minister of Agriculture until Churchill sent him out to govern Burma in 1941. He shared the convictions of his leader who had said "My ideal is narrow and limited. I want to see the British Empire preserved for a few more generations in its strength and splendour..."[3]

Confronting this formidable empire stood Aung San, aged thirty, leader of the Burma National Army which had changed sides to fight alongside the British only five months earlier. Before going to train with the Japanese to fight on their side he had been a student, active in a group of young, educated, radical Burmans who had formed the Thakin (or "Master") Party shortly before the war. In 1937 they had done very badly in Burma's only general election, winning only 3 out of 132 seats in the Parliament. When the war began they were proscribed owing to their hostility to the Allied cause. There had been no public protests. Now he had, at most, 7,000 men rather precariously under his command — men whom Dorman-Smith wanted to disband as soon as possible; men who would melt away or take to banditry if they were not paid. They were the armed wing of the Anti-Fascist People's Freedom League, a fragile assembly of nationalist groups put together a few months earlier.

That must have seemed a puny power base from which to confront the imperialists, many of whom believed the AFPFL would follow the usual Burmese pattern and fall apart pretty soon. But Aung San was a dedicated patriot and a shrewd politician, determined to hold his quarrelsome colleagues together, and to prevent the British from recreating the habits of obedience they depended on. Although moody, a poor speaker and subject to ill-controlled bouts of anger, he lived a spartan life and was untouched by graft. He met Slim in May and Mountbatten in June, and convinced both these experienced appraisers of men that he was to be treated seriously.[4]

Meanwhile, fundamental shifts in the foundations of power were taking place which the British authorities had not yet fully understood. The Japanese might be humiliated by defeat, but right across South-East Asia they had destroyed for ever the authority of Western Empires – French, Dutch and Portuguese as well as British. In Indonesia they handed over their arms to the rebel leader, Soekarno, to ensure the Dutch would have no easy return to power. In Burma they had not only demonstrated that the British could not defend the country; they had trained and armed, for the first time in sixty years, an Army of Burmans. It was still in being. Although it turned against the Japanese late in the day, this Army (Vernon recorded in a volume of official history) had then "fought courageously…and suffered severe casualties in full scale operations"[5]. They got to Rangoon two days ahead of the British forces. Meanwhile the British, working through Force 136 of their Special Operations Executive, had been sending them arms and radio sets, and promising to liberate their country. These changes in the political climate could not be reversed.

Equally profound changes were going on among the British. In July 1945 they had elected the first Labour Government to win an absolute majority – a massive one that owed a great deal to voters in the armed forces. (Vernon was one of those who voted Labour – probably for the only time in his life. "We must not go back to the unemployment of the 'thirties" was his explanation to his son David.) Attlee's new Government was committed to giving India and Burma independence. Their first priorities were not imperial but to maintain full employment in Britain and create there the kind of welfare state that had been called for in the Beveridge Report.

Meanwhile the soldiers were yearning to get home. It was for good reason that Louis Allen called his book '*Burma. The Longest War*'. Slim – always sensitive to the morale of his men – says that, by the end of it, many of them "had served continuously for four or five years in the East, most of them in the often heart-breaking conditions of the Burma front" … suffering "the soldier's dumb pain of separation". "When I asked a man sitting in his foxhole or beside the track what he was, he would often, instead of answering 'I am a Lancashire Fusilier'… or 'the Bren Gunner of this section', say 'I am a four and two' or 'Three and ten'. He meant that was the number of years and months he had served in the East, and the unspoken question in his eyes was 'How many more?' I could not answer him." Those "who had served longest were our key men. If we sent them home without replacement, neither our British nor our Indian formations could continue to fight efficiently." Their commanders, from Mountbatten downwards, appealed in vain for replacements. As troop ships were assembled, the men began going home. None of them had ever refused to fight, but Slim makes it clear that he could not rely on their loyalty for much longer.[6]

The reluctance of the Westminster Government to send soldiers – and later many other resources required to rebuild an empire – was not due just to negligence. The overseas investments that Britain had long relied on to remain solvent had been disposed of to pay for the war. Lend-Lease, the American programme of aid that had kept Britain in the war, was cancelled one week after the Japanese surrender. The Americans were not going to help the British rebuild their empire. It would be two more years before aid under the Marshall Plan brought help to the countries of Western Europe. The men coming home to

Britain would need jobs, and soon their growing families would need health services and schools. Above all, they needed homes. With 200,000 of them destroyed in the blitz, another 250,000 so badly damaged they could not be lived in, the building of houses had to be a top priority.[7] Britain might look like a victorious imperial power, but she was exhausted, broke and struggling to survive.

CIVIL GOVERNMENT

This brief sketch owes a great deal to hindsight. The situation was not so clear at the time to people who were dealing as best they could, day by day, with a chaotic world. Vernon, as the fighting ceased, was sent back from Rangoon to Meiktila where he became a "territorial", no longer a "formation", Civil Affairs Officer. That is to say, he was looking after an area, no longer moving forward with an advancing army. It was a very large area, for he was coordinating four Commissioners (as they would have been called in peacetime) and linking them to the military commander responsible for the whole of Upper Burma. He described his new job as being "like the lethargic plains after the keen, rarified air of the hills." Messervy, his Commander in Fourth Corps, had been a "redoubtable fighter" and Cobb, the brigadier on his staff with whom Vernon had worked most closely, was a classical scholar at Winchester and "had a brain like quicksilver". Major-General Snelling, his new Commander, was "known throughout the Fourteenth Army as 'Grocer Snelling' — a nickname honoroubly gained by his feat of keeping the Army fed and supplied by air from India and Arakan throughout its advance down the length of Burma. A line of communications headquarters has to be concerned mainly with grocery and hardware, and Snelling was pleasant enough to me; but I can recall nothing about him or any of his staff officers." Vernon's predecessor in this job had been the redoubtable Denis Phelips, so warmly appreciated by Slim, but now showing signs of the stress he had undergone in recent years. He was "living it up and beating it up so riotously that if you wanted to talk business with him you had to do it before 6 pm. I could not see how he could last."

Vernon, who drank little and felt he needed to keep in touch with the more sedate senior staff officers in A Mess, feared he must be regarded by some of his colleagues as "putting on airs". He got around the country as much as he could, making contact with people he had known before the Japanese invasion. There was a massive amount of work to do, getting essential supplies flowing again and rebuilding an administration, often with inexperienced staff.

Burma was devastated and Burmese leaders were in confusion. A correspondent writing to the Foreign News Editor of The Times described the situation. "Rangoon is in a shocking mess still and dacoity (banditry) is rife up-country, the dacoit leaders often being ex-members of Aung San's Burmese Forces. The whole country presents a great contrast with Malaya where things are much more normal and peaceful. The political Parties are splitting up, the Communist Party into two groups with a third group calling itself the Burma Socialist Party.... those of the Left under Aung San, and those of the Right, under U Saw... Prospects for the rice crop are not good."[8]

After months of argument with Mountbatten, who was reluctant to let the civilians return, Dorman-Smith got back to Rangoon in October, 1945, and civil government was re-established. Vernon took off his uniform and awaited a posting, with a wild hope that he might be sent up-country to Taunggyi and his beloved Shan States. But he was made Commissioner of the Pegu Division — the most demanding in Burma, which included Rangoon and all the political hot spots in and around the capital. His offices were in Rangoon because he had to keep in touch with events there and talk frequently with the Governor. He took with him Robert Lucas, who had succeeded Pat Rathbone as his Assistant: a loyal and effective young man who had become a valued friend, sharing his interest in music. It was to be another friendship that lasted for the rest of their lives.

Seeking somewhere to live in Rangoon, they were immediately confronted by the new realities. Finding that an attractive
house that he and Ruth had once lived in was empty, Vernon took
possession of it and, with his own hands, got down to cleaning the
lavatories which were in a filthy state. But all accommodation was
allocated by the military authorities and when he went to seek
permission to move in he was told, with some embarrassment,
that this house had been reserved for Aung San and the high command of the Burma National Army. Although he was convinced
that they were unlikely to use so European a house, far from markets and the homes of the Burmese community, there was
nothing for it but to seek shelter in an officers' mess. (He could not
have foreseen that the future head of the civil service had been
cleaning the lavatory of the future prime minister. But I think he
would have appreciated the joke.)

Ruth had returned with Annis to England in March 1944.
They had a few days with David before he joined the Navy. After
launching Annis into secondary education at Benenden School,
Ruth made a study of probation services, remand homes,
approved schools and juvenile courts in England, and wrote a
report laying out plans for the juvenile justice system to be set up
in Burma. Encounters with her mother and her mother-in-law
were as unrelaxed an experience as they had always been. Having
found another set of foster parents to leave Annis with, she eventually returned with her report on a troopship bound for Calcutta,
arriving there in November 1945. Apart from a short home leave
Vernon had been given before heading back into Burma with the
Army, they had been apart for seventeen months – the longest
separation they had ever endured. When she returned to Calcutta,
Vernon got ten days leave to see her – rather guiltily putting his
Brigadier's uniform on again to get a flight there and back – and
they had a blissful week of walking in the mountains around
Darjeeling. She rejoined him next month, coming in another
troop ship to Rangoon.

Among the people whom Vernon and Ruth rediscovered at

this time were Renee Vachet-Beeston, their French dentist, and his wife. When on leave in Britain they had always relied on a London dentist — a formidable figure who became President of his professional association. (I remember him only too well: swift, effective — and painful.) He would usually start by pulling out and replacing any dental work placed in Donnison mouths since the patient's last visit — probably years ago. The only work he respected and left in place was done by their man in Burma. Vachet-Beeston (so far as their well-connected London dentist could discover) had never qualified anywhere. Vernon and Ruth guessed that he had become a dental assistant while serving in the French Army and had learned his skills at the chair side. They were glad to find him safe in Burma, but distressed to learn that his wife had been paralysed by a stroke. Ruth asked to see her and, sitting by her bedside, found that she could communicate by blinking an eyelid. Holding a card on which the alphabet had been laid out, Ruth moved her finger from letter to letter, watching for the blink with which she gradually spelled out her message. To her horror Ruth found that the sentence taking shape before her said "My husband is poisoning me... killing me..." She departed, unsure whether this was a paranoid fantasy or the cold truth. The lady died soon after. (Perhaps Renee believed it kinder to bring her life to a close, rather than see her languish helplessly in this ruined country?)

Before long, David was able to get to Rangoon for a few days from a naval base in Ceylon. His naval career had been a constantly frustrated pursuit: first of action. He had been in a training barracks when the D Day landings took place. Then he wanted to get into submarines; an ambition encouraged by the only shots he saw fired in anger — against one of our own submarines which was depth-charged to the surface and then narrowly survived some rather wild shell-fire. To show there was no ill-feeling, her captain invited David and two other midshipmen to join his crew on a brief exercise. But the best he could do in Europe was to be in the first ships to get to Oslo, and the second group to get to

Copenhagen – where they received a great reception and the girls were marvelous, but the war in the West was over. So he strove to join the Pacific Fleet, got as far as Australia – and then the atom bombs fell. His main achievement in a dusty barracks on the edge of Sydney was to spend a blazing hot week-end going through all the records to find out how many men they had in the camp. Three figures emerged: the smallest being the number allocated to working parties, while a larger number held the cards which entitled men to a few hours "shore leave" down town, and twice as many were getting a daily rum ration – much of it being sold by enterprising petty officers to Australian civilians.

Finally, still searching for something useful he could do, he began running discussion groups on "current affairs" for sailors, with hopes of becoming an education officer. Their favourite topics, he found, were "politics" followed by "religion". But, as the war petered out, every opportunity was closing down. Which is perhaps why he survived. Had he been born a year or two earlier he would have served in the Battle of the Atlantic – alongside Ray Hale, a friend of his who had been sunk five times, twice surviving days and weeks in open boats, throwing shipmates over the side as they died (and, at the end of the war, still being unable to swim).

One hot night in a cruiser, steaming through the Indian Ocean, news came over the radio that Labour had won the 1945 election – massively. Although, at nineteen, David had been too young to vote, this was a transforming moment for him. The good guys had won at last. There was hope for the future. He must get home to help them.

David ended up in another naval barracks in Ceylon. From there, and later from Singapore, he managed to hitch lifts to Rangoon – first on a tug, crossing the Bay of Bengal soon after the city was liberated, and later on aeroplanes flying to Rangoon via Bangkok. A day or two in Siam (now Thailand) was a revealing experience: a country which had not been part of a European empire seemed busier, cleaner and better organized than those

Able Seaman David

that had been. He returned to Singapore in a Dakota, one of whose twin engines failed. As the 'plane dropped lower and lower, he and another young man crouched beside an open door throwing cargo into the void till the 'plane just made it across jungle tree tops to the airfield at Penang. But he had managed to see his parents for two long week-ends, which was why he had joined the Navy in the first place. And the Navy taught him a lot – about ships and about people. His diary is littered with drawings of ships and their gear. As for men: the same sailors who were so hard-faced in transit camps, giving no help to anyone and stealing the hair brush your mother sent you to war with, were also rock-solid comrades on small ships. In the right conditions, human nature is perfectible – which was the basic argument for socialism.

In Ceylon David made friends with the Kularatnes, a Singhalese family whose sons – bright boys about his own age – had taken jobs as labourers on the Colombo waterfront to mobilise dockers to join the movement for independence. Rather tactlessly, he spoke admiringly of them on his visit to Rangoon, until his mother's sharp response reminded him that his parents were the kind of people his friends were mobilising against. On his second visit, in the summer of 1946, his father was clearly under strain, but never said anything about his work. He talked instead about his hopes of going home, and sailing with David some day on the Norfolk Broads

Vernon and Ruth had found a house in Rangoon and invited two good friends to share it. They had even managed to acquire a baby grand from an Army mess which had lost its pianist and wanted to replace their piano with a cocktail cabinet. Since Vernon and Ruth had given their own to an Air Force mess when they left Rangoon four years earlier, this seemed a fair exchange. There was music again in the evenings – Vernon still playing his flute.

Solomon, the great concert pianist, came to Rangoon on a tour organized by ENSA, and because the Donnisons were the only

120

in one of the two
steam drains from
the nozzle box through
which steam enters
the HP turbine.
It was
repaired by
making a hole.
and screwing in
a plug.

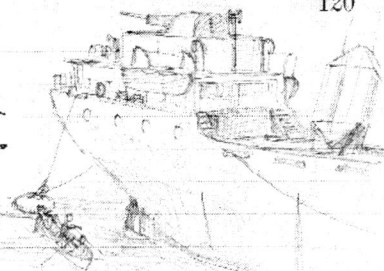

OLD. FASHIONED
COUNTER STERN.

27.8.45.

We got the gunroom paintwork
scrubbed down this forenoon; it makes a great
difference. At stand-easy – between radar
lectures – the Strathnaver passed us, eastbound
She is 22,300 gross tonnage; 27,600 displacement
Twin screw, turbo-electric. 23 knots. They were
supposed to carry 1170 passengers in peace
but as troopers hold 7,000 or so.

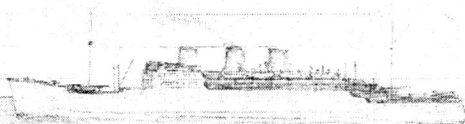

SS. STRATHNAVER. RED SEA 27.8.45.

28.8.45:

We reached Tewfik at 0600 but

~~Thursday dawn~~

There is the dawn. It does not come perceptibly. You are suddenly aware of a change: a slight greying of the shadows.

Why does everything look so different at night? A street at night is just the same, in fact, as it is in daylight, but there is an indescribable air of mystery and excitement about it. It is not only in the darkness or the silence or the solitude. I can't describe it

people known to Government House as being interested in music Dorman-Smith asked them to look after him. Vernon recalled "someone of great modesty, sensitivity, friendliness and charm. Government House may not have heard of him but a lot of the troops had. The hall was packed for two concerts, and he said to us afterwards that, notwithstanding the awful piano he had to use, he had never enjoyed playing so much as on this journey. 'No-one is here because he ought to be, or because it's fashionable. Only those come who are thirsting to hear the music.'"

Like many other Europeans, Vernon and Ruth were burgled. "Burma had for years been deprived of crockery, cutlery, cooking utensils and, above all, clothes. If you put up curtains they were likely to be stolen to make longyis and eingyis" – skirts and shirts. David found on his visit that everyone slept with a revolver under the pillow. A dead man was found one morning in the road outside – a marauder shot by the police or the Army.

Even the elements were threatening. One night, Vernon and Ruth "were awakened by the roar of a tremendous wind. Our big mosquito net was whisked from us and streamed out horizontally. The rain began and soon it was pouring through holes blown in the roof. There was no electric light, and all we could do was to find the driest part of our beds and shelter under raincoats till dawn. Our room seemed lighter than usual as day returned, and soon we could see why. Nine full-grown trees around the house had been blown flat. When we went out we found a heavy metal shoe scraper that rested by the front door had been carried right round to the other side of the house. Mercifully, no trees had fallen on our servants' quarters: they would have been smashed to matchwood. One other house in the street had been slightly touched, but the rest were completely undamaged. We saw the looks of incredulous amazement on the faces of the servants next door as they came out into the dawn." It was the Donnisons' private cyclone. Government House offered them a refuge, but they managed to find another house large enough to shelter themselves, their servants and the two friends staying with them.

Hugh Wilkie was Chief Secretary, in charge of the Home Department and head of the whole civil service. He was a sick man and due to retire soon. It became clear that either Denis Phelips or Vernon would have to take over his job. "I hoped that it would not be me" Vernon recalled, "for the post was clearly going to become a very hot seat, and I doubted whether I had the qualities for it. I felt that Denis had a better brain and more personality than me. But, as far as we could tell, he was busily drinking himself to death as Commissioner for Mandalay. The choice fell upon me, and when I went to take over from Wilkie his first words were, 'Thank God it's to be you'." That was in February 1946.

Vernon was 47. This was to be his last and most testing job in Burma. Since elections had yet to be held, he worked not to a Minister but to the Home Member of the Governor's Executive Council: Sir Paw Tun, one of the two Burmese Ministers who had chosen in 1942 to escape with Dorman-Smith to India. Vernon was responsible for law and order, the recovery of arms, the police, the magistracy and much else. He had to give leadership to all Departments, and had direct access to the Governor on subjects which were reserved to him. But this familiar power structure soon began to crumble.

MURDEROUS TIMES

Burma was full of fresh and terrible memories of the things done by all sides during the invasion, occupation and reconquest of the country. During the Japanese assault, Aung San and his men had tortured and killed Burmese officials who tried to remain loyal to the British. One of these was Abdu Raschid, a village headman, who was locked up for days without food or water and then taken to the public square in a cart with a pig in it – a calculated humiliation, for he was a Muslim. There he was subjected to a brief show trial, crucified, and finally bayoneted to death by Aung San himself. There was no denying what had happened. Witnesses to the event were calling for prosecution of Aung San who eventually wrote an article for the Hanthawaddy newspaper of April 7th, 1946, in which he argued that his action had been necessary at the time. Next day the headman's widow sent a petition to the Governor, asking that he be tried for murder.[9]

This case posed in the sharpest way all the most difficult questions about the role of the British in Burma. They needed to find people all over the country who would run the public services which had long been manned largely by local recruits. They were reviewing the cases of officials and police officers who had stayed in the country through the occupation to see if they had gone beyond the normal requirements of their duties to help the Japanese. If so, they would not be reappointed, and might be prosecuted. But those who had stayed in Burma felt they had suffered worse things than their colleagues who had escaped to India – and the vetting process seemed to be taking a painfully long time. Meanwhile nationalists, who had actually taken up arms against the British and committed atrocities against loyal officials, were gaining power and recognition. By Mountbatten's order, their Army's flag had been flown alongside the Union Jack at the victory parade through Rangoon. In one of his reports from the Pegu Division, before he became Chief Secretary, Vernon had said "the lower-paid Government servants are terrified of the forces of disorder and unable to live on the pay they are given. All Government servants are apprehensive of the future. ...The economic disability can and should be removed at once. The others are more difficult to cure. I am continually surprised by the loyal service that is still being given by many people in these circumstances."[10]

Efforts were being made to prohibit public drilling by private armies – Aung San's was not the only one. The Government tried to persuade him to merge his forces with theirs but he had insisted they would only come in as whole units. These, the Government knew, would continue to respond to his orders. Finally he conceded a merger on an individual basis, but withheld 3,500 of his most loyal men who were to work on "welfare" duties. Before long they were drilling with weapons and became, in effect, the private army of his political movement, the AFPFL.[11]

Aung San had his difficulties too. He was trying to hold his coalition of competing nationalist groups together. The Communists had already been instructed by Moscow that all Governments in the liberated territories were to be opposed — even those led by local nationalists — and they too had their private armies, intent on creating chaos if they could not win power. Aung San was also trying to persuade the minority groups and hill tribes to join with Burmans in an independent Burma. They had always been more loyal than the Burmans to the British, more likely to become Christians and to join the Army, and they had been much more effective in fighting the Japanese — killing 12,500 of them in the course of the campaign. Thus far, British plans for Burma always stipulated that these people should remain under British rule unless they chose to join an independent Burma; but Aung San was not prepared to leave the British in control of some 43 per cent of his country's territory and 15 per cent of its people.

In May 1946 the police were ordered to prevent an armed demonstration at Tantabin by Aung San's men who were plainly flouting the prohibition against drilling. There was firing between the groups; four demonstrators were killed, five injured and many arrested. During the uproar that followed, Vernon wrote a minute to the Governor in which he said "I agreed reluctantly to the release of all persons concerned... provided that this did <u>not</u> mean that they should not be sent for trial after investigations, if these showed ground for doing so..." "...it cannot possibly be argued that the orders of the Commissioner of Police or the Deputy Commissioner... were not legal". Indeed, he pointed out, the Governor himself had instructed them to take firm action. If officers were let down in so clear-cut a case, "it is my considered opinion that we shall not in future be able to rely upon the magistracy and police doing their duty". Most important, perhaps, was his conclusion that "what we need to do... is <u>not</u> to stop

making arrests <u>but</u> to get our revised order for the whole of
Burma as quickly as possible."[12] There would be people determined to make the country ungovernable as long as the future
power structure remained uncertain.

An Inquiry followed, and meetings between Dorman-Smith,
Vernon and Aung San. Reporting to Lord Pethick Lawrence, the
Secretary of State for India and Burma, the Governor described
their fruitless attempts to find a compromise that Aung San would
accept. "Aung San's pet argument is that he does not wish 1942 to
be experienced over again. Then, the inability of villagers to
defend themselves made it possible for the Japanese to operate all
too freely." His argument was hard to refute, even if the Governor
knew that its main purpose was to enable him to hang on to "his
own private army"[15] The British response to these events was
complicated by the need to look over their shoulders to the
Indians, now negotiating for independence and unwilling to allow
their soldiers to be used to suppress nationalists in other countries.

The strain was telling on Dorman-Smith who suffered from
amoebic dysentery during these months. His telegrams became
longer, more frequent, more incoherent, and went increasingly
over the head of Pethick Lawrence to Attlee himself, urging
sometimes the prosecution of Aung San for murder, sometimes
that he be given power; sometimes tougher action against the
paramilitaries, sometimes conciliation. He was looking always for
allies against the AFPFL among the old guard of Burmese politicians, younger moderates, the ethnic minorities – anyone but the
Communists. Vernon had never liked him, describing with distaste "his politician's toothy smile, his readiness to slap your back,
and his cleverness of a bright but immature undergraduate. I did
not feel that I could trust him." But trying, as ever, to see both
sides of the question, he added that Dorman-Smith was of course
quite right: Aung San had either to be tried for murder or made
Prime Minister. "Nothing in between was any good."

Attlee could stand this no longer. On 7 May, 1946, he wrote to
Pethick Lawrence in characteristically pithy sentences: "I have

received another long and incoherent telegram from Dorman-Smith. It is obvious that he has lost his grip. He changes his position from day to day and has no clear policy. I am convinced he must be replaced. ...Subject to your views I propose to recall him for consultation at once."[14]

George Appleton, one of Vernon's friends who was public spokesman for the Governor at this time, gave a kinder glimpse of Dorman-Smith on one of the last tours he made of Burma before he was recalled. Their boat got stuck on a sandbank so he went ashore to chat with local farmers. "He was at his best, and became a farmer once more. The headman too was bright and intelligent, and they had a cheery conversation, with me as interpreter. ... back on the boat he talked about the soil as the common link between people of all nations, and spoke almost lovingly of husbandry and caring for the soil, almost as if it were a human being."[15] But Appleton also said that when Dorman-Smith had summoned him, a few weeks earlier, to ask him to prepare a public announcement that Aung San would be prosecuted for murder, he was "deeply disturbed" and after "a troubled night" went to see "H.E." (His Excellency) to say "it would be a disastrous step and if it was decided to take it I must resign on the spot and announce in public my reasons for doing so".[16] Vernon, in a long memo to Dorman-Smith dated 30 March , had already said "Whether we like it or not, the prosecution of Aung San for murder is off. ...I am personally inclined to the view that it is better so."[17] The Governor eventually backed off.

While high-level discussion continued about Dorman-Smith's successor, an Acting-Governor was brought in: Sir Henry Knight, an experienced I.C.S. official from India. He began by visiting Government offices, talking with clerks and messengers, and seeing for himself the appalling conditions in which they were working – in dirty and decayed buildings with leaking roofs, no lights and no glass left in the windows. Vernon described him as "a diminutive figure – but with the heart of a lion. He had ability, shrewdness, common-sense, a twinkling sense of humour and

great courage." Knight said that Burma needed "more administration and less politics". As for the Aung San murder charge, he
used the power he held — before elections had created a parliament — to proclaim that crimes committed during the years
between the Japanese invasion and defeat could not be prosecuted
without the Governor's permission. Aung San and the widow of
the murdered headman were promptly informed that no further
action would be taken on his case. (Problem solved — in magisterial fashion!) For the brief spell of his time in Burma everything
quietened down — largely, Vernon recognized, "because everyone
knew that he was not the permanent Governor and therefore it
would be foolish to waste ammunition on him."

It was unusual for H.E. to dine outside Government House, so
the Donnisons felt honoured when Sir Henry came one evening to
have dinner with them. Their cat, who was accustomed to bringing a dead rat into the house to display to diners on such evenings,
brought two for Sir Henry. "We felt that tribute was being paid to
a great man".

Sir Hubert Rance, the next Governor, was a soldier whom
Mountbatten had pressed for. He took over at the end of August
1946. With no previous experience of Burma, scant respect for the
I.C.S., and bringing no imperial "baggage" with him, he was
determined to get the British out of the country with as little
bloodshed as possible. A police strike began a few days after he
arrived. Later, other strikes brought more public services to a halt.
Aung San had cut his political teeth by organising a strike of students at Rangoon University which ultimately compelled the
Rector to resign. Now his men took to the streets of Rangoon,
directing traffic at the main crossroads as the police withdrew.
They placed appeals in the newspapers "To All Bad Hats" — to
desist from robbery and other crimes during the strike. "The lull
in crime was unnerving but merciful" commented Vernon.[18]

Rance forced the resignation of the nominated Executive
Council that advised him, and on 28 September appointed a new
one which became effectively a national government, with Aung

San as its leader and his men holding all the posts they asked for. A week later the police strike was settled.

Reflecting later on the strike and its aftermath, Vernon wrote "… it was a defeat which marked the effective passing of power from British to Burmese, though the formal transfer did not take place for another 15 months." The Governor could no longer "disregard the advice of his Council on any matter which the Council decides to make an issue" for he "has no alternative Council to fall back upon…."[19] The police, the civil service and everyone else knew their loyalty now lay to the AFPFL. Senior officials transferred their most sensitive papers – like those dealing with the prosecution of Aung San for murder – to Government House. But for most purposes they were now accountable to Burmese "Councillors" – effectively Ministers – who were Aung San's men. Difficult though life was in the central Secretariat, it was much harder for Burmese officials out in the districts who were constantly hassled and threatened by local nationalists who were more brutal than their leaders in Rangoon.

Vernon recognized the difficulties this situation created for imperial officials, of whatever ethnic origin, who had been accustomed to serve the Crown. In a letter to the India Office he said "I consider … that the time has come for the winding-up of these Services with all possible speed… The administration will never function smoothly until these Services have been eliminated. They are… an obstacle to the running of the country by the Executive Council or its successor in the way it wishes to govern. Whether we like this or not is now immaterial."[20]

These tensions were not confined to Burma. In London, at the end of September, 1946, the Chiefs of Staff Committee had considered a paper from Lord Montgomery who said they needed "a reserve ready to be committed should the situation in India, Burma, Malaya or Palestine seriously deteriorate". Otherwise, they "were approaching the position when we would no longer be able to meet our commitments".[21]

In November 1946, Rance was telling the Secretary of State:

"There is a new spirit of nationalism abroad – tempered and restrained, but quite unyielding. His Majesty's Government must either make terms with it quickly, or prepare without delay to hold the country by military force."[22] He was establishing more productive relations with Aung San, but the Communists were constantly raising the stakes, demanding faster progress towards independence, and, next month, collaborating in a small revolt staged by 300 armed dacoits.

By December, the General in charge of Burma Command was telling the War Office that he could not call on his Indian or Ghurka troops "for political reasons" and he urgently needed two British Brigades, together with a large administrative "tail" of drivers, mechanics and others. "Consider imperative" he concluded, "that political action be directed towards maintaining peaceful situation or we may be in serious military position".[23]

Keeping the peace was what Rance was trying to do, but an imperial machine, spread all around the world, moves at a lumbering pace as the realities of its situation seep at varying pace through the minds of all concerned. Churchill, now Leader of the Opposition, was still making speeches in Parliament deploring the way in which Burma was being handed over to "Quislings" after the loss of so many British lives in the campaign to recapture the country. Pethick Lawrence, the Secretary of State, and his Cabinet colleagues were more generous towards nationalist aspirations, but reluctant to move as fast as Rance was urging. Rance, in letters to Pethick Lawrence in November and December, 1946, said that Aung San's Socialist Party controlled much of the police and public services, and they would all disintegrate if the Party resigned from Government. There would then be bloodshed. "Every endeavour must be made to keep the AFPFL in office as there is no other practical alternative Government."[24] Yet in November the Burma Office sent out 20 young British recruits to join the civil service in Rangoon. All were sent home a few months later.[25]

One of Vernon's friends, Nick Larmour, a talented Irishman

(later a diplomat and "Sir Nicholas") had similar experiences. He had originally been flown out from Calcutta to join the civil service in Burma in the summer of 1942. Arriving at Myitkyina, by then the only airport still held by the British, he was greeted, to his surprise, by the Governor and his staff who invited him to have supper with their party. Next morning they had all disappeared to India on the same aeroplane, leaving young Nick to walk out through the Hukawng Valley – a 200-mile route on which thousands died. He made it – 30 pounds lighter – and returned to Rangoon at the end of the war, after a spell in the Civil Affairs Service, to work as an assistant to Vernon. When Nancy, his young wife, came to join him, Ruth swept her up and told her she must get into teaching in a local school or helping in a children's home – the kinds of things she had herself done before the war. She was busy preparing her own plans for child care, probation services and juvenile courts. Nancy and Nick found all this heartwarming but rather awful, for they knew that Burma was not going to be like that any more. Nancy loyally signed up to work in a school, but soon had to abandon this because it became unsafe for Europeans to go down town.[26]

At a meeting of the Supreme Council of the AFPFL, held at the beginning of November, the Communists were finally expelled from the League. Demands were formulated for elections to be held in the following April and full independence to be conceded a year later. Soon negotiations for a meeting with Attlee began. He announced in Parliament on 20 December that there would be talks with Burmese leaders, and Aung San set off with his team for their first visit to London in mid-January 1947. The British had accepted that they had to concede independence, and to back Aung San because he was the one man who might be capable of holding the country together. They hoped he would keep open the possibility of Burma joining the Commonwealth, and eventually reach some agreement with the ethnic minorities that would protect their interests. Meanwhile, his men had each been assigned British officials whom they would kill if their leaders returned empty handed from London. Vernon and Ruth, Nick and Nancy Larmour, and many of Vernon's friends were on the list.

It was an anxious time for Vernon. The Larmours were of a younger generation. Irish by origin, they had a different attitude to empire; and, as Labour supporters, they were confident that Attlee would make the right decision. They noted that Vernon had an increasing tendency to sweep his hand around the back of his neck, which they had come to recognize as a sign of stress.

Recalling these weeks, Vernon later wrote: "The C.I.D. warned that the AFPFL were planning outbreaks of violence in the event of their delegation's demands being refused, and that these outbreaks were likely to include attacks upon Europeans. We overhauled our plans. In extremity Europeans were to concentrate in Government House and its compound which would be held with such police, military police and Burma Army forces as remained loyal. All European males were to be armed and the defence of this stronghold would if necessary be undertaken by them. I began to feel that I could take no more, and that all I wanted was to get out of Burma with Ruth and myself alive. I suppose I was tired. I am not proud of my conduct at this time, but I felt that my nerve was going." The Donnisons left Burma shortly before Aung San's delegation set off to London where Attlee reached an agreement with them that enabled them to return to Burma in triumph at the end of January 1947.

POWER TRANSFERRED

The AFPFL ratified the London agreement on 4 February, and gained a great victory in the April election for a constitution-making Assembly. Henceforth they had an interest in restoring public order, but other groups were still intent on disrupting government, or simply on brigandage. Ian Wallace, Vernon's successor as Chief Secretary, stepped aside to make way for a Burman and became Commissioner for Pegu. There he realized that his

District Officers were receiving instructions direct from Rangoon that he knew nothing about. "...I found it frustrating and embarrassing" he recalled, "and was glad to leave Burma..."[27]

The main problem the British had failed to resolve — and it is still unresolved today — was the status and future of Burma's minority groups. Aung San was growing into statesmanship, and seemed genuinely determined to find a solution that they could accept. Saw Shwe Thaik, the Shan whom Vernon had chosen to recommend as the new Sawbwa of Yaunghwe back in 1928, was made Burma's first President. For a while, some progress was made towards restoring order. Sir Gilbert Laithwaite, Deputy Under-Secretary of State for Burma, and a former I.C.S. official, was sent out by the Cabinet to meet politicians and officials and write a report on the whole situation. He said he "had been struck by the difference between the attitude of the European element in the Civil Service and that of the same element in India. They seemed all to take the view that AFPFL's demands would have to be met, and this not for defeatist reasons. ... The Executive Council [they said] was an effective, austere and hard-working body... not corrupt...[and] well spoken of by the civil service."[28]

But there had long been rumours of armed uprisings and assassination plots against the Government. In June, a large consignment of Bren light machine guns and Sten sub-machine guns was to be handed over to the Police from Fourteenth Army stores to equip them to deal with these threats. The uniformed Burmans who came with all the proper documentation to collect this armoury disappeared without trace. The weapons had been hijacked.

They were used on 19 July, 1947, when Aung San and seven of his Cabinet Ministers were murdered by a group working for U Saw, leader of the principal opposition Party. Nick Larmour, who had been asked to stay on by the Burmese, was working in a neighbouring room as gunfire broke out. Later that day the Governor spoke on the radio together with U Nu, one of Aung San's old friends and the most senior of the surviving Ministers, with whom Rance had already built a firm working relationship. U Nu took over leadership of the Government.

The Burma Independence Act passed through the British Parliament in November, despite the opposition of the Conservative Party, and Burma became an independent Republic, outside the Commonwealth, on 4 January, 1948. Soon after, the opposition parties and the ethnic minorities joined forces in open rebellion against U Nu's Government.

Before leaving, Vernon and Ruth borrowed an Army staff car that was to be handed over to a Deputy Commissioner up-country and delivered it to him after a tour that took them round many of the places they had known best. "I know we felt this was a wonderful farewell journey" wrote Vernon, "but I can scarcely remember a thing about it. I was too exhausted. Since then, life has been happy and far from dull. But it no longer has the quality of our Burma life – of being something that has ended, that cannot come again, and cannot be experienced by those now growing to maturity."

NOTES

1   Hugh Tinker (ed.) *The Struggle for Independence. 1944-1948.* Documents from Official and Private Sources, London, H.M.S.O. (two volumes) 1983.

2   Louis Allen, Burma. *The Longest War, 1941-1945;* London, J.M.Dent and Sons, 1984; page 640.

3   Quoted in Allen, 1984; page 632.

4   Aung San Suu Kyi, *Freedom from Fear and Other Writings,* Harmondsworth, Penguin Books, 1992; page 37.

5   F.S.V.Donnison, *British Military Administration in the Far East, 1943-46,* London, H.M.S.O., 1956; page 354.

6   William Slim, *Defeat into Victory*, London, Pan Books, 1999; pages 520 et seq.

7   D.V.Donnison, *The Government of Housing*, Harmondsworth, Penguin Books, 1967; page 163.

8   Tinker, 1983, Vol.I; page 761-62.

9   Tinker, 1983, Vol.I; pages 725-28.

10   Tinker, 1983, Vol.I; pages 1003-04.

11   The whole story of Britain's negotiations with nationalist movements in Burma is well told by F.S.V.Donnison in *British Military Administration in the Far East, 1943-46;* Chapter 19.

12   Tinker, 1983, Vol. I; pages 815-16.

13   Tinker,1983, Vol.I; pages 831.

14   Tinker, 1983, Vol.I; page 773.

15   Tinker, 1983, Vol. I; page 983.

16   Tinker, 1983, Vol. I; page 986.

17   Tinker,1983, Vol.I; page 716.

18   Tinker, 1983. Vol.I; page 1009.

19   Tinker, 1983, Vol.I; page 1011.

20   Tinker,1983. Vol.I; page 1010-12.

21   Tinker, 1983,Vol II; page 56-7.

22 Tinker, 1985, Vol.II; page 144.

23 Tinker, 1985, Vol.II; page 190.

24 Tinker, 1985, Vol.II; pages 144 and 196-97.

25   Tinker, 1985, Vol.II; page 890.

26 Personal conversation with the Larmours.

27 Tinker, 1985, Vol. I; page 897.

28 Tinker, 1985, Vol.II; page 167.

XI

IN CONCLUSION

Before saying goodbye to Burma and the people who played their parts in this story I should try to reflect on empire and the marks it left on them all.

Vernon and Ruth travelled homewards on a crowded troop ship, thankful that his recent status entitled them to a small cabin instead of having to sleep in separate dormitories for men and women as most people did. During their last months in Burma they had made friends with Salah Tyabji and his wife Akhtar. Vernon recalled him as "a fiery nationalist before the war – the acknowledged leader of the Muslim community in Burma. He had suffered shocking indignities at the hands of the British who frequently sent him to prison. He and his wife had founded a school in Rangoon and conferred other benefactions on the city". When Burma fell to the Japanese Salah walked out to India: Vernon had seen him on the track. When he got back to Rangoon he found, "to his dismay, that the Burmese didn't like Indians any more than they liked the British. We struck up a warm friend-ship."

The Tyabjis had pressed Vernon and Ruth to visit their relations who lived near Bombay; so when their ship called in there they spent an evening with Hassan Ali and his wife Kumoo, who was Akhtar's sister, along with a circle of their family. "We were charmingly entertained, and – to our shame – taken quite by sur-prise by the civilized atmosphere and surroundings we encountered. Here were cultured, educated, traveled people living among exquisitely beautiful things, with fastidiously high standards of workmanship and cleanliness – beyond the appreciation of the Burmese, and of all but a very few of the Europeans in Burma. It was a happy but sobering experience."

David, meanwhile, had got demobilized in Australia where he spent six months, working on sheep farms and in a children's home in Sydney, staying with his father's sister and her family in Canberra, and hitch-hiking around that friendly and robustly egalitarian country (egalitarian if you paid no attention to the aboriginees). The Australia of that time offered him a glimpse of comradeship and the dignity of labour in a nearly classless society: a hope for the future. He worked his way home to Britain as a merchant seaman and had his week sailing on the Norfolk Broads with Vernon before starting at Oxford. It was the first time he had really talked with his father since they had gone canoeing for a week-end on the Thames, ten years earlier.

THE NEW BURMA

If this sounds like a story that ends with everyone living happily ever after we should remember that life was not so rosy in Burma. The Government was beset by various rebel bands and, on the Thai borders, by the remnants of a Chinese Nationalist Army, funded by the opium trade and by the American and Taiwan Governments who saw them as a useful threat to the Chinese Communist regime. Burma gradually descended into a chaos in which it was inevitable that the only remaining unifying force – the Army – would eventually take over. (Cromwell, Napoleon and many other strong men before and since had shown the way.)

Ne Win, one of the 30 young comrades who had gone with Aung San to train in Japan at the beginning of the war, was Prime Minister and Army Chief in 1960. He had always been on the semi-Fascist Right of the nationalist movement. Going to China that year, he visited their leaders and admired what he saw. In 1962 he led an Army coup, jailed most of his Ministers, abolished Parliament, the constitution and all rival Parties, and prohibited private enterprise, nationalizing land and property of every significant kind. His slogan was 'One blood, one voice, one command'. Saw Shwe Thaik, the President, was jailed and soon died in the Insein prison. Rumours still persist that he was murdered. Myint Thein, Vernon's old friend who had dug up for him the bottle of whisky he had buried for the day of his liberation, had become Chief Justice of Burma. Ne Win imprisoned him too, and would not even let him out to visit his wife when she was dying. The media and University students were terrorized into silence. Tourists and foreign enterprises were, so far as possible, kept out. Before long, Burma, which had been the world's biggest exporter of rice, could barely feed itself. Income per person fell from $670 a year in 1960 to $200 in 1989, making the country one of the poorest in the world.

At length, in 1988, Ne Win said he was going to retire and a surprisingly free general election was held in 1990. It was won, with a massive majority, by Aung San's daughter, Aung San Suu Kyi, and her Party. The group of generals who had taken over from Ne Win responded by placing her under house arrest and shooting down or imprisoning many of her followers. Meanwhile, armed rebellions in the hill country continued. Ne Win died in 2002.[1] Since then, cease-fires, conceding power to various ethnic groups, have been negotiated; but warfare continues in many parts of the country, and there are more than 20 armed groups fighting the Government. Suu Kyi remains under arrest.[2]

Vernon, writing at the end of the 'sixties, said that all the things the British had tried to bring to Burma – democracy, constitutional government, an uncorrupt and effective judicial and administrative machine, a free press, an independent university, productive private enterprise – had been swept away. "They need not be overmuch lamented for they did not thrive in Burmese soil. And it is probably better that the Burmese should create and develop something of their own." "Of the British contributions, it is probable that the only one that survives in vigour and is of unmixed benefit to the people of Burma is... Western medicine and... the medical services."[3] J.S.Furnivall, writing 40 years earlier, had predicted all this and more, saying "after a period of anarchy, more or less prolonged, our descendants may find Burma a province of China." Then a capacity to play football may be the only "inglorious, if not unfitting, memorial of British rule in Burma."[4]

What went wrong? It is not enough to say that democracy and free enterprise "did not thrive in Burmese soil". Why did they fare so much worse there than in the soil of India? Malaya? Singapore? Hong Kong? Books have been written about that question. I shall only draw briefly on a few of the insights this one has given me.

The British came to Burma, in every sense, from India – to protect India from Burmese marauders, and bringing with them their Indian soldiers, clerks, servants, and later Indian money lenders, traders, lawyers, doctors and many more. Most of Burma's trade was with India. Indians and Anglo-Indians, who have sometimes been described as "mediators" between the Burmese and the British, were in fact a barrier between them. They stole their country from the Burmese. It was not a conspiracy. It was just what happens when people who had for two centuries lived and worked with the British, learning their ways and speaking their language, were brought in to help run another country. The British did much the same in other places on the fringes of India.

The charm of the Burmese to British people who got to know them arose from their friendliness, gaiety, wit and self-confidence – all characteristics of a society much more equal than India's. That equality meant that, in this fertile land, no-one starved, most people could read, and there were no big land-owners, no nobles or tycoons. But it also meant that very few people gained higher education or went abroad. There were no people like the Tyabjis or the Alis – or Gandhi, Nehru, their families and friends. When Aung San took his team to meet Attlee and negotiate the independence of his country, scarcely any of them had been to Europe before. So if the Burmese were ever to become business leaders, soldiers or members of the more learned professions, the British would have had to educate them, send them abroad, and give them the opportunities they would need. But Rangoon University, founded in 1920, did not teach its students much about economic development or business management, or send more than a hand-ful of its graduates abroad. It was seven years before it began teaching Burmese. When they conquered the country in 1885, the British had burned down the great royal library in Mandalay and destroyed what was left of the Burmese aristocracy. They came to believe — David was reared on the myth — that "the Burman will never be a businessman, a soldier" — or various other things the modern world requires. They did not feel that Burmese religion, culture and tradition had much to offer the modern world. Neither did they offer an alternative vision that gave Burmese people leading roles in shaping their country's future. That would in any case have been difficult for the British, for they and their politicians were deeply divided about the future of their empire.

The British did recruit and train Burmese and mixed-race administrators and magistrates, but these soon became a small social class — a class speaking English, who naturally used their relatively high salaries to give their children opportunities to enter the same exclusive group. Meanwhile the Burmese lan-guage dwindled into the speech of cultivators, village craftsmen and the family. When bright youngsters like Aung San, with poor English and no academic or professional background, found their way into Rangoon University and learnt that it was unlikely to open up great opportunities for people like them, it is not surpris-ing if they turned their energies to revolution and the expulsion of foreigners. Neither was it surprising that the Government they eventually formed treated capitalists as their enemies. Foreign investors had done little for Burmans.

Like other Western countries, the British had built parliamen-tary democracy for themselves over long centuries within a society which already had its land-owners, its nobility, its soldiers, clergy, bankers and industrialists. Democratic institutions were rooted in – created, shaped, funded and manned by – this broader apparatus of civil society. Trying to plant a parliament, political parties and a free press into a society where such civil society as there was belonged mainly to people of other ethnic origins, the British should not have been surprised to find that politics became corrupt, violent, and focused on getting the foreigners out. Since this was the only experience the Burmese had of parliamentary democracy, and it only lasted four years, it is not surprising that they gained little enthusiasm for it. Neither is it surprising that Burmese soldiers – when they eventually took over – had no sense of the restraints that democracies usually impose on the military. They may have trained briefly in Japan; but not at Sandhurst.

The very idea of Burma as a country with clearly defined borders was a British invention, designed as much to keep the Chinese and the French out as to meet Burmese needs. Two-fifths of this territory was occupied by ethnic minorities – people with their own languages, cultures and proud traditions, and long histories of conflict with each other and with the Burman majority living in the plains. Only the British and their soldiers kept this explosive mix under control. It would call for strong and astute leaders to hold the country together once the British left, and such hopes perished when Aung San and most of his cabinet were murdered.

The best of the British were at their best when walking through the jungles and mountains, talking with local farmers and their Headmen, attending their celebrations, and leading the native people who staffed the public services – acting, in short, as Plato's Guardians. This was the life that Vernon and Ruth most enjoyed and always remembered. They were less sure of themselves in Rangoon and the larger towns, and more inclined there to withdraw into clubs and social rituals that were confined to white people. Vernon and Ruth were among those who did invite all kinds of people to their various homes; but the music, the hospitality and celebrations they offered them would have been enjoyed only by those capable of entering into an essentially European culture. Meanwhile it was in and around Rangoon, among young students, talking their own brands of Marxism and Fascism in garbled English, that the future of Burma was taking shape. They had no time for Guardians.

To these thoughts of mine Vernon added the reminder that "The British connection was extremely short, a passing and brief connection on the scale of history..." lasting "only 62 years. There must have been not a few Burmans living in 1948 who could remember the time when a Burmese king and court existed in Mandalay."[5] This connection ended with two campaigns that passed from end to end of the country and back again, burning up its wooden towns, looting and raping, and reinforcing belief in the old Burmese proverb that there are "five great Evils – fire, water, foes, robbers and rulers".

So we should not be too surprised that the Burmese withdrew into extreme isolation from other countries, into a world of village life (such towns as they had were neglected and stagnant) living under a tyrannical regime that was suspicious of foreigners and their enterprises, and accustomed to shedding a good deal of blood when power changed hands – all familiar features of the old Burma.

A FRACTURED FAMILY

Ruth and Vernon were 47 and 48 when they left Burma. They had spent a quarter of a century working for this piece of the British empire. What marks did that experience leave on them and their family? They returned to a battered and tightly rationed country under Labour government.

Ruth, who had hardly ever made a meal in her life, bought the pamphlets produced by the Ministry of Food and learnt to cook. Very well, too. She endeavoured to maintain the housekeeping standards that her mother, with lots of servants at her command, had taught her. (Years later, when Vernon was in his nineties, we found him still wrestling to shake out his bedding and turn his mattress every morning.)

Like most of his colleagues, Vernon was invited to apply for a job in the Home Civil Service, but could not bear the thought of becoming a cog in so vast a bureaucratic machine. Moreover, after many years following his own career path he felt it was Ruth's turn. So they found jobs together as house master and mistress in a training school for boys who had been in public care. After a year in this rural setting, they were thirsting for something that made more use of their knowledge and experience. So he joined the Historical Section of the Cabinet Office to work on official histories of the war – moving to a house in East Hagbourne, handy for visits to his mother nearby and for Didcot trains to the Cabinet Office in London. David was now a student at Oxford – also nearby – and Annis, his sister, would join him there before long. Meanwhile Ruth, once she had got the house and garden in order, became a magistrate, served on a hospital management committee, sang in a choir and was hostess to their friends and neighbours.

After so many years of anxiety and separation, all members of this family looked forward to a settled future in which a good deal of love and fun would be shared. Not for them the conflicts so many maturing families have to go through. But Ruth, who was the dominant, loquacious leader of the family's social life, carried until her death the scars of her nagged and neglected childhood. The censorious demands she made on her own children, and later on their children too, re-enacted much of her childhood experience.

All this owed nothing to empire. But the family's failure to grow through these difficulties and resolve them did owe something to long separations, and to the suppression of feelings taught by years of institutional life – in foster homes, boarding schools, the navy, and now in Oxford colleges. David and Annis treated their mother with courtesy but kept a prudent emotional and physical distance from her. David was soon staying in Oxford during vacations as well as in term time, and burying himself in work — interspersed with bouts of rowing. He and Annis gave each other a good deal of rueful, jokey mutual support, but were not well equipped to confront and resolve emotional turmoil. Nor was their mother an easy woman to confront.

Meanwhile Vernon's life was divided, as ever, between work, Ruth, music and occasional holidays — usually spent visiting friends in Germany or Scotland and exploring the forests and mountains of these countries. When he retired from the Cabinet Office, after writing three good books for them about military government in South East Asia and Western Europe, he and Ruth bought themselves a Landrover and — with Barbara Donnison, a younger cousin — drove to India, Burma, and on through Malaya, Australia and New Zealand, returning by boat to Greece and a shorter drive home across Europe. Demanding though these nine hard months of exploration must have been for two people in their early sixties, they returned more fulfilled and serene than ever before. This was clearly their ideal way of life.

On the way out, they arrived from Iran at a frontier post on the Pakistan border in the middle of the night. There a sergeant, sitting under an oil lamp, pushed an immigration form across the table and told them to start unloading the densely packed Landrover for inspection by Customs officers. Uncertain how his old service would be regarded in the new Pakistan, Vernon decided to chance it and wrote "I.C.S. retired" as his occupation. The sergeant, from the other side of the table, immediately spotted this and called out "He is old I.C.S.! Wake the Major!" Their gear was replaced in the car without inspection and the Major emerged from his quarters to welcome them to Pakistan. Visiting Srinagar in Kashmir, where, seventeen years before, they had a healing holiday on the lake after their escape from Burma, the man on whose houseboat they had traveled recognized them in the street, ran after them and insisted they come with him again for a weekend. It was to be like this all the way. In Burma they were welcomed and cared for, wherever they went, by Burmese friends, and their former colleagues and servants.

Ruth's relationship with her mother remained spiky. Childhood conflicts with Eleanor, her nearest sister, had never been resolved, and when Eleanor brought her new husband, Michael Barratt Brown, to meet the family, Vernon and David had to do the honours: Ruth refused to come downstairs. She even quarreled with her sister Barbara, a woman so kind and loving that no-one else had ever fallen out with her, so far as I know. As their mother, Isabel, drifted towards her death, these conflicts calmed down and relations between the sisters became more friendly.

Meanwhile, Ruth gave much love and kindness to other people's children: to Kelly Isaacs, the young violinist they had befriended in Rangoon – now working in London – and to a succession of German au pair girls who came to help them at Hagbourne and remained lifelong friends. With their aid and Annis's, she and Vernon gave great parties there for the playing of music, and for the usual festivals at Christmas and birthdays.

But Ruth's relations with her own son remained frail. He gave her a copy of his first book, "*The Neglected Child and the Social Services*", a pioneering study of all the work done by statutory and voluntary services for a large group of families whose children eventually came into public care. Could their break-up have been prevented? was the central question asked. He thought the book would interest a woman working as a magistrate in the juvenile and family courts. (It did not occur to this neglected child that this might be a disturbing subject of research to chose – and a disturbing title to lay before his mother.) She made no comment on the book, or on any of the others he sent her over the following years. Some forty years on, when his parents' library was divided up, he found his mother's copy of "*The Neglected Child...*" – the pages still uncut.

Ruth died of cancer in 1968. Vernon nursed her devotedly to the end. The last words she spoke recalled some movingly beautiful music they had heard together, years before. After her death,

Vernon – numbed by grief – stayed on in their home, completing his book on Burma, and going for long walks. Other women came to stay and to take holidays with him, but no-one could replace Ruth. After two years, he gradually emerged as a charming host and companion, with devoted friends who came to play music and golf and to share holidays with him. People from Burma and from Germany were often among his guests and hosts, and his longest holiday took him back to Burma again where Burmese friends were as delighted as ever to welcome him. Aung San Suu Kyi, standing with Vernon and her husband Michael Aris in the Hagbourne garden, can be seen in the accompanying photograph.

David's career, after Oxford, threaded a route between the academy and the state, with recurring involvement in research and in public inquiries dealing with housing, education, urban and social policy. He did a five-year stint in the chair of the Supplementary Benefits Commission which had a general responsibility for Britain's last-resort, income maintenance system. Meeting and talking regularly with some of the poorest people in Britain, and writing reports about their plight and the policies advocated by his Commission gave him the mix of insider and outsider roles for which he seemed best fitted. His childhood and youth had taught him a cautious relationship with women, a habit of seeking refuge from troubles in ever-more-intensive work, and a capacity to find support in a "family" of working colleagues – which helped to see him through emotional difficulties, but not to resolve them.

And Annis…? It will be for her to write her own story some day, and she too may want to reflect on the price that empire exacted from its children. She was a constant source of care and comfort for Vernon in his last years. A few hours before he died she and David were with him in the nursing home to which he had eventually to move. A buoyant young doctor had come, proposing to rush him into hospital to arrest the pneumonia that threatened to carry him off. Vernon said "Thank you – but no. I've had a good life." He was nearly 95.

*Aung San Suu Kyi, her husband and children between
Vernon and his grand-daughters*

COUSIN TED

The story of empire is not only about imperialists – the conquerors and law-enforcers. In a country like Britain, which sent
millions of people overseas, most of us still have relatives – people
of various cultures and colours – living in distant parts of the
world. Usually unknown to us, these cousins are descendants of
the migrations, and the relationships between masters, friends
and lovers, brought about by empire.

Vernon's cousin Ted was one such relative of mine, but I have
many more. I told his story to the point where he served in Africa
during the second world war, and found and married Margaret in
the course of a fortnight's home leave. He brought her and their
two daughters back to England after the war, and went on working as a mechanic. Margaret did a clerical job till they both
retired, and Ted did most of the cooking for the family. I recall
great curries. He was a loyal husband, and a loving father to both
their girls. Margaret had been a devout Catholic since the nuns
befriended her when – unmarried – she had her first baby. Ted
drove her to mass every Sunday and waited to bring her home
again, but never went to church himself. There was a hard and
private kernel of strength within that gentle exterior. (How else
do you survive what Ted had gone through?)

Ted's mother, Anne, came back from India to live in London
and occasionally visited them. His girls recall a powerful, dark
lady who was warmly welcomed by their mother, but treated with
reserve by their father. When she died there was a big family row
between Margaret, who said he should come to his mother's
funeral, and Ted who refused to go. His sister Daintie, who had
come all the way from her farm in Rhodesia to be there, refused
ever to speak to him again.

Ted's daughters and their children still travel the world, picking up jobs wherever they go. It is as if some thirst for exploration
– some determination not to be pinned down to one place – still
runs in their blood. It has not been easy to learn their story, for

Ted at Hagbourne

theirs has been a family overshadowed by secrets. They discovered, a little while before their father died, that he had once been in Burma – but for what purpose was never said. Then Daintie's daughter, now in Cape Town, revealed all to them on one of their world tours, and I was at last able to speak freely with them. They have helped me put this story together.

Ted was a skilled worker and a kindly, loyal, lovely man. Given the hand he was dealt by fate, that was as great an achievement as becoming head of the civil service in Burma.

CONCLUSION

In a country where Britain left so scant a legacy, was the imperial project just a terrible waste of time and talent? Did Vernon and Ruth throw away their lives – abandoning their country and their children for no great purpose? Vernon, I think, would have said that you can only do your best in life – drawing on the knowledge, the opportunities and the traditions of your own time. I add a few thoughts of my own about the way in which we should respond to these difficult questions.

First – as Mao might have said – it may be too early to give a confident answer. When Aung San Suu Kyi, who had lived most of her life in England, led a political party with a classic democratic platform in the first general election held since her father's death, the people of Burma had not forgotten these liberal values. They voted overwhelmingly for her. Many of those now striving most bravely and creatively to find a way forward for Burma draw in various ways on these liberal traditions.

Second – we should remember that the choice for Burma during the years when she was conquered, piece by piece, in three wars, was not between imperial domination and independence; it was between domination by Britain or France – and later by Japan. Siam only remained independent because the British and the French agreed to leave it as a buffer state between their spheres of influence.

As for David and Annis, we should not assume that if Vernon and Ruth had lived cosily in England they would have devoted much more of their lives to caring for their children. I think David was much loved in his first years. But thereafter, whenever his parents came home to England they would be off to the wilds of Germany or Switzerland after paying brief visits to their mothers, leaving their children in someone else's care. They were no better at caring for their grandchildren. The long separations from children compelled by life in the I.C.S. suited them pretty well. Ruth, in her later years, recognized her limitations, saying, after an unhappy encounter with Annis's two small daughters, "I know I'm not good with little ones. I'll make it up to them when they're older". Cancer deprived her of that opportunity. But if this story has a message about parental love it is that, after many years absence, you may be able to create a new relationship with your child – as if with a new friend, as Vernon did in his old age with Annis's girls. But you cannot recover the lost years, or recreate the kind of relationship that more fortunate children have with their parents.

Yet, within the imperial culture of their day, Vernon, Ruth and many others like them did not do too badly. The loving welcome they received on their visits to Burma, and – more surprisingly – from total strangers all through Pakistan and India, showed that the "Guardians" had not been forgotten. When, on his last visit, Vernon asked the Headman of a remote Burmese village whether he still received the kind of visits he used to make as a District Officer he was told "No Government officers in Burma have ever visited such parts, other than the British"[6]. Later still, when David and his wife visited Burma in 1984, they were generously and kindly cared for, and handed on from one Burmese family to another – all talking about "Uncle Vernon" and "Aunt Ruth". Vernon continued till the end of his life to write to old friends in Burma, and to be visited by those who could get to Europe. Myint Thein, eventually released from jail, continued to correspond with Vernon with the help of a secretary when both

Vernon aged about 90

men were blind and in their nineties.

Vernon's conclusion about empire, looking back on its history in his last writings, was that people prefer to be ruled by members of their own nation, no matter how appalling the regime; and it is better that they should be.

Finally, we must remember that each generation has to ask itself the same hard questions I posed for Vernon and Ruth: everyone, that is, who wants to help roll the rickety cart of history forward in particular directions, and cannot rest content with teaching their students, treating their patients, building some houses, clearing the drains or pursuing whatever trade they follow. In 1948, at the point when this story ends, David – or I (for this is where first and third person must come together) – hoped to help in building, not an empire, but a fairer, healthier, better-educated, more equal Britain. Millions of others shared that hope. William Watson wrote poems about it a hundred years ago – and was ostracised by an imperialist society for doing so. Here is one of them.

THE TRUE IMPERIALISM

Here, while the tide of conquest rolls
Against the distant golden shore,
The starved and stunted human souls
Are with us more and more.

Vain is your Science, vain your Art,
Your triumphs and your glories vain,
To feed the hunger of their heart
And famine of their brain

Your savage deserts howling near,
Your wastes of ignorance, vice, and shame,
Is there no room for victories *here*,
No field for deeds of fame?

Arise and conquer while ye can
The foe that in your midst resides,
And build within the mind of Man
The Empire that abides.[7]

Living now in a society that is in many ways as deeply divided and as unfair as the one my generation inherited – a society engaged yet again in wars of conquest against brown skinned people – can those of us who have tried to create a better world claim that we have done anything more than pass on to a few people some of the kindness, the hopes and the ideals that others gave us?

NOTES

1 Obituary, *The Economist*, 14 December, 2002.

2 Martin Smith, *Border Minorities Revisited*; a lecture given to the Britain-Burma Society, London, 27 June, 2000.

3 F.S.V. Donnison, *Burma*, Ernest Benn, London 1970; pages 243-245.

4 J.S.Furnivall, *An Introduction to the Political Economy of Burma*, Rangoon, Burma Book Club, 1931; page xxiv.

5 Donnison, 1970; page 45.

6 Donnison, 1970; page 99.

7 William Watson, *The Poems of Sir William Watson*, London, George Harrap, 1936. Reprinted in Chris Brooks and Peter Faulkner (eds.) *The White Man's Burdens*, Exeter, University of Exeter Press, 1996; page 340. Italics added.

SOURCES

The main sources for this book were the memoirs, journals and letters of my family, and the conversations I have had with relatives and friends involved in the story. The evolving historical context of their lives I have had to learn from books, and I want to thank helpful librarians at the London School of Economics and Political Science and the School of Oriental and African Studies where I spent many days reading them. These were the most important.

LOUIS ALLEN, *Burma. The Longest War 1941-45*, London, J.M.Dent, 1984.

J.RUSSELL ANDREWS, *Burmese Economic Life*, Stanford, Stanford University Press, 1948.

AUNG SAN SUU KYI, *Freedom from Fear and Other Writings*, Harmondsworth, Penguin Books, 1992.

CHRIS BROOKS AND PETER FAULKNER (eds.) *The White Man's Burdens*, Exeter, University of Exeter Press, 1996.

JOHN F. CADY, *A History of Modern Burma*, Ithaca, New York, Cornell University Press, 1958.

MAURICE COLLIS, *Trials in Burma*, London, Faber & Faber, 1938. New edition, 1945.

JOSEPH CONRAD, *Heart of Darkness*, Ware, Herts;
Wordsworth Editions, 1995. First published 1902.

NORMAN DAVIES, *The Isles. A History*, London, Macmillan 1999.

F.S.V.DONNISON, *Public Administration in Burma*,
London, Royal Institute of International Affairs, 1953.

F.S.V.DONNISON, *British Military Administration in the Far East, 1943-46*,
London, H.M.S.O., 1956.

F.S.V.DONNISON, *Burma*, Ernest Benn, London, 1970.

BERNARD FERGUSSON, *Beyond the Chindwin*,
London, Collins, 1945.

H. FIELDING, *The Soul of a People*, London,
Macmillan, 2nd. Ed. 1898.

J.S.FURNIVALL, *An Introduction to the Political Economy of Burma*,
Rangoon, Burma Book Club, 1931.

EVERETT E. HAGEN *The Economic Development of Burma*,
Washington, D.C., National Planning Association, 1956.

G.E.HARVEY, *British Rule in Burma 1824-1942*,
London, Faber & Faber, 1946

ERIC HOBSBAWM, *Age of Extremes. The short twentieth century*.
London, Michael Joseph, 1994.

LAWRENCE JAMES, *Raj. The Making and Unmaking of British India*,
London, Little, Brown, 1997.

SOURCES

MICHAEL JOLLES, *Samuel Isaac, Saul Isaac and Nathaniel Isaacs,
A monograph*. 78, Greenfield Gardens, NW2 1HY, 1998.

DESMOND KELLY, *Kelly's Burma Campaign. Letters from the Chin Hills*,
London, Tiddim Press, 2003.

WILLIAM MACKENZIE, *The Secret History of SOE, the Special
Operations Executive, 1940-1945*, London, St. Ermin's Press, 2000.

U MAUNG MAUNG, *From Sangha to Laity. Nationalist Movements
of Burma, 1920-1940*, Delhi, Manohar Publications,
A.N.U. Monographs on South Asia, No.4, 1980.

G.E.MITTON (ed.), *Scott of the Shan Hills*,
London, John Murray, 1936.

GEORGE ORWELL, *Burmese Days*, Harmondsworth,
Penguin Books, 1944. First published in the U.S.A., 1934.

PLATO, *The Republic*, trans. Desmond Lee, Harmondsworth,
Penguin 2nd ed. 1974.

JOSEPH ROTH, *The Wandering Jews*, (Trans. Michael Hofmann),
London, Granta Books, 2001.

EDWARD SAID, *Culture and Imperialism*, London,
Chatto and Windus, 1993.

GEOFFREY L. SHISLER, *The Life of the Rev. Simeon Singer*,
London, New West End Synagogue, March 28th, 2004.

BALWANT SINGH *Independence and Democracy in Burma, 1945-1952.
The Turbulent Years*, Ann Arbor, Michigan,
University of Michigan, 1993.

WILLIAM SLIM, *Defeat into Victory*, London, Cassell, 1956.

MARTIN SMITH, *Burma: Insurgency and the Politics of Ethnicity*,
    Dhaka, The University Press, and Zed Books of London,
    2nd. Ed.,1999.

IZUMIYA TATSURO, *The Minami Organ*, Tokyo, Tokuma Shoten, 1967.
    Translated into English by U Tun Aung Chain of
    Rangoon University.

THANT MYINT-U, *The Making of Modern Burma*,
    Cambridge, Cambridge University Press, 2001.

HUGH TINKER, *The Union of Burma*, 4th edn.,
    Oxford University Press, 1967.

HUGH TINKER (ed.) *The Struggle for Independence. 1944-1948.
    Documents from Official and Private Sources*,
    London, H.M.S.O. (two volumes) 1983.

FRANK N. TRAGER, *Burma. From Kingdom to Republic*,
    London, Pall Mall Press, 1966.

FRANK N. TRAGER, (ed.) *Burma: Japanese Military Administration,
    Selected Documents, 1941-1945*, Philadelphia,
    University of Pennsylvania Press, 1971.

DOROTHY WOODMAN, *The Making of Burma*,
    London, Cresset Press, 1962.

PHILIP WOODRUFF, *The Men Who Ruled India. The Guardians*.
    Jonathan Cape, London, 1954.

LEONARD WOOLF, *Growing. An autobiography of the years
    1904-1911*, London, Hogarth Press, 1961.

INDEX

Chick, Harriet, 18
Churchill, Winston, 43;
　years of disaster, 208, 233, 238;
　the tide turns, 265, 281;
　and Civil Affairs Service, 271,
　287;
　in opposition, 305, 309, 329
Clark, Joe, 276
Clive, Robert, 115
Cobb, Brigadier, 312
Collis, Maurice, 167
Conrad, Joseph, 116
Cooper, Charles, 194

Das, C.R., 166
Dawkins, Enid, 121
Day Lewis, Cecil, 217
De Bruyn, Daintie – nee
　Donnison 39, 134, 278, 348, 350
De Valera, 166
Dee, Arthur, 231
Di Conti, Nicolo, 72
Disraeli, Benjamin, 15
Donatello, 273
Donnison, Anne, 39, 44-45,
　133-34, 348
Donnison, Barbara, 344
Donnison, Edith (nee Phipps or
　Moore) 40-43, 129, 141, 177-78,
　190, 233
Donnison, Edward;
　in childhood, 39, 44-45;
　in jail, 133-34, 184;
　later life, 278-79, 348, 350

Donnison, Frank, 24-25, 36,
　39-40, 42, 44, 109
Donnison, George, 36, 39, 44
Donnison, John, 36, 39-40, 133-34
Donnison, Keith and Margot, 188
Donnison, Margaret, 279, 348
Dorje, Riksin, 58
Dorman-Smith, Reginald;
　in Simla, 270-71, 283, 289-90,
　305, 309;
　back in Burma, 313, 321,
　325-26
Doupe, John, 151
Dumble, 221
Dunkley, Mr. Justice, 161
Dyer, General, 80

Edgerley, Leo, 300, 306
Eliot, T.S., 210
Elsom, 151
Emrick, 106
Engels, Friedrich, 275
Ewing, Major, 102

Fielding Hall, 55
Fincham, 41
Fleet, Bill, 52
Foliere, Father, 105
Ford, Frank and Mrs., 240
Fowler, 106
Franklin, Benjamin, 273
Fullerton, Admiral, 154
Furnivall, J.S., 163, 339

NAMES OF PLACES

This index is based on the names
in the book; modern names for
many can be found on the map on
page 66.

General Council of Burmese
Associations, 164

Government of Burma Act, 1935,
193

Government of India Act, 1919,
165

"Guardians" of Plato's Republic,
applications of the tradition,
32, 46, 59, 61, 72, 136, 341, 351

Grenadier Guards, 51, 61, 117, 134,
277

Gymkhana Club, 84

Home Guard, 277

Indian National Army, 266

Indian National Congress, 263,
268

Insein Jail, 133-34, 338

Irrawaddy Flotilla Company, 87,
108, 120

Karen people, 65, 110, 209,
244-46, 281, 302

Kachin people, 65, 246, 265

Labour Party, 20, 142, 234, 316

Magdalen College, Oxford, 52

Marlborough College:
in Vernon's day, 45-50, 84, 117;
in David's, 204, 206, 210, 229,
230-31, 273-5

Marshall Plan 311

Mon people 65, 70

National Council for Civil
Liberties, 145

Newnham College, Cambridge,
26, 58

Oldfeld School, 178-79, 190

Pegu Club, 84, 195

Rangoon General Hospital, 197,
204

Rangoon Gramophone Society,
220

Rangoon Juvenile Courts, 199

Red Cross, 297

Refugees:
Jewish from Germany, 190-91;
escaping from Burma, 249;
feeding the starving, 243;
British refugees in India, 242,
267-68

Royal College of Organists, 40

Saya San Rebellion, 162, 166, 193

Shan people and the Shan States:
65, 111, 313;
Donnisons work there, 119,
123-24, 136, 149;
buy a cottage there, 220;
Shan servant joins them, 269

Somerville College, Oxford, 122

Special Operations Executive,
280-81, 310

Sudan Political Service, 59